Borders and Berwick

AN ILLUSTRATED ARCHITECTURAL GUIDE
TO THE SCOTTISH BORDERS AND TWEED VALLEY

NOT BEING A NATIVE OF THE BORDERS, but originating from further north, my impressions of the Borders varied with the routes that we followed south. The coastal route with its memories of Fife and East Lothian to Georgian Berwick; the simple and yet strong rural architecture of Lauder, Greenlaw and Coldstream; the Victorian richness of Peebles, Innerleithen, Selkirk and Hawick. The Borders appeared as separate north/south corridors of style.

However, when we moved to the Borders I became aware of the influence of the River Tweed and its tributaries, not so much as strands of style but as generators of industry. On the river banks sit the great woollen mills surrounded by their workers' terraced houses, and in the rural areas the *big* houses with their home farms and their workers' cottages – all tied together by the river and creating a rich tapestry of interwoven interests which includes Berwick with its Georgian houses and its bridges.

Charles Strang has captured this richness with buildings as diverse as Traquair, the oldest continuously inhabited house in Scotland, to Manderston, swansong of the classical house; from the dramatic clifftop setting of Fast Castle to the unique cast-iron *pissoir* at Walkerburn. The challenge is thrown down to us all to maintain this tradition.

J ANDREW LESTER
Chairman
Border Architects Group, 1991

© Author: Charles A Strang
Series editor: Charles McKean
Series consultant: David Walker
Editorial consultant: Duncan McAra
Index: Oula Jones
Cover design: Dorothy Steedman, Almond Design

The Rutland Press
ISBN 1 873190 10 7
1st published 1994

Cover illustrations
Main: View of the new bridge over the River Tweed at Kelso, Scotland.
Aquatint by William Daniell, c.1802 (National Library of Scotland)
Inset: Neidpath Castle (Borders Regional Council)

Typesetting and picture scans by Almond Design, Edinburgh
Printed by Pillans and Wilson, Edinburgh, Glasgow, London and Manchester

INTRODUCTION

Berwick Borough Museum

Union Suspension Bridge, Norham

*In 1552 the **Debateable Land**, a district in dispute between the two realms and consequently a notorious haunt of criminals, was partitioned by agreement, ... but the governments of both countries found it was hard to impose order, and in times of war found disorder and raiding a positive advantage. Men therefore had to build for defence and protection. On the English side of the border the bastle-house, a fortified farmhouse, made its appearance, while in Scotland the tower-house remained the favourite fortified dwelling, often protected by a stone enclosing wall or barmkin ... Bastles and tower-houses were still being built in the early 17th century.*
DoE, *Border Warfare* from Fuller's *History of Berwick*, 1799

Aikwood Tower, Selkirk

RCAHMS

While the administrative whims which have led to the present local authority boundaries can be more lightly dismissed, it was a brave man indeed, in days gone by, who would ignore a national boundary, whether for reasons of love, war, hunger, greed, family ties, patriotism, or sheer cussedness. Yet for many centuries the Border between England and Scotland was in dispute and brave men, and not a few brave women, existed there who would make their own way in the world, owing allegiance to their own folk, or occasionally their own (small) settlement, before contemplating a national perspective to their own brief existences. The Borderer grew up over the ages self-reliant, fiercely competitive (if occasionally a little small-minded), basic and practical as befits someone close to the land. Such front-line troops on both sides in national boundary disputes were bound to suffer grievously, and the fate of their architecture was no less bloody, buildings which might conceivably give succour or support being destroyed by attacker and defender; and the depredations of the military damaged the civilian economy, making rebuilding even more difficult and temporary in nature.

Little early architecture has survived the military periods beyond medieval burgh plan forms, while the great set pieces (sometimes literally) of Border abbeys, towers and the earlier brochs, the land through which swirl the rivers Tweed and Teviot still provides a rich architectural inheritance. The Berwickshire Merse, that flat and productive (when improved) agricultural plain, sprouted a crop of great 18th-century houses for wealthy landowners. And the central Borders, with its incised valleys, plentiful water and wool, developed its textile industry from cottage to multi-storey factory and single-storey shed in the 18th, 19th and 20th centuries.

Dominated by no single settlement worthy of the name city, the area of this guide may be none the worse for that, although the Border rivalry which is particularly visible on the rugby field can occasionally appear somewhat sterile to the uncommitted. Essentially small in scale (only Berwick and Hawick have any genuine claims to urban architecture) and relatively simple in detail, towns, villages and hamlets are therefore vulnerable to large and/or unsympathetic development, and to more erosion of character by the introduction of replacement windows, new materials, or the Philistine application of inappropriate design standards for road design or parking layouts. Parochialism may also be detected in the architecture, where local connections sometimes mean more than quality of product: such an attitude would not sell many woollen goods outwith the Borders.

But proximity to Edinburgh (more architects per head of population than anywhere else in Scotland, and possibly in Europe) and Newcastle, and a number of enlightened clients (occasionally municipal ones) produced many good, and several great, buildings, and a number of local architects who made good too.

John Major, in 1518, described the Borders response to (English) incursions: *If twenty thousand of the enemy were to invade at dawn, a working day of twelve hours would hardly pass before the people were in action against them. For the nearest laird rallies the folk of his district at the first rumour of an enemy and by noon every man is ready in his arms, which he keeps to hand, and mounted on his horse: and they seek out the enemy's position, and whether they are organised or not, go at once into action. Thus they often destroy themselves as well as the enemy: but is enough for them if they drive him back. And if by chance the enemy comes off best, then the next laird gathers together another force, ready to fight: and all come at their own cost.*

Above *Joiner's glazing, Coldstream.*
Left *Thirlestane Castle, Lauder.*
Below *Gateway opposite the Crook Inn, Tweedsmuir*

Occasionally, the use of external architects has led to a lack of appreciation of context, both historical and physical. But in the same way that few appreciate a prophet in his own country, it can sometimes take an outsider to put an objective value on his surroundings. Whatever the reason, more informed discussion is required on the quality of our architecture and built surroundings. It is hoped that this guide, as well as being pleasurably stimulating to the eye, will be a contribution to that discussion.

While a publication of this format and size cannot include all deserving buildings, or even fully describe those included and their contexts, the guide's author would like to be made aware

3

Top *Interior, Channelkirk Church.*
Above *Doorway detail, Tillmouth
Dower House*

I am not wont to believe the
common Scots condemnation of the
English, nor yet English
condemnation of the Scots. It is the
part of a man with eyes in his head
to put aside all inordinate love of his
own folk and hate of his enemies,
and then to hold the scales of
judgement even and to keep the sett
of his mind well based on reason,
and temper his opinion accordingly.
John Major (the medieval Scots
scholar), *Historia Majoris Britannia*

Red Lion Inn, Kelso

of corrections required, supplementary
information available, or any constructive
observations on the architecture of the Borders
and Berwick as displayed in this guide: please
contact him c/o The Rutland Press, 15 Rutland
Square, Edinburgh EH1 2BE.

Organisation of the Guide
This guide addresses, through reference to its
architecture, something of the landscape,
history and character of Borders Region and
that part of Berwick Borough as far south as
Holy Island. The order of presentation works
from east to west: starting with Berwick-upon-
Tweed, the Berwickshire coast, and radial
routes from Berwick itself. West to Kelso, the
guide then loops southwards through Roxburgh
District, Jedburgh, Hawick, Newcastleton, and
then north to St Boswells and Melrose. After
taking the A68 north, and the A7 south to
Galashiels and Selkirk, the Ettrick and Yarrow
valleys are visited, and thence to Innerleithen
and Peebles, exploring the varied interests of
upper Tweeddale and ending at Carlops.

Text Arrangement
Major buildings are introduced by sequence of
name (or number), address, date and architect.
Buildings which are more lightly emphasised
are contained within text paragraphs. Buildings
which have been demolished or, more rarely,
which have never been built, are so identified,
and do not appear on the maps: the maps
themselves contain numbers which relate to
those adjacent to the text, not page numbers.
Quotations are printed in italics, and a list of
references is given on page 260, along with
photographic credits, acknowledgements,
glossary and index.

Access
While many of the buildings featured in this
guide are open to the public or visible from the
public road or footpath, some are private and,
particularly in the more rural parts, readers are
asked to respect the occupiers' privacy.

Sponsors
The generous support of Scottish Borders
Enterprise, Borders Regional Council, Dawson
International PLC, Berwick-upon-Tweed
Borough Council, Berwickshire, Ettrick and
Lauderdale, and Roxburgh District Councils is
gratefully acknowledged.

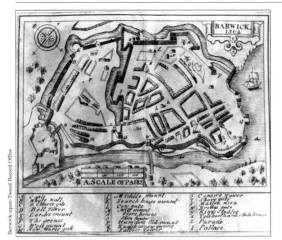

Berwick, 1564

Berwick-upon-Tweed Record Office

Berwick-upon-Tweed Record Office

BERWICK-UPON-TWEED

England's most northerly town, further north than Brodick, at the mouth of the Tweed, 155km (97 miles) from source to sea. Sloping, exposed site north of the river has been built over with a wealth of fine-grained townscape, full of unexpected pleasures. The whole is much more than the sum of its parts. Worth a weekend's walking within the walls alone.

In the 13th century this richest and most prosperous of Scotland's burghs, one-time chief sea-port of Scotland, was sacked by Edward I following Balliol's alliance with France. In the Wars of Independence it was much fought over. In 1482 Berwick was finally relinquished by the Scots after changing hands 13 times in 300 years; yet by 1551 it was transformed into an independent burgh, neither English nor Scots. The Crimean War declaration in 1854 was made in the name of Victoria, Queen of Great Britain, Ireland, Berwick-upon-Tweed and all the British Dominions, while the eventual peace treaty did not mention the town, arguably leaving it still at war with Russia.

In the 13th century, 15 religious houses had warehouses in Berwick, then Scotland's premier port.

In 1292 **John Balliol** was declared King of Scots by Edward I of England. Balliol was viewed as the English King's puppet (his nickname was Toom Tabard) but even he rebelled, in 1296, unsuccessfully, ending in his public humiliation, following the English slaughter of the inhabitants of Berwick.

It would give us pleasure could we say with truth, that a proper attention to the laying out of the streets in a regular manner had originally been attended to. All of them are not only irregular, but intolerably ill paved ... The principal street, however, and one through which there is constantly a very considerable throughfare, is shamefully cramped at the bottom, by the Town Hall being injudiciously placed in the middle of it ... A similar obstruction is occasioned by the building called the Main Guard.

Berwick is pleasantly and beautifully situated on the north side of the river Tweed, long celebrated both in history and in song ... Fuller's *History of Berwick*, 1799

Below Berwick from Tweedmouth: note the quay walls. Bottom Berwick-upon-Tweed, 1746

Strang

Berwick-upon-Tweed Borough Museum and Art Gallery

BuTBMAG

Top *Berwick-upon-Tweed from the south*. Above *The Old Bridge at Berwick on Tweed*

Berwick Bridge
George Home, Earl of Dunbar, High Treasurer of Scotland, was James VI & I's trusted Scottish adviser, promoting the King's building of the bridge as a symbol of state unification and being made Governor of Berwick. Sadly, neither King nor courtier saw the bridge completed, Home dying in the year of its commencement and King James visiting Scotland only once, in 1617, despite good intentions proclaimed on his *journey to work* in 1603.

Three bridges and swans

Berwick Bridge, 1611-34, James Burrell
In length 355m, and 5m in width, 15 red sandstone arches with cutwaters carry Doric columns and busts, the arches at their highest (14m) at the north end, *the arches seem to be following each other across the Tweed like a herd of elephants* (Chamberlin).

Royal Tweed Bridge, 1925-8,
L G Mouchel & Partners
Four reinforced concrete spans of no great beauty, it alleviated the congestion on the old brig – it simply transferred it to Golden Square, Marygate and Scotsgate instead. Now itself greatly relieved by the 1984 construction of the A1 bypass which crosses the Tweed almost imperceptibly well to the west.

Royal Border Bridge, 1847-50,
Robert Stephenson
For the York, Newcastle & Berwick Railway, thus linking up the east coast main line, 28 high round arches in stone-faced brick on stone piers, 38m above the Tweed. A structure of genuine grandeur (built by 2738 men, 180 horses, and two Nasmyth steam-hammers to drive in elm piles) big enough to

Strang

Berwick-upon-Tweed Borough Museum and Art Gallery

absorb the detritus of 1990s rail electrification without flinching.

Town Hall, Marygate, 1754-61,
Samuel & John Worrall
The plans, two elevations and a section were supplied by the Worralls for some £31 10s, and Pattison and Dods carried out the work, Joseph Dods (builder, architect and town bailiff) cheekily signing the building. Restored 1857-8 and 1969 (Civic Trust Award). Dominant sturdy Gibbsian belfry 45m high, significant in the streetscape where it commands the lower end of the commercial centre, Marygate (the upper end unfortunately wrecked by the 1928 bridge access and the un-civic bus station). Streets slip past to both sides of its stepped approach and giant Tuscan west portico and frieze. Within is a Venetian-windowed Georgian assembly room, while on the top floor is the barred-windowed former gaol, now a museum of correction. Arcaded basement, stone-paved buttermarket open at the east end, closed arches to the west in commercial use, surprising glazed extension, hopefully temporary and fully reversible.

Royal Border Bridge

Murray's *Handbook for Travellers in Scotland described the town thus: [It] is best seen from the railway and is not worth entering.* The view is particularly spectacular coming from the south and the borough is certainly worth entering. Perhaps Murray was trying to encourage the traveller onward to Scotland.

The public buildings *of Berwick are not very remarkable. The town-house has a spire, which the church wants.* Robert Chambers, *Picture of Scotland*

The upper flat *is occupied as a common gaol, and is perhaps the most healthy and pleasant one in the kingdom. This is owing to the many large windows, from which the prisoners enjoy several excellent views ...*

Left *Corner of Hide Hill with view to Town Hall, 1800.* Below *Town Hall*

Berwick-upon-Tweed Borough Museum and Art Gallery

Berwick-upon-Tweed Borough Museum and Art Gallery

Town Stocks, Marygate, six leg-holes in a timber cross-bar, set in round-topped wooden uprights. Original stocks position was on the side of the Town Hall steps facing East Street. This version used to be railed around, just north of the Scotsgate; now they are relocated back to the Town Hall but so close to its wall as to be unusable were liberal values no longer to hold sway in the borough.

32-36 West Street, 1779;
restored Berwick Borough Council
Red sandstone, three-storey 3:1:3 bays, with moulded architraves and other Gibbsian details. Note the date of 1779 in halves, one on each skewputt. At the foot of this steep street linking medieval bridge with borough centre, **No 57** displays a noble pillared doorway.

Maltings Arts Centre, 1990,
Law & Dunbar-Nasmith Partnership
Deceptive single-storey fronting to one of the town's hollow cores of parking, a solid composition of pantiled roofs, stained timber, buff (rather than red) brick, and stone plinth, six-storey river elevation not high enough to obscure the hideous concrete-framed backside of the Co-operative store. RIBA Award, 1991.

Top *32-36 West Street.*
Above *Doorpiece, 57 West Street*

The Maltings burned down in 1979. *The potential theatre ... was a four-storey shell with a 10m drop from one side of the building to the other. Its sandstone walls were of variable thickness, with a significant lack of right angles.*
Architects' Journal

Great square masses *of sandstone oppress the eye wherever it may turn; massive walls, massive houses, a massive bridge, and massive quays and piers!*
Robert Chambers, *Picture of Scotland*

Town walls

Town Walls, from 1588, Sir Richard Lee, G Portinari & J A'Contio
These stone-faced earth artillery fortifications are what gives the town its present-day character, the Italianate designs incomplete (relying on the medieval south and west defences) despite being the most expensive Elizabethan government project. In the 1760s the walls were rebuilt incorporating artillery batteries. Gates include **Scotsgate** (widened 1815 and altered 1858, three arches, a large

Berwick-upon-Tweed Borough Museum and Art Gallery

one for the Great North Road, flanking smaller ones for the accompanying footpaths); **Cowport**, *c*.1596 with 18th-century timber doors on the outer side, portcullis groove, and with a stone, Welsh-slated **Gatekeeper's Lodge**, 1755, built into the walls; **Ness Gate**, 1816; and **Shore Gate**, *c*.1760, with original timber doors.

Lions House, 18th century
Named presumably for the lions couchant on the rusticated gate piers. A sad sight by 1971, it was repaired following intervention by the Berwick-upon-Tweed Preservation Trust formed that year. A prominent landmark on Windmill Hill, particularly in view of its three-storey five-bay form. Plain to severe elevation very sensible (rich detail could easily weather here), ashlar with rusticated quoins, scrolled gables and fine fanlight (see colour p.111).

The Magazine, 1749, adjacent, an oblong stone gunpowder store heavily buttressed, original interior, the stone enclosing wall's single opening a pedimented round-arched doorway facing the ramparts (and away from the town and barracks).

Bank Hill United Reform Church, 1835-6
Formerly the Presbyterian Church of England, ashlar, rusticated base and quoins, round-headed windows, Tuscan pilastered doorway with dentilled cornice.

8 Bank Hill, 1798
Stucco with stone cornice and quoins, large 24-pane sash windows reflecting its original role as the Corporation Academy.

BuTBMAG

Top *Berwick-upon-Tweed showing bridge and Edwardian walls, drawn and engraved by W Daniell, 1822.* Above *Scotsgate, 1937*

The women of Berwick are, without the exception of even Edinburgh or Inverness, the most beautiful to be found north of the Tweed. They are not only beautiful, in so far as bloom of complexion and regularity of features are concerned, but they possess the utmost elegance of form, and dress with taste at least equal to their native graces. The art of the toilette has here been carried to a height rare in this quarter of the island, or indeed out of the metropolis, on account, it is said, of the facility with which the belles of the last age procured the 'fashions' from London by means of the smacks.
Robert Chambers, *Picture of Scotland*

The buildings, which are of freestone covered with red tyles, extend in many places not only to the walls, but, in some part are really built on them. The houses, particularly in the High Street and Hide Hill, are, for the most part, three storeys in height and many of them are not only highly commodious within, but those of modern erection are handsomely fronted.
Fuller, *History of Berwick*, 1799

Bridge Street is narrow, as befits the medieval route into town, composed largely of intimate two-storey buildings, mostly now Georgian, many shopfronted: **50** (approached by close between **48** and **52**) is 17th-century, timber-framed, with the upper floor jettied over; **54-60**, an 11-bay building of *c*.1800, rusticated quoins and giant Tuscan pilasters; **62**, 18th-century clockmaker's shop, the roundel containing a timepiece; **64** is memorable both for its Victorian shopfront with slender fluted columns and decorated pediments over the doors, and as the original point of sale of Berwick Cockles, keeping dentists in business from 1801 (see colour pp.109/10).

A tragic loss of frontage opens the view of the car park just east of **Dewar's Lane**, a setted runnel to nowhere now, a battered **granary** of great character holding the line for the moment to the west (see colour p.111).

39 Bridge Street is art nouveau, ashlar, with decorative hoppers, rusticated quoins and a curved broken pediment, the centre doorway flanked by ogee-arched Venetian windows. The **Sally Port** links Bridge Street and Quayside, an old tunnel passage of intimate scale giving a sight of the backland granaries and older narrow gables.

35 Woolmarket, *c*.1830, riotously droved ashlar on ground floor, enriched window surrounds, doorpiece and stringcourse below moulded pilasters, cornice and gable scrolls. Home of George Johnston, founder of the Berwickshire Naturalists Club.

King's Arms Hotel, 43 Hide Hill
Georgian coaching inn, more like a country house than a pub, painted stucco, in three portions, the middle with Venetian windows, that to the right with rusticated quoins and gable scrolls. Stables demolished 1782, rebuilt 1845, to rear. Charles Dickens stayed here in 1858 and 1861, giving public readings at the Assembly Rooms, 1845, now part of the Hotel.

Butting on to the rear of Berwick's walled defences, the buildings of **Quay Walls** form a memorable group as the river frontage of the town. **No 1**, 1809, formerly bank; **No 3** early 18th-century former granary, pantiled with slate eaves courses, three storeys to Quay

Walls, four to the rear where a courtyard can also be entered from quay level via a passageway through the Walls themselves; **Nos 4 & 5**, 18th-century (No 5, 1770), stone three-storey and basement, the former with a fine doorcase with cast lead traceried fanlight; **No 18**, **Custom House**, 18th-century Adam style, two-storey five-bay ashlar. Doorway bizarrely painted sky-blue, with round-headed traceried fanlight, Tuscan fluted pilasters, Venetian side-lights; **Nos 19-23** a splendid 18th-century group, **No 21**, the home of Thomas Sword Good (1789-1872), painter and cartographer, with a Doric doorcase and Venetian windows.

The Chandlery, The Quay, converted into small units, 1988, Bain Swan Architects, pantiled and eaves-slated, whose extensions and fire escapes (though not the Velux rooflights) contribute to the cheerful jumble of quayside building (see colour p.109).

On the east side of **Palace Green**, a quiet little space with a dwarf walled and railed garden enclosure in its heart, is the **Governor's House**, early 18th century,

Top *Hen and Chickens Hotel, 15 Sandgate, 18th century.* Above *Former Corn Exchange, 1858, John Johnston, now a swimming pool.* Left *The Chandlery.* Opposite: Top *54-60 Bridge Street.* Bottom *Dewar's Lane*

Thomas Good, Honorary RSA in 1828, was a contemporary and imitator of Sir David Wilkie, painting many of Wilkie's favourite subjects: fishermen, agricultural labourers, and other simple folk engaged in simple tasks. Jane Bewick was not impressed: *A painter of some eminence he got out of his depth by painting in Wilkie's style; as soon as these would not sell he threw by the brush and married a Woman with money – and now enjoys the fruits of his industry ...*

Governor's House

As the military significance of Berwick dwindled in the 18th century the post of Governor tended to be filled by generals *en route* to civvie street. It was finally abolished in 1833.

Berwick-upon-Tweed Borough Museum and Art Gallery

Top *1,2,3 Wellington Terrace*. Right *Old Guardhouse, Palace Street*. Above *Avenue House, 4 Palace Street East*

Slate came to Border roofs from a variety of sources. *Stobo* slate (see Stobo) was thick and relatively heavy. *Scotch* slate was quarried mostly from Argyll, and came mixed so Scotch-slated roofs are usually graded, the smaller slates used towards the ridge of the roof. *Welsh* slate is thinner and more regular: entire roofs are slated with a single size of slate, reflecting their large scale of production from the consistent Welsh supply (most Welsh slate arrived as the railways appeared, but in the Borders around the Tweed there is some evidence of its earlier use, probably shipped in to Berwick). *Westmorland* slate is grey-blue rather than blue-black, and came into use at the end of the 19th century. Properly detailed, a slate roof will last for more than 200 years.

similar features to the Barracks (see p.15). Central three-storey five-bay roughcast block has armorials in cartouche over the door and ashlar pilasters at angles; flanking two-storey wings have gabled centres and crowstepped end gables. To the west harled, pantiled and slated two- and three-storey housing, 1976, Robbie & Wellwood, wraps around **No 18**, not unharmoniously.

1, 2 & 3 Wellington Terrace, 19th century, continue the Quay Walls group, ashlar houses, Nos 1 & 2, pre-1816, No 3, 1852, (Wallace Green Manse, lying-paned above, single-paned below).

The single-storey, Scotch-slated **Old Guardhouse**, 18th century, faces north down Palace Street, its simple Tuscan portico of four columns and pediment relating this small building to its much bigger brother in Marygate. There indeed the Guardhouse originated, being rebuilt, altered, as a reading room, on its present site in 1815. Within are a pair of guardrooms either side of a vaulted, windowless prison chamber.

Palace Street contains several late 18th-century houses, richly detailed, including **25/27** dated *HB 1782*, and **14**, fine wooden doorpiece, pediment on consoles over fluted pilasters.

Youth & Community Centre,
5 Palace Street East, 1754
Three-storey, six-bay, Welsh-slated with a pilastered doorpiece and an attractive spiral volute as the side boundary wall joins the gate pier. The Town's Grammar School 1866-1939. Schoolroom added, 1847.

2-20 Ness Street, 18th century
Fine group of two-storey, stuccoed, pantiled

houses with sash windows and brick chimneys; **No 18** has a pedimented doorpiece and a timber cornice at its wallhead.

The west side of **Ravensdowne** is almost entirely elegant 18th-century houses, although a disagreeable housing development, not quite infill, proves a let-down at the junction with Woolmarket. **No 5** Ravensdowne, **Boys' National School**, 1725, rebuilt and enlarged, 1842, ashlar, with channelled ground floor.

Military Hospital, Ravensdowne, 1745-6 Entered by a pedimented gateway, sadly close-boarded, through a stone boundary wall. It is ashlar, two-storey with attic in a steeply pitched slated roof. Built by the Board of Ordnance, one of the earliest surviving of its type.

On the east side **Nos 2 & 4**, early 19th-century ashlar pair, two-storey and basement, subtly different doorcases with pilasters, set *in antis* with frieze and cornice, within shallow segmental arches with fanlights. **Nos 6 & 8**, late 18th-century, a former manse in ashlar, with quoins, Gothick fretted parapet with pineapple and acroterion in centre, convex-friezed and dentil-corniced doorcase. **No 30**, late 18th-century group of stone rubble two-storey pantiled cottages restored by Berwick-Upon-Tweed Preservation Trust, to the left an archway, to the right 18th-century ice-houses (presumably part of the Tweed's salmon-netting industry) under allotments (see colour p.112). **Nos 52-56**, late 18th century, dry-dashed, two-storeys, with rusticated pilasters, paterae in a frieze, crenellated parapet and Chippendale-type ornament, **Nos 54 & 56** have good fanlights in an ashlar asymmetrical front. **No 64, St Cuthbert's RC Presbytery**, 1829, ashlar two-storey, good fanlight, through pend to rear simple Gothick-windowed **RC Church**, 1829, Ignatius Bonomi, later polygonal apse.

Church Street links Holy Trinity Church (and Barracks) with the Town Hall and Quay. **Police & Magistrates Court**, 1899-1901, R Burns Dick, following a competition, is ebullient but thoughtful baroque-nouveau which contributes positively to the townscape with its highly modelled frontage. An earlier example is **58-60**, roughcast and pantiled, with Elizabethan guts, straddling the cobbled

Elevation, Police Station, 1899

Berwick-upon-Tweed Borough Council

common lane to Nos 58 A-I, a terraced group of two-storey town houses restored 1990, the lane closed by the two-storey pantiled 58J.

Old Vicarage, 61 Church Street, early 18th century
Stately brick with stone cornice and plain parapet, end pilaster strips, and a moulded stone doorcase with rosettes on the frieze. The **Masonic Hall**, Church Street, 1872, two-storey, gabled, bears carved emblems.

Holy Trinity Parish Church, Wallace Green, 1650-2
Mason John Young of Blackfriars in London, details similar to that city's church of St Katharine Cree 1628-31. Rare survivor from the Commonwealth period, low key, especially when trees in leaf, since towerless, allegedly at Cromwell's command. Five-bay round-arched arcade of round Tuscan columns. Jacobean west gallery and pulpit, chancel and clerestory added 1855, reredos early (1893) Lutyens. Good Flemish or Dutch stained glass, some of it 16th-century, inserted 1855 (see colour pp.101/2).

Holy Trinity Parish Church

Berwick-upon-Tweed Borough Museum and Art Gallery

Church of Scotland, Wallace Green, 1858-9, J, J M, & W H Hay
Imposing Decorated style of kirk – prominent 38m spire with angle spirelets and patterned slating – as expected from these prolific architects. Draws the eye a little too much for the townscape good of Holy Trinity Church. Opposite is **1-9** Wallace Green, a stuccoed brick and stone late Georgian terrace, pantiled and slated roofs with chimneys of old brick.

Berwick-upon-Tweed Borough Council

Borough Offices, Wallace Green, 1848-9,
Thomas Brown of Edinburgh
Jacobethan former borough court and gaol
complete with lively chimneyed skyline and
castellated bays.

*Front elevation, Borough Offices
(Prison and Court Houses)*

A terrace of houses adjacent to the Barracks,
2-10 Parade, early 19th century, painted, some
lined render, three good doorcases, two-storey,
slated or pantiled roofs. **Nos 12-18**, 19th
century, symmetrical E-plan in ashlar, the
forward portions gabled, all below slate roofs.
Nos 20-22, a symmetrical late Georgian pair in
ashlar with pantiled roofs.

The Barracks, 1717-21, Nicholas Hawksmoor
Reputedly the earliest in Britain (frequently
attributed to Sir John Vanbrugh), with
accommodation for 576 men, built at a time
when Jacobite Rising fears were matched by
more basic grumbling by burghers having
soldiers billeted upon them.
   An open quadrangle with separate stepped
gabled buildings on three sides, that to the
north being closed by a high stone wall and
gatehouse, the round-arched gateway carrying

*View of the Barracks and Parade
from the Walls above the Cow Port*

Berwick-upon-Tweed Borough Museum and Art Gallery

Berwick-upon-Tweed Borough Museum and Art Gallery

Barracks Courtyard

Every apartment *is to have a new floor and new windows. The windows in the upper storey are to be enlarged and made square instead of being semicircular at the top as before.*
Fuller, 1799

Scots customs*, words, habits, and usages [are copied here] even more than becomes them: nay, even the buildings in the towns and in the villages imitate the Scots almost all over Northumberland.*
Daniel Defoe

Daniel Defoe had been a spy, an *ingenious person*, working towards the Union in 1706 (and reporting on the Anti-Union riots). *Some of the wisest and most discerning men wish two or three regiments of horse or dragoons were sent but near the Borders, as silently as might be.* Despite his patriotic endeavours, he was objective in his assessment of the Union seven years on: *[The Union] has brought the English Court to be the centre of all the wealth and ready money of Scotland, which should otherwise have circulated in a home consumption to the encouragement of trade and the enriching of their own people.*

a low square tower and four coats of arms, those of George I containing *the four quarters for Scotland and England, for France, for Ireland and for Hanover*; the shop formed to the right still sporting its VR letterbox.

The **southern (clock) block** replaced the original magazine in 1739 and since 1985 holds the Town Museum and that part of Sir William Burrell's collection given to the town in affectionate recognition, no doubt, of time spent in the area while based at his Berwickshire seat of Hutton Castle (see p.55).

In the **eastern block**, cement refaced like its western twin, an English Heritage exhibition tells the story of the infantryman's way of life and death, and this block also contains the regimental museum and headquarters of the King's Own Scottish Borderers. *English Heritage; open to the public; guidebook available*

North of the Golden Square roundabout the **Brewer's Arms** boasts a welcoming curved-glass ground-floor frontage (see colour p.112). Across the street in Walkergate the former **Baptist Chapel**, 1810, has striking 12-pane sashed pointed openings at first floor over shopfront.

Norham House, 15 Walkergate, 1976, Robert Rhind
Sophisticated brick office building (DSS) neatly detailed, surviving well in contrast with the ageing blockwork of **William Low's supermarket**, 1979, James Parr & Partners, across Hatters Lane.

Gateway Supermarket, 1985, David Fox & Partners
Mostly red brick though artless *non-frontage* to

Berwick-upon-Tweed Borough Museum and Art Gallery

Berwick Castle was where Isabella, Countess of Buchan, was imprisoned for four years following her crowning of Robert Bruce. Bruce was crowned in 1306 at a time when the Earl of Fife, who traditionally placed the new king upon the Stone of Destiny, was in English hands. The brave Countess was the Earl's sister.

Left Berwick Castle. Below Berwick Castle and Edwardian walls

Strang

Castlegate, better south elevation, almost marshalled against the superior forces of the Elizabethan wall, the car park holding them a decent distance apart.

Berwick Castle

Survives only in fragments, its recorded origin dating from the 12th century, with a bloody history and a consequently energetic series of repairs and alterations. The medieval walls begun by Edward I surrounded the town, the castle occupying the north-west corner. From 1604 a large country house was begun on this site by the Earl of Dunbar, but contemporary with the building of Berwick Bridge the castle area was left in ruins, much stonework being robbed to construct Holy Trinity Church (see p.14).

Final despoliation in 1847 when the greater part of the remains were swept away in the construction of the railway station on the site. Sections remain, however, of the curtain wall and river steps, and isolated lengths of the medieval town wall, punctuated in Northumberland Avenue by the **Bell Tower** (whose circular base dates from the period of Edward I, the octagonal upper storeys being Elizabethan), make its line still traceable.

Strang

The War Memorial, Castlegate, is a stone pedestal bearing a bronze winged figure by Alexander Carrick, and memorial plaques.

War Memorial

Church of St Mary, Castlegate, 1858, J Howieson

Early English, nave, clock tower with spire, transepts, chancel, organ chamber and vestry.

Free Trade Inn, Castlegate
Unspoilt interior; fine woodwork, glasswork and
partitioning matched in appeal by local banter.

11 Railway Street, 1844, ashlar, two-storey,
wallhead enriched with poetic busts, Burns and
Shakespeare being recognisable. Its rear wing,
48 Tweed Street, is a riot of Victorian
ornament, by William Wilson of Tweedmouth,
acanthus cornice carrying busts and birds,
masks at all window lintels and keystones,
attic window with carved and scrolled
architraves, and chiselled stone walls.

Railway Station, Railway Street, 1924-7
Red sandstone, classical style, centre clock in
curved gable above, rusticated pilasters, single-
storey flanking wings, and pyramid roof.
Located upon the Edwardian castle, this
building reflects its site less well than the first
(1844-6) station's castellated appearance.

Above *Front elevation, Bell Tower
School, 1902.* Below *Bell Tower*

Bell Tower School, Bell Tower Place, 1903,
J Landell Nicholson & Fred E Dolchin
Competition-winning Infants' School in red
brick extended with a long south-facing range.
County Middle School, Lovaine Terrace,
1927, red-brick, pantiled-hipped roof, ensemble
of organic nature with latest extension, 1991,
Taylor Philip & Hunter, pantiled but finished
in perversely buff brickwork.

The **Bell Tower** (there were 19 towers in
Edward I's walls) is in a prominent position
from which it was possible to spot invading
forces – Scots by land, French or Scots by sea.
Perhaps fortunately today the roofless shell
does not allow access, for much of the view is
dominated by the immense caravan site
towards the sea.

Castle Hills

Strang

Castle Hills, Paxton Road, before 1824
Gothic revival, castellated two-and-a-half
storeys, balconied and verandahed in copper-
roofed Chinese-patterned iron, with
asymmetrical four-storey square towers (with
Gothic tracery) at either end. Fragment of
sculpture from Berwick Castle, built into drive
retaining wall.

Corporation Arms Inn, Kelso Road, 1831
Ashlar two-storey and basement, hipped slated
roof, built just off the riverbank. Elaborate
painted relief of town arms (a play on the
words bear and wych(elm)) dated and with the
name of the mayor over the front door.

On 19 June 1308 Edward II, prior
to invading Scotland, wrote to his
chamberlain in Scotland *Whereas, to
conserve our royal right and with the
help of God crush the rebellion of
Robert Bruce and his accomplices ...
We command you to provide for our
enterprise, without delay, 3000
salmon, in the regions of Scotland at
the outgoing from that country, to
have them barrelled, and cause them
to be kept safely and securely until
our arrival in the said regions ...*

*Tweed Bank £5 note, depicting
Berwick from south*

Berwick-upon-Tweed Borough Museum and Art Gallery

Old Toll House, Lamberton

Leaving Berwick and striking north across the Border on the A1 coast road one comes quickly upon **Lamberton** where, from 1798 to 1858, keepers of the Toll used to marry couples in the same fashion as at the more famous Gretna Green. The now-demolished **Toll-house** is marked by a plaque.

In 1705 Joseph Taylor and friend visited Scotland: leaving Berwick *about a mile distance we came to a small dike, which is the boundary between England and Scotland: Upon our first Entrance into Scotland we embrac'd one another with all the friendship imaginable: We were now got into a very desolate Country, and could see nothing about us but barren mountaines and black Northern Seas: we often cast our Eys back at dear England ... : we had a great deal of cause to leave our Country with regret, upon account of the discouragements we receiv'd from every body, even upon the borders of Scotland, and by what I could gather from the discourse of all persons I convers'd with, I concluded I was going into the most barb'rous Country in the World.*

Lamberton Church
Where Margaret Tudor met the representatives of James IV (and traditionally is said to have married him here by proxy), thus leading to the eventual succession of James VI to the English throne. Only ruins of nave and chancel remain as the burial-place of the Rentons of Lamberton.

Mordington House, demolished 1973
Georgian mansion, centre block two-storey-and-basement, seven-bay front, pedimented doorway, hipped roof. Flanking wings originally two-storey Palladian pavilions and single-storey links, made monolithic and ponderous in late-Victorian times. The **Mordington burial vault**, dated 1662, with its rustic relief panel of the Crucifixion, stood originally against the east gable of the 1757 kirk which went out of use in 1869.

Mordington House

Edrington House, 18th century, recast 19th century
L-plan two-storey with basement, pedimented doorway, plain gables and skews, Victorian south bay battlemented.

Burnmouth

The ideal fishing village, with old white cottages hanging on the corners of cliffs, and a long, one-sided street of one-storey houses facing the sea (1930s description) is in two parts, the upper cluster close to both A1 and east coast main line. The real interest, though, is down the perilous ravine road to the old **Harbour**, improved 1879 (breakwater, pier extension, lighthouse), most recently inner basin constructed 1959. To the north Partanhall (a partan is Scots for a crab) is a string of cottages apparently left at the foot of the precipitous cliff by the same receding tide which has also deposited the rugged Annie's Rock. Fishermen's stores and 1950s houses are also notable with their metal balconies and giant order pilasters.

Above *Three-storey terrace, Burnmouth*. Left *Burnmouth Harbour and Partanhall*

Ayton Castle, 1851, James Gillespie Graham For William Mitchell Innes, Governor of the Bank of Scotland. Scots Baronial fantastic exercise (not unrelated to Graham's work on Brodick Castle, 1844) in red sandstone, previous castle burnt 1834. Drawing room extension and billiard room, 1860, David Bryce; further additions, 1864-7, James Maitland Wardrop. Extensive interior redecoration, 1875, by Bonnar & Carfrae, still

Margaret Tudor, 1489-1541, was the eldest daughter of Henry VII, and married James IV in 1503. Their child became James V just shortly after his first birthday, his father having died at Flodden. Queen Margaret found solace only temporarily in her marriage (1514) to Archibald Douglas, Earl of Angus, Duke of Albany, whom she divorced, and finally married Henry Stewart, Lord Methven, in 1527.

James Gillespie was born in Dunblane in 1776, and spent his earlier life as builder. But he was *ambitious, pushing, and none too scrupulous* and developed a large portfolio of work which included the laying-out of the Moray Estate in the Edinburgh New Town. No doubt his career was not hindered by his marrying an heiress (and adopting her surname) in 1815.

Left *Ayton Castle*. Below *Ayton Castle Tower*

Ayton Castle
The present Dining Room fireplace
was introduced in 1873 after Mark
Twain, on a Scottish tour, acquired
its predecessor, which is now in the
Mark Twain Museum, Hartford,
Connecticut, USA.

Before the 18th century, when
turnips and swedes were grown to
overwinter cattle and sheep and thus
fresh meat had a year-round
availability, pigeons (especially the
young, called squabs or in Scotland
peesers) were farmed via doocots.
Located in open positions (trees give
cover for winged predators) the birds
were largely self-reliant. Their
interest in food sources was
indiscriminate of ownership, however,
and in 1697 an Act restricted the
construction of doocots to those with
land in the neighbourhood.

Right West Lodge, Ayton Castle.
Below St Dionysius' Church.
Bottom 49 Main Street, Ayton Village

largely extant, with stencilled imitation silk
damask. The dangers and dilemmas of
architectural criticism, particularly by the
misinformed, are well illustrated by the
following comment on Ayton Castle's
exceptional architecture: *There may come a
time when, as with so many other Victoriana, it
will appeal to future ages; at present it is for us
but a curiosity* (Imperial Gazetteer). *Open to
the public*

In addition to the elaborate offices and stables
block, all in red sandstone, Ayton Castle boasts
a **doocot**, 1745, circular three-tiered beehive
type, and **West Lodge**, glorious red sandstone
Scots Baronial, archway and screen walls, seen
at their best in the rays of the evening sun.

Ayton Church, 1864-6,
James Maitland Wardrop
No doubt produced by Ayton Castle patronage.
First Pointed with 36m spire, stained glass by
Ballantine & Sons. Concealed from the
roadway, in the burial ground, **St Dionysius'
Church**, early 12th century, extensively
altered and rebuilt; now ivy-clad ruins.

Ayton (*Eyetown* after the river), c.1100, was
two settlements, Superior and Inferior. Now
virtually one wide street at the former crossing
of the A1 and the Duns/Eyemouth road. Few
buildings of outstanding interest, but many
attractive nevertheless, e.g. **St Andrew's
Square**, **Red Lion Hotel**, **43** and **49 Main
Street**, and **Hillside**.

Peelwalls, early 19th century
Classical mansion, two-storey (ground floor
rusticated) five-bay front, Doric pilastered
doorway, hipped slated roof.

Linthill

Linthill, early 17th century, L-plan, harled crowstepped, gabled three-and-a-half storey house.

Linthill was the site of a gruesome murder in 1751 of wealthy widow, Mrs Hume of Billy, by her butler, Norman Ross. Catching him in the act of theft, and despite having her throat cut, she rang an alarm bell, and the killer, trying to escape his fellow servants by leaping from a first-floor window, broke his leg, was captured and hanged. As if Mrs Hume had not suffered enough, her funeral cortège was en route for her last resting-place at Bunkle Kirk when it was realised that the coffin had been left behind.

Prenderguest, early 19th century Classical farmhouse, centre Palladian first-floor window over sophisticated round-headed door recess with decorative fanlight, in contrast window-panes square.

Down the Eye Valley stands **Netherbyres Mill**, originally a tweed mill, later meal, now ruinous following the 1948 floods, a surprisingly extensive pantiled range in the valley below the A1: two or three floors at one end, two cast-iron overshot wheels, wooden hoppers and machinery, roofless kiln.

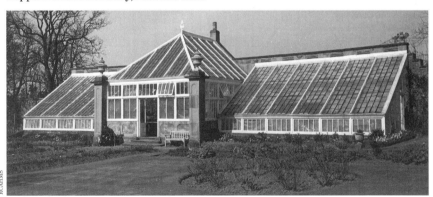

Netherbyres, c.1834-5, George Angus for Captain Sir Samuel Brown Unprepossessing mansion, with great rolling Victorian bargeboards, enlarged in the 1860s and 1930s. Now home for retired gardeners. Brown was **the** engineer of his time, and built a bridge over the Eye Water, now sadly lost. Notable elliptical **walled garden**, c.1730, laid out by William Craw, mathematician and horticulturalist.

Greenhouse in walled garden, Netherbyres

Berwick-upon-Tweed Borough Museum and Art Gallery

Eyemouth Harbour

We had here *[in Eyemouth] plenty of claret, and very cheap; but the cookery was so nasty, as also the women, and the town so stinking, the houses and inhabitants so miserable, that it was with sorrow I beheld them.*
Journal of an English Medical Officer in the Duke of Cumberland's Army, 1825

In the 1980s, archaeological investigations into a fishy midden gave extraordinary insights into the environs and habits of the medieval inhabitants of the town. Pollen analysis could give clues to the landscape, and studies of bones explained patterns of fishing, since the *season of the catch* as well as the number and type of fish could be determined scientifically.

Gunsgreen House doocot

Strang

EYEMOUTH

Fishing town and tourist centre which was once the principal port for the produce of Coldingham Priory lands and the fertile Berwickshire Merse. Free burgh of barony, 1597. Fragments of the medieval burgh can still be detected in buildings and spaces on the flat strip between the High Street and the sea, and on the headland signs of early fortifications are visible to the tutored eye. The beach was the first haven for fishermen before construction of the harbour proper. Expansion in Victorian times notably of the herring fishing saw the village become a town, a wave of Welsh slate roofs breaking over the harbour's hinterland, and the railway (now alas departed) serving the town along the valley of the River Eye. *Town Trail*

Eyemouth Harbour, Old Pier, 1747
First formally laid out by William Craw (presumably he of Netherbyres), and then substantially constructed 1768 by John Smeaton. The New Quay, 1843, canalised the Eye Water to the east, and provides convenient harbour berths on its west. Harbour extension, 1885-7, T Meek & Sons CE of Edinburgh.

Down this valley is one of the best views in the Borders, that to **Gunsgreen House**, *c*.1755, James Adam. Three-storey and basement five-bay Palladian villa with piended, platformed, slated roof about twin massive chimney stacks. Contained by (later?) curved, battlemented rubble retaining wall, pyramid buttresses alternating with blind oculi. Its **doocot**, 18th-century Gothick, battlemented rubble with blind crosslets and projecting stone cannon barrels, now a hard-done-to store which would amply repay restoration in view of its group

RCAHMS

Tales of smuggling were rife, although there is precious little evidence remaining. *The whole town still has a dark, cunning look; is full of curious alleys, blind and otherwise ; and there is not a single individual house of any standing, but what seems as if it could unfold its tales of wonder.*
Robert Chambers, *Picture of Scotland*

Left *Gunsgreen House from north-west.* Below *Old windmill, Gunsgreenhill*

RCAHMS

with the House, as would the **gates & gatepiers**, c.1753, the latter rusticated with cornices and pyramid copes. Beyond, on the skyline at Gunsgreenhill is the **old windmill**, of which only a circular stump in random rubble remains, the openings bricked up below a pantiled roof.

Marine Parade formerly an important frontage of narrow gables giving an insight into the traditional layout of plots end on to the sea. Now local authority housing, 1991, Bain Swan Architects, with similar scale if not consistent plan-form or materials.

Individual harbour frontage buildings are not outstanding until the **Fishermen's Mission** (the Hippodrome), Harbour Road, c.1833, four-storey, eight-bay former warehouse, erected as spacious granaries now Mission following sympathetic conversion, 1988, Bain Swan Architects.

Ship Hotel, Harbour Road, c.1730 Multi-gabled painted frontage to the Quay, great curvilinear skews and scrolled skewputts, probably pantiled but now slated roof.

Almost by definition, flooding is a hazard of most water-powered mills. The 1948 floods brought to an end a number of mills which were, at that time, just clinging on to their function.

Fishermen's Mission (Hippodrome)

Strang

Meek's and Dickson's Yards, Harbour Road, 19th-century frontage extensively rebuilt, 1987, BRC Dept of Property Services, as part of fishermen's stores and engineering workshops, neatly shoehorning redevelopment behind the frontage. The stores and net-mending area has a religious atmosphere and the courtyard form conceals the worst of the metal flotsam and jetsam. BRC Architectural Award, 1988; Civic Trust Commendation, 1989.

Brown's Bank, part of the Eyemouth Boatbuilding Co, mid-19th-century two-storey, three-house terraced block, rendered and lined as ashlar, stone dressings, brick end stacks and slated roof. **Eyemouth Boatbuilding Co & Marine Radio**, Harbour Road, later 18th-century two-storey three-house block, pedimented doors, pantiled roof with slate verge courses. **No 49** Harbour Road, late 18th-century three-storey, three-bay richly detailed Georgian house of considerable character tucked away below the main road.

Old Churchyard, between High Street and Albert Road, has been largely cleared of tombstones, many re-erected against churchyard walls. The sloping site was raised 2m in 1849 to enfold victims of the cholera epidemic. In centre, memorial to the **Great Disaster** of 1881 when 191 fishermen (129 from Eyemouth alone) lost their lives off Eyemouth in freak storm. **Watch-house**, also 1849, built from ancient gravestones, many richly carved and atmospherically weathered.

Top *Meek's and Dickson's Yards.*
Middle *Brown's Bank.* Above
Eyemouth Boatbuilding Co.
Right *49 Harbour Road*

The Great Disaster occurred in circumstances where there had been bad weather for some days, and the east coast men were keen to fish. They were caught by an immense storm which blew up with great speed, a number of Eyemouth boats being wrecked and their crews drowned within sight of land and their loved ones waiting in vain on the shore.

St Ella's Place (formerly General's Wynd), a delightfully formal little square dominated by the gable (**No 12**) to the north.

4 & 6 Market Place, 1735
Dated on marriage lintel, two-storey three-bay house with shop opening to the right, rendered and painted.

Top *St Ella's Place*. Left *Auld Kirk from west*

The Auld Kirk, 1811, Alexander Gilkie
Handsome stone tower a decorative addition to the Eyemouth skyline, the Kirk has been passed to the east by Manse Road, a product of the 1960s road obsession which removed actively or passively a considerable amount of Eyemouth's burgh architecture. Alterations in 1836 to steeple and west front by *Mr Elliot* (Walter Elliot of Kelso?), enlarged 1902, and in 1980 sensitively yet firmly converted by Borders Regional Council to **museum** (principally local history and fishing) and **tourist information centre**.

Below *Waddell's, Fish Merchants, Mason's Wynd*. Bottom *Saltgreens Old Folk's Home*

Waddell's, Fish Merchants, Mason's Wynd, 19th century
Fish-smoking house with wooden ridge ventilator, the wynd slipping furtively past to Chapel Street.

Saltgreens Old Folk's Home, 1989, Borders Regional Council Architects
Pantiles, red guano-streaked brickwork, and high-tech glazed core. Very high quality *helicopter architecture* uneasy in Eyemouth's historic street plan. In **George Street** the old street pattern was replaced by **Swan Court** housing, 1984, for the Royal British Legion Housing Association, while a similar, smaller, blockwork project of **District Council Housing**, Chapel Street, 1987, Bain Swan

27

Above *Burgh Chambers*.
Right *Chester House*

Architects, on an island site, at least
maintained the building line.

Burgh Chambers, 1880,
probably David Rhind
Two-and-a-half baronial storeys of former
Commercial Bank of Scotland, carrying at its
central gable head a fishing boat, *Supreme*, in
relief, and fish-scale slating in places too.

Chester House, Church Street, *c*.1760
Two-storey, five-bay elegant house with former
pavilions sitting modestly behind its rubble
screen wall. Further south the street frontage,
a stone boundary wall, has been pierced by a
pack-horse arch.

The pack-horse arch is a most
unusual feature: despite now being
filled in, its form is still visible,
being a chunky T-shape, with the
head of the T being framed by a flat
or depressed arch. A horse with
panniers could therefore walk
straight through, while (presumably)
only one man at a time could enter
or leave, a not insignificant factor in
unsettled times when valuable
cargoes were housed and
transported from here.

Above this, at *Holy Corner*, stands the
Eyemouth Parish (built as Free) **Church**,
Victoria Road, 1878, stugged ashlar English
Decorated Gothic, five-bay church with tower
and octagonal spire.

St John's House, 12-16 Albert Road, *c*.1825
Large classical three-storey three-bay villa set
into a sloping site, the centre bay to the river a
segmental bow. Subtly proportioned, with
slender sidelights on the bow windows.

Health Centre, 1986, Robbie & Wellwood
Nautical undertones but uncomfortably
beached on its restricted site.

Armitage Street is an attractively huddled
later 19th-century pair of terraces stepping up

the hill from the High Street via a pend at the top to Albert Road.

Reston is a long straggle of a village where the railway line branched to Duns. **Mid Town House**, *c.*1810, modest two-storey, three-bay house in rubble with ashlar quoins, round-headed doorway with fanlight, and attractively emphatic raised wallhead framing the front gate. **Berryhaughs**, dated 1706, T-plan, crowstep-gabled farmhouse at the head with a tail of rubble-pantiled farm buildings.

Stoneshiel, near Reston

Stoneshiel, *c.*1840
Two-storey, three-bay and two-bay asymmetrical ashlar house with hood-mouldings and battlemented skyline.

Sunnyside (Auchencrow)
A thriving settlement until the 18th century, despite (or because of) its reputation as a centre for witches, the *Edincraw* of Border ballads. **Sunnyside Farm**, late 18th century, harled, three-storey, three-bay T-plan with a pilastered doorway, slated roof and skews.

Houndwood House, dated 1656 on an inscribed tablet brought from Fulfordlees, oblong with vaulted basement, refronted and altered 19th and 20th centuries with baronial crowsteps. **Houndwood Church**, 1836, severely square kirk body with belfry and additions of 1903. **Press Castle**, early 19th-century battlemented house with Gothick

In the summer of 1649 some 350 commissions against witches, mainly in East Lothian and Berwickshire, were issued.

Scots agriculture before the improvements of the 18th century was notably inefficient, at least according to John Major. The Scots scholar and historian, *c.*1470-1550, recognised that this was not down to mere primitive technique (although ploughing with a great wooden plough behind eight oxen cannot have been easy or perhaps frequent) but rather more because of the system of three- or five-year leases, or *tacks*. Writing in his *History of Greater Britain* he observed: *If the landlords would let their lands in perpetuity, they might have double or treble of the profit that now comes to them – and for this reason: the country folk would then cultivate their land better beyond all comparison, would grow richer, and would build fair dwellings.*

Press Castle, 1897

St Ebba was a daughter of the (Christian) King of Northumberland, who escaped by boat from pagan Mercians, and reached shore at St Abbs. Apparently founding *the religious home of Coldingham, next ... when the cruel Danes came on shore, the religious lady, who was wondrous beautiful too, it seems, cut off her nose and upper lip, and made all her nuns do the same, to preserve by that means, their chastity. But the barbarous Danes, enrag'd at them for their zeal, fir'd their nunnery and burnt them all alive ...*
Defoe, 1723

Latterly, from 1535, **the King of Scots** was able to nominate to the Pope the heads of religious establishments James V provided for five of his (infant) illegitimate sons thus: the Abbeys of Kelso and Melrose, the Priories of St Andrews and Pittenweem, the Abbey of Holyrood, the Charterhouse at Perth, and the Priory of Coldingham. Although the Pope was no doubt keeping in with King James (he had just fallen out with Henry VIII, remember) such practice was unlikely to benefit the Church, which, of course, broke from Rome in 1560.

In 1616, in anticipation of James VI's visit to Scotland the Privy Council *ordered that part of the way in the Parish of Coldingham should be enlarged and mended by the people of Coldingham and Oldcambus, and later on decreed that horses and carts from every Berwickshire parish should be made available for the royal progress. But ... the work was still not begun a month before the King was expected, and threats of being held to be rebels had to be made against the people to hurry them up.*
Gordon

The Statistical Account for Coldingham suggests that landowners sought improved roads because only by such canalisation of travellers would damage to their **enclosures** be avoided.

Coldingham Priory

features, to the rear a range of offices and rectangular two-storey **doocot**, battlemented and ornamented, bearing date of 1607.

COLDINGHAM

Set just south of the bleak Coldingham Moor in a little valley back from the sea, the old village is no more than three or four streets around the market cross, a classical column surmounted by a square stone block bearing the Home crest. The **Manse**, 1801, repaired 1828 and later enlarged, is a two-storey, four-bay house, harled with stone margins and slate roof. **Thorburn**'s is 17th/18th century, two-storey harled, pantiled roof and crowstepped gables, with picturesque one-storey outbuildings; **Sunnybank**, an 18th-century two-storey slated house with pantiled outbuildings to rear, coach-house to left; and **Abbey Cottage**, richly decorated two-storey house with voluptuous porch, twin bays, and mannerist quoin details. Other buildings of note in the irregular village include the pantiled **Sunnyside**, **Glencourt Cottage** (formerly a Dame's School), **Burnside Cottage**, and **post office** with its rolled skews.

Coldingham Priory, 12th century
A pale shadow of its pre-eminence, set off to
the south, its physical presence diluted by the
architectural salvage of centuries with the
result that *there is not a house in the village
that has na a kirk stane in't*. Chambers reports
that the double monastery (monks and nuns)
here founded by St Ebba, *c*.661, was the first in
Scotland, and with a chequered career, for on
one occasion the *disorderly lives of its tenants*
brought destruction by fire from heaven.
Refounded 1098 by King Edgar. Sacked in 1216
by King John, burnt in 1544 by the English,
most of the remains demolished 1648 by
Cromwell; reconstruction, 1661, of choir *by the
sight of John Milne master mason or other they
shall bring to visite the same after finishing
thereof*, west and south walls partially rebuilt,
1835-58, to form **Parish Church**, William J
Gray (Gray & Paterson). Heraldic stained
glass, 1904, Robert Home.

ST ABBS
Picturesque fishing village, its harbour offering
welcome relief on a section of coast with
spectacular cliffs, birdlife, and smuggling
stories. The **Harbour**, 1833 and later, can still
be lively, particularly with divers of the human
variety. Note the pantiled **fishermen's huts**
along Sea View Terrace. **St Abbs Head
Lighthouse**, 1862, David & Thomas
Stevenson, stands on its headland above
smugglers' caves.

Fast Castle
Levelled 1515, rebuilt 1521, its remote ruins,
set on a precipitous promontory, approached by
drawbridge over a 6m wide chasm, correspond

It was pure fluke that the
Stevensons became the premier
lighthouse designers and engineers:
Robert Stevenson (1772-1850) as a
child lost his father, and was 14
when his mother remarried, to
Thomas Smith, first engineer of the
Lighthouse Board. Robert went into the
business, and in 47 years built or
planned 23 Scottish lighthouses.
David and Thomas were Robert's
engineer sons, and in turn Thomas's
son was R L Stevenson, a more
literary light.

Below *St Abbs Lighthouse*.
Bottom *Fast Castle*

RCAHMS

RCAHMS

The Gowrie Conspiracy was an alleged attempt to murder or kidnap King James VI in 1600.

almost exactly to a 1549 plan. Recognisable in Sir Walter Scott's *The Bride of Lammermuir* as the model for the keep of Wolf's Crag, *the solitary and naked tower, situated on a projecting cliff that beetled on the German Ocean. ... A wilder or more disconsolate dwelling it was perhaps difficult to conceive.* Formerly occupied by Logan of Restalrig, a Gowrie Conspirator, Fast was apparently intended to be the place of captivity of King James VI.

Right *Renton House.*
Below *Pavilion, Renton House.*
Bottom *Co'path Church*

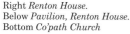

Renton House, very early Georgian (perhaps 1715, the date of the sundial) Plain classical three-storey mansion in whinstone with dressed sandstone margins, steeply pitched roof, and later two-storey, pedimented, stepped portico. The vertical division of the elevations, with very shallow pilasters in the entrance front and flush rustication on the garden front, is most unusual and unparalleled. Best feature is charming walled late-Stewart type forecourt complete with flanking symmetrical single-storey four-bay, bellcast-roofed pavilions.

COCKBURNSPATH (*Co'path*)
Ancient village originally formed about its market square, the medieval cross (repaired 1908) still surviving with thistle and rose motifs, its shaft standing on a three-tiered irregularly stepped base. Picturesque pantiled single-storey outbuildings line the east side of the kirkyard, and indeed pantiled vernacular buildings characterise the rest of the old village.

Parish Church, 16th century or earlier, extensively restored 19th century, a narrow rectangular building with angle buttresses (a sundial terminating that to the south-west) and a round truncated tower in the centre of the west gable; to the east abuts a small burial vault.

Old Manor House (Sparrow Castle), 16th century, two old houses at right angles, the one with moulded window openings, the other a vaulted basement and outside stair.

The narrowing of the coastal strip, and its crossing by steep deans (ravines) made the manoeuvring of armies difficult and time-consuming. The deans also led to a family of bridges, **Tower Bridge**, **Dunglass Bridge**, c.1930, reinforced concrete bridge carrying the A1, **Old Tower Bridge**, 18th-century, stone, single-arch bridge and **Pease Bridge**, 1786, David Henderson mason/architect, four tall brick arches, nearly 39m (130ft) high over the Pease Dean, the highest bridge in the world at the time of construction.

South-east of the village is **Cockburnspath Tower**, 15th century, ruined 10 x 8m tower-house with later outbuildings in courtyard entered by arched gateway.

St Helen's Kirk is a 12th-century Norman ruin, 1.5km east of Co'path, on the coast, its west gable rebuilt c.1400. Within the kirkyard are some hog-backed monuments.

Cove Harbour
Entered by a 55m tunnel from the cliff-path. A landing-place in the 17th century if not earlier, the harbour form remains that of 1831, by which time at least two earlier ones had succumbed to the elements. Cove was one of the great romantic experiences until the headland was removed (see colour p.60). The fishermen's cottages are built off the rock, from the sea at low tide atop a boiling rock formation. Caves in the cliffs hold tales of smuggling but may also

Co'path Tower

In **1762** the construction of Smeaton's Coldstream Bridge was justified on military grounds because *the hill called the Pees* (the Pease Dean) was pretty well impassable for artillery.

The *Glasgow Boys* flourished in the 1880s/90s as a reaction against the (Edinburgh-dominated) art establishment, numbering James Guthrie, Joseph Crawhall, E A Walton, amongst them. Initial realism of style and subject developed into the more vigorously decorative work of such as George Henry and E A Hornel. As many rebels before him, Guthrie conformed eventually, being elected President of the Royal Scottish Academy in 1902, and knighted.

Left *Cottages, Cove.* Below *Cove Harbour*

Above *Abbey St Bathan's Church.*
Right *Edin's Hall Broch.* Below
Detail, Edin's Hall Broch

reflect the existence of coal seams. At the top of
the harbour track is the fishing hamlet which
accommodated a *Glasgow Boys* artists' colony in
the later 19th century.

Abbey St Bathans

Site of a 13th-century small Cistercian priory
dedicated to St Columba's successor. Post-1560
the Priory Church became the **Parish
Church,** and today its basic rectangular shape
has had a stubby tower with broach spire and
square porch added in the late 19th century.
The Church (just opposite the Southern Upland
Way Rest House) contains a recumbent effigy of
one of the prioresses.

Edin's Hall Broch, 2nd century

Type of building more commonly associated
with the north of Scotland, 22m internal
diameter, with walls 5m thick, set in oval fort
130 x 70m overlooking the Whiteadder. Fort
(east half *overlain by open settlement of
stonewalled houses*) of about the time of Christ,
the Broch conceivably constructed between
Roman occupations. Traditionally a giant's lair.
Scheduled Ancient Monument. Objects retrieved
in the course of its excavation are held in the
National Museum of Scotland (see colour p.59).

A copper mine opened at Ordwell
on the Whiteadder, adjacent to the
flimsy footbridge to Edin's Hall, in
1828, but was soon abandoned.

The Retreat

Late 18th-century circular building (originally
symmetrical composition with one-storey wings
and screen walls), two-storey, harled, with
Gothick windows and conical slated roof topped
by central chimneystack. A hunting-seat of the
Earl of Wemyss *highly ornamental to the scene.*

Ellem Lodge, Ellemford, c.1800

Renovated cottage which may have originated
as circular lodge or tollhouse: **Inn Cottage,**
formerly an inn, incorporates its stables.

The Retreat

Old Shooting Lodge, Byrecleugh, was one of the Duke of Roxburghe's shooting boxes, *a curious old house adjacent to a farm hamlet.*

Cranshaws Castle
Smallish but elegant round-cornered five-storey tower-house, 12 x 8m in plan, 14m to the parapet, corbelled and gargoyled, occupied and in a good state of preservation.

Cranshaws Farm Gateway
Pedimented archway carrying inscription **A L L C A N L E A R N O N T H I S G A T E W A Y W H E N E D W A R D W A S C R O W N E D K I N G**, the work of Andrew Smith (later of Whitchester). See p.37 for the answer.

Cranshaws Castle

Cranshaws Parish Church, 1899, George Fortune
On site of earlier church of 1739, from whence was incorporated a mural tablet of arms of the Royal House of Stewart, installed apparently in an even earlier version as a pointed reminder by King James VI to the Revd Alexander Swinton who omitted, in the King's presence at a service, to pray for the Royal Family.

Cranshaws was supposed to have been haunted by a brownie which had the reputation of being helpful almost to an unreasonable degree. The brownie had its breaking point, though. Having for a number of years gathered and threshed the corn, unwisely a comment was passed that it had not been very neatly piled up at the end of the barn. The next day the grain was found in the Whiteadder at the foot of the Raven Craig, a precipice two miles away.

In 1832 *the stables of many gentlemen were in better repair than Cranshaws Kirk*, according to the minister. As at Ettrick, the shepherds brought their faithful companions to their Sunday observances, prompting a saying that *this is like Cranshaws Kirk – mair dogs than folk.*

Left *Cranshaws Parish Church.*
Below *Detail, Cranshaws Parish Church*

Whinstone, with red sandstone dressings, four-bay with apse, Westmorland slate roof, with delightful detailing – sundial on south-west corner held up by a grotesque (Time), apse decorated with corbels as masks, and a curved door to the laird's loft. The church is set within its walled enclosure, as is the adjoining manse, no doubt reflecting the shepherding which also went on outside the kirk.

Longformacus House, early 18th century, attributed to William Adam, but possibly by James Smith
Simple seven-bay rectangular house, rusticated

RCAHMS/L B Chappell

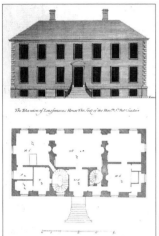

RCAHMS

Top *Longformacus House*. Above
Elevation and plan, Longformacus House

James Smith (*c*.1645-1731) was a mason by trade but had been to Italy: an educated man, his was an early Grand Tour before they became fashionable, and may have been initially prompted by religious rather than architectural preoccupations. To become a mason in the 17th century was not simple: in addition to the apprenticeship it was necessary to pass a design test or *essay*. Smith's essay in 1680 was to design *an hous of thre storie high, of one hundred foot of length and fifty foot wyde overalle, with ane skaile staire eighteen foot square. And the stone work to finish pavilion way with ballaysters together with one dorick yett of ane different skaile.* Records of St Mary's Chapel, Edinburgh, in H Carr *The Mason and the Burgh*

Foulden Village

quoins, pedimented be-urned central addition later 18th century, late Victorian north wing now demolished. U-shaped **stable range** on the site of an earlier house, and cylindrical red sandstone rubble harled **doocot** with ogee-curved roof of fish-scale slates.

Longformacus Parish Church, rebuilt 1730 On old foundations (part of the south wall may be medieval). Basic rectangular form and bellcote, repaired *c*.1830 and renovated 1892-3, west aisle 1894, fine stained glass especially the Landale memorial window, post-1943, depicting Poverty, Chastity and Obedience.

FOULDEN
One of the most striking village ensembles in the Borders, the picturesque range to the west, incorporating the former **school**, 1881, by John Lessels, who designed the rest of the terrace. Patterned rosemary tiles and other decorative detailing provide a richness more usually associated with Continental practice, and this work (probably piecemeal renovation of an existing cottage row rather than an architectural *tour-de-force*) was put in train by John Wilkie with other estate improvements.

RCAHMS

Foulden House

Foulden House, *c.*1800 (demolished)
Main block 1-3-1 bay three-and-a-half-storey, giant order pilasters rising from a rusticated ground floor, flanked by peristyled and porticoed two-storey pavilion wings.

Tithe or **Teind Barn**, Foulden
Origins obscured by major renovations 18th/19th century, rubble sandstone, two-storey and basement, external stair, crowstepped gables, slated roof. The barn stored produce collected by the church as teinds. *Historic Scotland property which can be open to the public, on application locally*

Teinds were a form of tax levied by the church on its parishioners, being one-tenth of all agricultural production. There are only two surviving tithe barns in Scotland, both post-Reformation (1560); the other is at Whitekirk in East Lothian.

Left *Foulden Tithe Barn.* Above *Cranshaws Tower and farm gateway*

Cranshaws farm gateway puzzle (p.35): Edward (I and VII) was crowned king in 1902 (give underlined letters their Roman value (W = VV) and add)

Foulden Church, 1786 (first recorded 13th century)
Graveyard with primarily 18th/19th-century stones the exception being that of Ramsay of Dalhousie, d.1592: *Hier lyeth ane honorabil man Georg Ramsay in Fulden Bastel who departit 4 Jan 1592 and of his age 74.* **Foulden Manse**, 1841, L-plan two-storey house, the upper openings with ornamental pediments; possible 18th-century core.

Chirnside
T-plan all but hilltop village, the Duns/Ayton road occupying its straggly head, the junction at Crosshill historic site of annual sackcloth sale.

Toll roads were enormously unpopular with the general public. *We have had more disturbance and riot in the county about establishing the toll-gates ... Seven gates that were erected have been pulled down and burned or thrown into the Tweed ... The whole town of Chirnside, man woman and child, I believe, were concerned in the riots. The sheriff went from Dunse last Sunday night with a party of dragoons, but they had scouts out everywhere to give them intelligence, and not one was taken.* Letter from Ninian Home of Paxton House, 13 July 1792, in Gordon

Chirnside Primary School

On a windy hillside, *set some way below a historic village, this school stands like a beacon which the (architectural) profession considered rather overdone for a tiny Borders hill-top cottage ... It looks as modern now as it must have done the day it was opened.*
McKean

The kirkyard was the site of a famous resurrection, when the second wife of the Revd Ebenezer Erskine was laid to rest with a valuable ring on her finger, and the sexton, having buried her shallowly, then tried to remove the ring with a knife. At this assault the corpse sat up, then rose to dash across the kirkyard to the manse door, which she implored the minister to open *for I'm fair clemmed wi' the cauld*. The fate of the sexton is not recorded.

Ninewells, birthplace of David Hume (1711-76), the philosopher, although his home was replaced by another house, 1839-41, William Burn, Scots Baronial, which itself was demolished in 1964.

Ninewells Doocot

Chirnside Primary School, 1937,
Reid & Forbes
Sits against the hill as an unexpected period piece, harled, whinstone dressings, in the modern Scots revival, focused upon the stair-tower, with great elegance of composition and detailing which is taken through to the entrance gateway.

Chirnside Church, from 12th century
The only 12th-century feature remaining is the chevron-patterned Norman doorway at west end of south wall. Sundial dated 1816 set on skewputt. Rebuilt 1878, extensively restored and altered 1907, A G Sidney Mitchell & Wilson, with fine gateway approach. **Ninewells Doocot,** 16th century, circular beehive type of rubble doocot in a garden adjacent to the kirk. Near the kirk also stood a tower-house (demolished 18th century) of the Earl of Dunbar.

Whitehall was a large mansion, of which only a two-storey range remains, complete with Palladian windows and rustic porch. In open fields stands the now ruinous **Whitehall Doocot,** an impressive rectangular-planned two-chamber doocot with stone skews defining its monopitched roof.

Chirnside Bridge Paper Mill (Dexter's), 1842 & 1857, David Cousin; additions 1897; reductions 1971-3
The Italianate administrative block was built

as a house for the owner of the mill: there was an earlier mill and house on the site, and the porter's lodge, now store, Gothick octagonal single-storey-and-basement, probably dates from this period.

Allanbank House, 1848, David Bryce; demolished 1969
One of three small manor house commissions executed by Burn and Bryce while they were partners in the 1840s. *Large mullioned windows, plain gables and high chimneys, contrasting strangely with the more vigorous Scottish Baronial work Bryce was beginning to develop.* Survived by **stable block** and Gothick bridge-shaped *eyecatcher* built into a nearby hill.

ALLANTON
Confluence of Whiteadder and Blackadder nearby and, as a consequence, the site of two bridges, one over each, dated 1851. Allanton is a picturesque village incorporating in its street a pair of splay-fronted **lodges** (defining the entrance to Blackadder House), the **Old Fire Station** (a stable opening complete with entablature, ornamental scrolls, and rainwater head dated 1815) and a cast-iron water-pump. Across the street a voluptuous cast-iron wall fountain. (See colour p.60.)

Blackadder House, 18th century, demolished *c*.1925
Symmetrical three-storey, seven-bay front including angle towers, possibly incorporating the remains of Blackadder Castle. Unexecuted plans, 1782, for alterations by James Playfair, superseded by Robert Adam proposals which gave the house its final profile. Remodelled and extended, *c*.1853, John Lessels, who rebuilt *with balustraded terraces and wallheads, a large asymmetrical wing, the addition of strapwork patterning suggesting a Transitional style.*

Blackadder Mount, 1785, Alexander Boswell
Court of farm buildings, the centre archway supporting a clock tower and urn-flanked spire, similar to those of Penicuik and Tarvit (see *Fife* in this series).

Bunkle Church, 1820 (date on bellcote)
Plain rectangular building with Romanesque Gothic features, probably later insertions, unlike the **Old Kirk**, late 11th century, a genuinely Norman, simple semicircular, semi-

Cast-iron wall fountain, Allanton

The *Scotch plough* was a large, clumsy, wooden wedge which required up to a dozen oxen to force it on its (crooked) route through heavy soils. **James Small** (*c*.1740-93) a native of Berwickshire, was apprenticed to a carpenter/ploughmaker, then made wagons and carriages in Doncaster. Setting up business at Blackadder Mount, he developed *Small's swing plough,* a light narrow plough ideal for the lighter improved soils.

Below *Blackadder House.* Bottom *Bunkle Church from the south*

Blanerne House

Buncle, Billy, and Blanerne,
Three castles strong as airn;
Built when Davy was a bairn;
They'll a' gang doon
Wi' Scotland's croon
And ilka ane shall be a cairn.

At **Edrom Church** *one named
MacGall was laid to rest in 1825,
only to become the victim of
'resurrectionists'. His body was
dressed in clothes and propped up in
a seated position between the two
grave-robbers on their horse-drawn
gig. Caught by a farmer and innkeeper returning from Gifford Fair,
the corpse and gig were taken to
Duns, the corpse for reburial, the gig
(when the townsfolk found out about
events) to be smashed up and burnt
by a mob despite a reading of the
Riot Act.*
Dane Love

domed stone-slab roofed apse left in the
churchyard, the remainder of the older
building demolished in 1820.

Blanerne House, 1895
Although William Burn prepared plans *c*.1830,
this house is late 19th century rebuilt after
fire. Gabled H-plan two-storey and basement.
Blanerne Castle, adjacent on a plateau above
the Whiteadder, now simply ruinous remains,
one wing of a tower-house with a shot hole
guarding the entrance doorway, and a two-
storey building with an oven at its south end.

PRESTON

Within this small village stands its **Market
Cross**, two stone steps, a square pedestal and
a square broken cross shaft. Just west of the
road to the Whiteadder Bridge, **Preston
Church** is rectangular, a medieval ruined nave
and chancel, with piscina, going out of use in
1718 when the parish united with Bunkle.

Preston Bridge, 1770, over the Whiteadder,
has three arches with round recesses in the
spandrels: **Nell Logan's Bridge**, with its **cell**
is a *cuddy gaol* set below a single-arch bridge.

Cumledge House, 1834
Classical, two-storey, three-bay, ashlar house
with splayed wings and centre porch.
Crowstep-gabled stable block to rear.
Cumledge Mill, *c*.1800 was originally a
blanket mill.

Edrom Church, 1732
Incorporates late 15th-century aisle said to
have been founded by Robert Blacader,
Archbishop of Glasgow, 1499. His coat of arms
is on the buttresses. T-plan kirk, major
alterations, 1886, including open timber
scissor-truss roof structure. Bellcote and

Edrom Church

patterned slate. In graveyard 12th-century Romanesque doorway (probably rebuilt) of **Old Kirk** is now burial-vault entrance, with chevron and fret-patterned semicircular arch set on capitals.

South elevation, Edrom House

Edrom House, early 18th-century Five-bay, two-and-a-half-storey-and-basement house of James Smith school, smaller than Renton, in ashlar with rusticated quoins, good baroque doorpiece, brick central stacks over bellcast roof. Remains of short canal garden feature on the axis of the house, as at Mavisbank. **Edrom Newton**, a late 18th-century courtyard farm, has a central double-storey block, single-storey wings, and Venetian-windowed gable-ends. **Edrom Newton Farm Buildings**, 1874, are a solidly symmetrical Dutch-gabled ball-finialed farm court, entered by central archway with doocot over.

Edrom Newton Farm Buildings

Manderston, 1903 (principally), John Kinross A Home estate, and with a designed landscape still largely as shown on General Roy's map of 1750, the present house originally from *c.*1790, built for Dalhousie Weatherstone. Victorian remodelling for Sir William Miller (spending some of the fortune he made trading with the Russians during the Crimean War).

General Roy's military survey, in many cases, provides the first (reasonably reliable) mapping of the Scottish landscape, and its topographical content was supplemented by the skills of its draughtsman, artist Thomas Sandby (1725-1809), *father of the watercolour school.*

41

Manderston
John Kinross had designed a boathouse, stables and home farm in the 1890s for Sir James Miller, and clearly had the confidence of his client. When asked how much Manderston's transformation budget should be he responded, *It doesn't really matter.* Sadly, Miller survived the works and completion celebrations, a ball in Nov. 1905, by only three months.

Reconstructed by Kinross for Sir William's son, James, (to remind Sir James' wife of her family house, Kedleston Hall) to the fastidious standards of this practice (also responsible for The Peel (see p.221)). Sumptuous interiors. See particularly the world's largest collection of Huntley & Palmer's biscuit tins, dating back to 1868. *Open to the public; guidebook available*

Country Life Ltd

Manderston Stables, 1895, John Kinross Classical courtyard range with pedimented arched entrance and splendidly preserved detail of pampered equines. **Buxley**, to the north, is a model group, *c.*1900, of estate buildings – with the dairy, interior religiously marble-faced, implausibly pretending to the status of a tower-house. **Manderston Kennels** a crowstep-gabled house, the **West Lodge** an earlier single-storey bay-fronted house built into the 20th-century neoclassical ensemble of ornamental iron gates and urn-topped piers.

Right *Manderston Dairy.*
Below *Doorway, Nisbet House*

RCAHMS

Nisbet House, 1630
Four-storey Scots Baronial house (combination of Z- and T-plans), harled and spattered with gunloops suggesting someone at least was not entirely persuaded by the unifying rule of the Stewart monarchy – the mouldings around and hooding over the main door are particularly fine

– with great tower addition, 1774, making no real concession to context: Venetian windows, Gibbsian corners and wonderful plasterwork. Earlier castle and moat (the first Nisbet was knighted in 1092 – by William II of England for protecting him from the Scots) cleared to make room for the present house (see colour p.58). 18th-century U-plan **stable range** and contemporary red brick **garden wall** to the east.

Above *Nisbet Hill Doocot with its unique, pentagonal plan, battlemented around a ribbed stone roof terminating in a ball finial.*
Left *Kimmerghame*

Kimmerghame House, 1851, David Bryce Scottish Baronial exemplar destroyed by fire, *c.*1947, partly rebuilt, partly now sunken garden. Gothick **water-tower. Court of offices**, 1790, Alexander Gilkie. **Lodge**, 1835, by George Smith.

Smith was an Aberdonian, sometime assistant of William Burn: in 1834 Smith had won the Highland Society's competition for the design of *Cottages for the Labouring Classes*

Wedderburn, 1771-5, Robert & James Adam Superintended by James Nisbet. Battlemented three-storey elevations Adam Castle Style, the apparent symmetry conceals a courtyard originally filled by the 17th-century castle, cleared out in the early 19th century, of which only a heraldic panel remains. Wedderburn contains several fine chimneypieces, the best being by Piranesi. **Wedderburn Stables**, 18th century, are a square court entered through a

Wedderburn was built for the sad Patrick Home of Billie (*see Paxton House*) who, having built one house for a girl he was unable to marry, built Wedderburn for his new bride only to catch her *in flagrante* with a Mr Moore in Rome on their combined honeymoon and Grand Tour.

Giovanni Battista Piranesi (1720-78) was a Venetian artist renowned for his architectural etchings. His studies of Roman architecture and archaeology were pivotal to the development of neoclassicism in the 18th century.

Principal front, Wedderburn

John Baxter II was the son of the builder of Mavisbank. He studied architecture in Italy from 1761-7 before returning home to run his architect-mason father's practice. Unfortunate, in as much as he was working in the Adams' heyday, he nevertheless managed to lay out Fochabers and design the Town House at Peterhead, under the patronage of the Duke of Gordon.

At the completion of Gillespie Graham's Castle work a *New Song* of *quite remarkable awfulness* was presented: verse one went thus:
Mr Hay's building Dunse Castle on Mr Gillespie's plan
But still there's a part of the old Castle to stand
Where it will relate its ancient name Where many good families of Hay's (sic) did remain
It is hoped that the unsuspecting workmen's banquet was well on in drink before the ode was unleashed.

Gillespie Graham's client, **William Hay**, was a spendthrift but improving owner, a fan of the Picturesque in architecture and landscape, who was said to have designed the Episcopal Church in Duns.

Right *Duns Castle.* Below *Duns Castle stables*

pedimented archway. Good gates, the northern **Lion Gate**, 1794, a classical archway with lion couchant, the **West Gate** another archway but defined by screen walls and gabled lodges.

DUNS
This small burgh acts as administrative capital of the shire, although Duns' case for even this legal, if not practical, significance has not gone unchallenged, with Greenlaw playing the role from 1696 to 1853. The original settlement, burgh of barony, 1490, probable birthplace of Duns Scotus (1265-1308), medieval philosopher and theologian, was around the Castle on southern Duns Law. The new town developed, *c.*1545 (following English destruction of Old Duns), around the medieval church, with Market Square and Cross at the foot of Castle Street, no doubt, once the need for defence diminished, to the benefit of the policy setting of the Castle.

Birthplace of Thomas Boston, 1676 (in 11-13 Newtown Street, rebuilt 1893), and of Joseph Paxton, designer of the Crystal Palace, in 1803. In modern times Duns' townscape has suffered badly through unselective demolition and the construction of an unnecessary inner relief road, further fragmenting the settlement.

Duns Castle, 1818-22, James Gillespie Graham
Building in a parkland setting upon earlier drawings of Richard Crichton who died in 1817, this be-gargoyled Gothick castle has at its core an L-plan peel tower of *c.*1320, built for Randolph Earl of Moray. Gothick interiors, too, with ecclesiastical and secular details in rich combination. **Stable Range** entered by Gothick arch with octagonal spire over, 1792-4, John Baxter II, linked by screen walls.

Excellent lodges: **North Lodge**, *c.*1820, with panelled piers, Gothick tracery and flat pointed arch, **Pavilion Lodge**, 1774-7 & 1791, John Baxter II, a tall Gothick archway with flanking castellated towers, and **South Lodge**, *c.*1820, even more picturesque, asymmetrical, its gateway defined by a round tower to the left and a smaller square turret to the right, with curved screen walls.

Above *South Lodge, Duns Castle.* Left and below *Market House*

Duns Scotus, having become a Franciscan friar, and been held in captivity by Edward I, studied and then taught divinity at Oxford. He defended so well the doctrine of Immaculate Conception at a theological dispute in Paris that someone who had not met him remarked at his eloquence, *This is either an angel from heaven, a devil from Hell, or John Duns Scotus.* The Subtle Doctor, as he came to be known, died in Cologne.

Market House, 1816, James Gillespie Graham; demolished 1966
A new structure that does equal credit to Mr Gillespie as Architect and to Mr Waddell of Gavinton as builder. The tower which surmounts the buildings is a fine object, and gives great additional beauty to the external aspect of the town. A spire rising from the tower presumably was never carried out.

Its demolition left a void, which the surrounding buildings are too well mannered to fill. Even the now returned **Market Cross** used to shun the largely 19th-century Market Square, standing relegated to the Park to the south, where also is the **Duns Scotus statue**, 1966, Frank Tritchler, in bronze.

Prominent buildings still standing in Market Square include the Italianate **Bank of Scotland**, 1857, Peddie & Kinnear, **No 43** Market Square (three-storey with Ionic doorway, originally the town house of the Cockburns of Langton), and the **Mechanics'**

Top *Teindhill Green*. Above *Christ Church, Teindhill Green*

J P Alison, a confident exponent of art nouveau but also a gifted architect who responded equally to site and surroundings, came originally from Dalkeith. He practised for most of his working life from Hawick. The present-day firm of Aitken & Turnbull is the successor of his practice Alison & Hobkirk.

Adam Dickson, minister at Duns, published *A Treatise on Agriculture* in 1762, and a companion volume in 1769, over 1000 pages. He argued in 1764 that *small farms are hindrance not only to improvements, but to the raising of the value of lands* – his preferred size was not less than 100 and no more than 200 acres.

Duns Parish Church and its graveyard have to be sought out, and reached through an opening between shops and offices. And when we arrive there we are, architecturally speaking, too late. For the minister of Duns, as late as 1874, insanely pulled down the original chancel of a Norman Church *to improve the churchyard*. The only vestige is a lintel stone from the Wedderburn aisle, inscribed *Death cannot sinder ... 1608*.
Lang, 1957

Institute, 1840. Just off the Square in Walter's Wynd an original bow window – the sole remaining in the Borders.

Castle Street has good terraced ranges – with much surviving detail including pilastered and pedimented doorways, and cobbling – to both sides. **No 18**, Old Court House, 18th century, now lawyer's office with flat over, two-and-a-half-storey, hipped slated roof with two attic gabled dormers. **No 62** is an excellent corner building, with its subtle but important pedimented projection, in coursed whinstone with hipped slated roof and dominant central brick stack at the junction with Teindhill Green. Further east stands Norman **Christ Church** Teindhill Green, 1854, its tower effulgent with machicolations.

Wellfield, early 19th century
Two-storey and basement house set in its own grounds featuring gabled Victorian wings with Palladian windows. Alterations and additions, 1895 & 1905, J P Alison.

The Clouds, Rosebank, 18th century
The restrained public front of this building, aptly named *The Clouds*, faces north, and its main front, with Venetian windows, pilastered and fanlit doorway, and external staircase, has a sunny aspect down the sloping garden.

28 Newtown Street, possibly 17th century and later refronted, its steeply pitched slated roof showing evidence of crowstepping and original thatching. Reputedly the oldest house in the Burgh. **No 43** is dated 1843 as the Boston Free Church School, an ornamental gabled façade, complete with decorative panels and shell heads (perhaps indicative of the pearls of wisdom to be found within) to doorways.

Duns Parish Church, 1790 steeple, the rest rebuilt 1881, after fire in 1879
A chancel which had survived from medieval times, latterly as a burial vault in the churchyard, had been demolished in 1874.

In **Station Road** there are a number of fine 19th-century villas, most standing back from the road. **Blythe Bank**'s features include entrance flight, classical doorway with fanlight, rusticated quoins and centre pediment, while **Southfield**, one-time offices of the County

Council, has a later formality, coupled central
window above the coupled columned porch
flanked by Victorian bay windows. Rightly does
Groome describe Duns as having *pretty
suburbs, studded with tasteful villas*.

West from the Burgh, by the roadside, is
Scotston, 18th century, a single-storey, long,
humble building which exudes agricultural
history from its slated and pantiled roof and its
fine rolled skew gables.

Gavinton Church

Gavinton, laid out 1760
Mr Gavin, *parvenu lord of the manor*, relocated
the ancient hamlet, presumably too close to his
house of Langton, when the policies were being
remodelled. Several 18th- and 19th-century
buildings have not yet been despoiled by
improvement.

Gavinton Church, 1872,
James Maitland Wardrop
Langton church set above the village, with
square tower and spire. The earlier **St
Cuthbert's Church** is vestigial, to the north-
west on the pre-clearance site, although its
walled graveyard remains with monuments
and vault.

Langton House

Langton House, 1862, David Bryce;
demolished *c*.1950
Elizabethan strapped mansion for the Marquis
of Breadalbane complete with picture gallery,
one of Bryce's most costly designs
(spectacularly detailed, built entirely of ashlar
masonry, and the only Bryce house in this style
– think what he could have come up with after
a little more practice) of which only the once-

Polwarth Church

*At **Polwarth** on the Green*
If you'll meet me the morn,
Where lasses do convene
To dance around the thorn,
A kindly welcome you shall meet
Frae ane that likes to view
A lover and a lad complete,
The lad and lover you
Allan Ramsay, *Polwarth on the Green*

Marchmont House

noble **gateway**, 1877, with its heavily rusticated piers and curved screen walls, remains, itself sadly in need of attention.

POLWARTH

Once an extensive settlement (*rather a field powdered with cottages than a village* – Chambers, *Picture of Scotland*) boasting no less than 14 cobblers. **Polwarth Thorn**, central on the Green, is not one but two, the elder and younger, thus ensuring the continuation of the ritual marriage dance around the trees, no doubt with fertility in mind. A handful of ruinous cottages survives around the Green, one retaining a stitched wheat straw-thatched piended roof covered by later corrugated iron.

Polwarth Kirk, 1703

Built over the burial vault, fine tower, harled and painted, but otherwise not dissimilar to Greenlaw Kirk. Internally renovated in 1928 (see colour p.60). Elegantly proportioned former **Polwarth Manse**, early 19th century, Doric-pilastered doorway.

Polwarth houses were *all old-fashioned, having stupendous chimnies of catton clay, and each provided with a respectable knocking-stone (a mortar and pestle?) at the cheek of the door, with which the barley used by the family was wont ... to be cleansed every morning as required.*
Robert Chambers, *Picture of Scotland*

At Polwarth Kirk Sir Patrick Hume hid in his ancestral burial vault from the wrath of the King, succoured by his 12-year-old daughter Grizel's clandestine sorties with food and drink from Redbraes Castle. Sir Patrick escaped to Holland, returning with King William to become 1st Earl of Marchmont.

Marchmont House, 1750-4, Thomas Gibson, attributed William Adam
Conceivably Gibson could have been only draughtsman and clerk of works, for this Palladian house owes much to Houghton Hall in internal planning and elevations, and it is known that the 2nd Earl subscribed to *Vitruvius Britannicus*, in which Houghton appeared, in 1725. Alterations, 1834, William Burn, and 1913-20, Sir Robert Lorimer, who added top storey and removed external entrance stair, creating an uncomfortably robust external proportion, indeed a monumentality which the original did not possess. Internally though, the house is of seamless quality from eighteenth century to twentieth. High point of the former is the

salon, with its Chinese Chippendale mirror-framed portrait (by William Aikman of the 1st Earl as a Chinese sage) and contemporary plasterwork. The latter boasts all the richness of detail of the best craftsmen in Scotland within the new carved-panelled Music Room formed as the west pavilion, and on the new main internal stair.

Criticism of the fact that Marchmont was being built with a rubble facing (and a brickworks was established west by the Fangrist Burn for the core) did not daunt the 3rd Earl, who rejoined that he intended to live on the inside, not the outside, of the edifice. In a letter to his wife he hoped *beside the lodging my Betty has in my heart, to place her in the best house in Britain.* Now Sue Ryder Home. *Public access in part.*

Above *Marchmont Doocot.*
Left *Marchmont House*

The grand scale of landscape setting with its 1.5km avenue, terminating upon the circular **doocot**, 1749, built by James Williamson, was probably the responsibility of William Adam, who drew plans for a new house and for the upgrading of **Redbraes Castle** and estate. Improvements took place *c*.1726-35. Redbraes survives as a sad architectural fragment of one wing (no evidence even of the *encircling moat*), awaiting the archaeologist, penned in a paddock adjacent to the **stables block**, partly remodelled by Lorimer, which has a battlemented Gothick corner tower (see colour p.58).

Fogo, like Polwarth, a place of importance formerly: *Ye're just the cooper o' Fogo* – a better man than your father, apparently, indicates the main trade and its developing excellence; that thriving village now only an attractive farm, at **Caldra Mains**, late 18th-century square courtyard range with pedimented corner pavilions. On the bank of the Blackadder is **Fogo Church**, 1755, repaired 1817, enlarged 1853, 17th-century burial aisle and good pulpit,

In 1690, **Redbraes Castle**'s hearth-tax return was 17 hearths, a fair-sized mansion.

Marchmont household books (1720-1817) refer, in 1720-1, to the purchase of thrushes, pistachios, tongues, hams and *twenty-three sheep from Pomerania.*

William Adam prepared plans and estimates in 1724 for a new house and a modernised Redbraes Castle. The 2nd Earl stressed that *what is necessary must be preferred to what is only convenient and both, in my opinion, to what is only magnificent.* After much consultation, involving Colen Campbell, James Gibbs, and probably the Earl of Mar in exile abroad, only minor upgradings took place until 25 years passed.

The Marchmont Estate Papers describe its agricultural development, 1730-88, under the 3rd Earl Hugh Hume (1708-94). Over this period between 30 and 50 labourers were permanently employed on the land, *making roads, tending thorns for the hedges, spreading lime, marling, levelling, making hay, ploughing and harvesting.*
James Handley, *Scottish Farming in the Eighteenth Century*

Greenlaw Parish Church

while spanning the river is the graceful single-arched **Fogo Bridge**, dated 1641.

GREENLAW

Grouped on the north bank of the Blackadder, its market place (framed by mostly humble buildings) large and green, around the **Market Cross**, a Corinthian column, 1881, capped by a lion carrying the Earl of Marchmont's blazon, reflecting his hand in its becoming the county town (1696-1853) (see colour p.59). At the top of the square green, **Parish Church**, **Tolbooth** and **Court-house** used to stand in a line. A wry couplet describes this ensemble thus:
*Here stands the Gospel and the Law,
Wi' Hell's hole atween the twa.*

Greenlaw Kirk
In 1834 the last public execution by hanging took place here, and the victim – an Irishman who had been found guilty of assault and robbery – was buried inside the gaol.

Cunningham was born the son of a builder in Leitholm, and was a pupil of Thomas Brown, Superintendent of City Works, Edinburgh. Cunningham's handsome Greek Revival work was in contrast to his later oeuvre, his Romanesque churches being variously described as *laughable* (*The Ecclesiologist*) and *bizarre* (Nikolaus Pevsner).

County Hall

Greenlaw Kirk, 1675

Lengthened 1712, to join the originally separate tower of 1696, and north aisle, 1855. Weathered red sandstone square tower and steeply pitched crowstep-gabled roof over the body of the kirk. Magnificent iron yett no doubt to guard *Hell's Hole*. To the north-east the monogrammed **gravestone** of a tutor to the family at Marchmont, its decoration reminiscent of Marchmont plasterwork. The **Old Market Cross**, 1609, a Corinthian column, used to stand centrally on the green, but was dismantled, 1829 (when the County Hall was built), and now stands just west of the kirk, indifferent to the upstart version by the road below.

County Hall, 1829, John Cunningham
A chaste yet elegant Grecian edifice, ... highly ornamental to the town, and whose position is less liable to satirical remark. Greek Revival,

hall (converted to swimming pool, 1960s, and then back, 1980s) with Ionic portico and raised dome, flanking pedimented pavilions. Its dome held the fire-proof room ensuring the conservation of legal documents.

Castle Hotel, probably contemporary with the Hall (in a remarkable civic ensemble for so small a town) for after all, then as now, would not the lawyers and judges demand transport, board and lodgings as befits their station? Symmetrical courtyard, flanking coaching wings and flight of stairs to pedimented main entrance in pilastered façade.

At the corner of High Street/Duns Road stands **Fairbairn Court sheltered housing**, 1984, a large group opened by HM The Queen, at least two-storey, stepped and slated, rendered, with some cosmetic sandstone implants, and perhaps set back rather far and with a bland skyline which, surprisingly, stands out.

By Greenlaw are **Whiteside Farm**, inserted Palladian windows and pilastered doorway taken from a lodge at Marchmont; **Roweston Cottage**, 18th-century Gothick, itself formerly a Marchmont lodge, octagonal, conical slated roof and central chimney; and, to the south, **Gordonbank**, possibly 17th century, experienced-looking, two-and-a-half storey, 1-3-1-bay L-plan house with crowstepped gables.

Top *Thatched Cottages, Greenlaw.*
Above *Castle Hotel*

Left *Gordonbank.* Below *Old Kirk, Westruther*

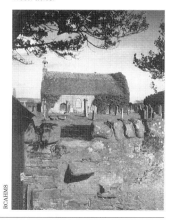

Westruther (struther = swamp or marsh) **Parish Church**, 1840, Gothick pointed windows, corner finials and bellcote. Ruin of the **Old Kirk**, 1649, altered 1752, stands in the graveyard. **Old Thistle Inn**, 1721, harled two-storey, five-bay, slated roof with rolled skews on one gable.

Spottiswoode House

RCAHMS/Brig Gen Sir J Swinton

The various inscriptions are the works of Lady John Scott (Alicia Anne Spottiswoode), a noted antiquarian who excavated a number of burial mounds in the area: she was also apparently renowned for her *refined version of Annie Laurie*.
Love

George Home of Bassendean was one of those who, having escaped to Holland, masterminded *The Revolution* which brought William and Mary to the Scots throne in 1689. The monarchs' gratitude may well have given Home the wherewithal to extend Bassendean.

On both sides of the border men *became resigned to unending conflict, and all those who could afford to do so built themselves fortified dwellings. Security was the overriding consideration in the architecture of the period. Houses built without defences ... were hastily fortified; church towers were built or rebuilt with an eye to defence, and some vicars built themselves fortified dwellings, the so-called vicars' peels. For lesser men, the characteristic form of fortified dwelling was the peel tower or tower house, a rectangular or square building often protected with a palisade (Latin* **pilum** *from which the term peel is derived). The great lords built themselves massive fortifications ... The peasantry, on the other hand, who could not afford stone towers or peels, had little alternative but to accept raids as another hazard of life ... In 1323 the inhabitants of Bamburgh apparently dismantled the timber frames of their houses at the approach of the Scots and took them into the Castle.*
Border Warfare, Department of the Environment

Spottiswoode House, 1832-4, William Burn; demolished 1928
Jacobethan, *a splendid modern house recently finished, and built in the old English style, with an encincturing and architecturally ornamented terrace, and partly the old family residence repaired, altered, and worked into proximate harmony of character with the new edifice* (Imperial Gazetteer). Signs of its existence abound, however, within the beautified and enriched policy landscape, including the rustic **Gothick archways** at Pyatshaw and Bruntaburn. There are **inscribed texts** at field openings on the approaches past Pyatshaw, **West Lodge** carries an inscription, too, and **Eagle** (or **Clock**) **Lodges** are Gothick set between battlemented pylons. The **Old Stables** are dated 1796, U-shaped with a Gibbsian two-storey, three-bay block at its centre, with Venetian window at first floor, and a cylindrical **doocot**, its upper half brick, completes the incomplete ensemble.

Bassendean House, 17th century
A neatly modernised plain old building, in the midst of tastefully embellished ground (Imperial Gazetteer). This long, narrow, three-storey house probably began life as a squarer tower. Note sundial at south end dated 1690 and porch dated 1862.

RCAHMS

Wedderlie, 1680 (*above*)
Once a seat, now a mere shooting-box ... an ancient edifice in a state of disrepair. Late 17th-century mansion added to an earlier tower-house, a corbelled crowstepped *unimproved Traquair*, its coach buildings made from gabled barns, originally thatched, one sporting a corner sundial. Wedderlie was owned by the Edgar family for over 400 years from 1327.

Evelaw Tower, late 16th century
L-plan massively fortified house with rounded
angles and shot-holes, still substantially vertical.

GORDON

Many attractive vernacular buildings *improved*
to their own detriment and that of their
neighbours. The plain **Gordon Church**, 1897,
is rebuilt on an older site, set back off the main
street, standing within the old graveyard.

Spectacular even in ruins **Greenknowe
Tower**, 1581, built for the Setons of Touch,
stands on a knoll (originally defended by
marshy surroundings) to the west of the
village. L-plan block 7 x 9m, vaulted ground
floor, in red sandstone (probably harled) topped
by corbelled angle turrets and crowstepped
gables, with an iron yett. Nothing remains of
the fine gardens which were the setting for
Greenknowe: the proposed golf course and/or
speculative housing developments are unlikely
to make amends for this loss (see colour p.57).
Open to the public; guidebook available

Hume village was the original seat of the
Humes/Homes.

Hume Castle dates from the 13th century, a
frontier defence, captured 1547, 1549, 1569, and
lastly demolished in 1651 (by Cromwell's
artillery under Colonel Fenwick), despite the
Governor's defiant statement: *I, Willie Wastle,
stand firm in my castle; and a' the dogs o' your
toun will no' pull Willie Wastle down* (see colour
p.58). Presumably his military judgment was as
bad as his poetic one. Current outstanding form
raised 1794 by Earl of Marchmont on line of
earlier work. Major medieval settlement on the

Top *Evelaw Tower*. Middle
Greenknowe Tower. Above *Yett,
Greenknowe Tower*. Left *Hume Castle*

Hume Castle was the key to the East
March. In 1547 Lady Hume held it,
with limited numbers: she conceded
when the English leader began to hang
her young son before her eyes. Two
years of occupation followed with
Hume being fortified by the English
assisted by locals specifically planted
to gain knowledge of the castle's
hurried extra fortifications and sentry
regime, knowledge which was used to
good advantage in a successful night
attack by *Milord Hume* and his forces.

Hume Castle

Robert Reid was almost exclusively a public sector architect (in Edinburgh), and Paxton was possibly his only country house commission. Responsible for buildings such as Perth Academy, Leith Customs House, Parliament Square and some of Edinburgh's New Town, and King's Architect, he retired to live at Lowood near Melrose which he bought in 1839.

The banks of the Tweed are dotted with fishing shiels. Most are simple one-room buildings (providing basic accommodation for the fishers) and a fish-house (to keep the fish cool) either cut into the bank like an ice-house or built on to the shiel as a cool-box with thick walls, stone floor and no windows. Some shiels also had a farding box (a hut or platform on stilts where the fishermen could watch for fish running up the river). Fish were caught by nets strung across the river, of course, and not by rod and line.

Paxton House

south-facing slope around and below the castle can be glimpsed only with some effort and the aid of imagination. Little of interest remaining in the village, much of which was probably thatched at one time, but ridges and eaves sloping parallel to the fall of the road seem characteristic. Adjacent is the white-painted Palladian-windowed but rambling **Hume Hall**, early 19th century and later, and **St Nicholas's Churchyard** with the gracefully decaying **Earl's Aisle** and old monuments (Hume parish united with Stichill, 1640).

Paxton House, 1758-66, possibly John & James Adam
Built for Patrick Home of Billie under the supervision of James Nisbet, interior work, c.1773, Robert Adam. Central four-column porticoed villa, quadrant corridors, U-plan flanking wings. Wonderful south-facing setting overlooking the Tweed. Built to house a Prussian heiress whose marriage could not be attained by the son of the murdered Mrs Margaret Home (see Linthill). Best Scottish Palladian mansion, in red sandstone, kitted out with Chippendale, most of which has fortunately survived, east wing, 1812-13, Robert Reid to form library (furniture by Trotter of Edinburgh also preserved) and picture gallery. Entry through the estate walls is effected between **Palladian lodges**, and the approach to the house crosses Paxton Glen by a masonry **estate bridge**, c.1770. Preserved by Paxton Trust, the gallery now an outstation of the National Galleries of Scotland. *Open to the public*
The grounds of Paxton were laid out by Robert Robinson, one-time assistant of 'Capability' Brown, from 1767, extending to **Paxton village**, to the north, a little-distinguished organic ensemble of more-or-less picturesque cottages, many pantiled, for Paxton estate housed a brick, tile, and drain manufactory.

On the banks of the Tweed below Paxton are the remains of **salmon fishing stations, icehouse, boathouse, fishing shiels** and stone flagged **tow-path**, punctuated by timber watch-towers.

Tweedhill House, early 19th century Two-storey with high oversailing-eaved slate roof. Courtyard stable range entered via pedimented archway.

Top *Tweedhill House.*
Above *Tweedhill House stables*

On one occasion, an entire English army is said to have kept itself fed for two or three weeks on (peas) growing in the Merse region round Berwick.
Hope

Left *Hutton Castle, 1961.*
Below *Hutton Castle, 1880*

Hutton Hall or **Castle**, from 16th century
A square tower of remote but unascertained antiquity, and an attached long mansion of patch-work structure and various dates even before Sir William Burrell acquired it (from Lord Tweedmouth in 1915) and set some of his collection here. The south-east end of this rambling house, set high above the Whiteadder is the tower, and although Lord Tweedmouth had not sensitively adapted it for his use, some of Burrell's treatment was cavalier, enlarging, extending, and removing the ground-floor vaulting. Burrell's addition and alterations were Robert Lorimer, 1916, and Reginald Fairlie, 1926, after Lorimer's schemes, including one for a new home incorporating the old tower, failed to inspire Burrell's imagination, and he and Lorimer, previously friends, fell out terminally. After Burrell's death, in fulfilment of his Will, the resulting principal interiors were removed and

Burrell's Trustees were originally charged with locating the collection well outwith Glasgow, the thinking being that the polluted urban environment was not suitable for museum objects. But with cleaner air and a commitment to *rural inviolability* of the Pollok Estate, where the National Trust for Scotland's first conservation agreement held sway, the Trustees realised Sir William's ambitions for a setting which is worthy of his years of astute collecting.

Above and right *St Mary's Church*

Broadmeadows House (*c*.1811, dem. *c*.1915) had *a Grecian front of fine white-coloured sandstone*, probably by David Hamilton. Court of offices, 1807, Alexander Gilkie.

Ladykirk was originally known as Upsettlington. James IV is said to have built the church here (on or near the site of its predecessor) and changed the name in gratitude to Our Lady after his near-drowning in the Tweed in 1499: the ford was in use until 1839. George Ridpath, Minister of Stichill (see p.167) and author of the *Border History of England and Scotland*, was born, 1717, in the manse here.

William Elliot, architect, was still practising in Kelso in 1824, at which time he had nine children surviving. His son Walter also became an architect, based in the town.

Ladykirk House

reconstructed in Pollok Estate, Glasgow, as part of the Burrell Collection. The husk left in Berwickshire nudged perilously close to demolition, but is now a private dwelling again.

Hutton Church, 1835
Plain Norman Gothic features, notably an ungainly square tower, but its setting has much of interest in gravestones and monuments.

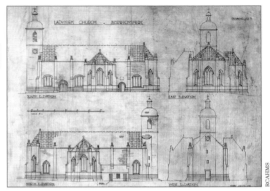

St Mary's Church, Ladykirk, *c*.1500
Triapsidal cross kirk, aisle-less, stone-flagged roof, with distinctive belfry, added 1743, attr. William Adam, *greatly disfigured by alterations* in first half of 19th century (when the west end was divided off for use as a school), thoroughly repaired, 1861.

Ladykirk House, 1797, William Elliot; demolished 1966
Central block (centre pedimented above four Corinthian pilasters) and symmetrical wings. A simplified version of Sir William Chambers'

Top *The Tweed at Coldstream*.
Above *Roundhouse, The Lees*.
Left *Greenknowe Tower*

Top *Stained glass, Hawick Library.*
Above *Detail, Redbraes Castle.*
Above right *Hume Castle.* Right
Nisbet Castle. Middle right *Metal
can clad shed, Greenlaw.* Far right
Aerial view of Edin's Hall broch

59

RCAHMS

Dundas House (now Royal Bank of Scotland) in St Andrew Square, Edinburgh (see *Edinburgh* in this series). Alterations and additions, 1845, William Burn.

Ladykirk Stables & Riding School, from *c.*1846, George Tattersall (the stables) and H F Ridley (the riding school)
Large U-plan range entered through an arched opening topped by a drum-mounted octagonal ribbed dome. **Ladykirk West Lodge**, 1799, spectacular lion-topped Corinthian archway, columned screen walls and lodge pavilions with niches.

Whitsome Parish Church, 1803
Gothick, altered 1912, stands on Hardie's Hill at the west end of the village. When Thomas Boston preached in the old kirk 250m to the north-west *the crowds who could not obtain access to the small thatched edifice, climbed to its roof, and tore away part of the straw, that they might hear and see him from above.* Perhaps unsurprisingly, that kirk has not survived, but in the old churchyard is a **watch-house**, 1820.

SWINTON
A planned village around its rectangular green, upon which is positioned the *12th Man of Swinton*, the village Cross, 1769, a classical, sundialed column in a defensive position on the football pitch. **Swinton Church**, 1729, extensively rebuilt on an earlier site, medieval fragments, 1782 aisle, later additions. **Swinton House**, burnt *c.*1797, and replaced by ashlar two-storey classical mansion with central bow.

Simprim Church
A small ruin (since Swinton and Simprim united in 1761), rectangular nave and chancel, with its graveyard. Thomas Boston was

RCAHMS

Top *Ladykirk West Lodge and lion gateway.* Above *Ladykirk stables*

Tattersall, the son of the proprietor of the equine auction mart, was also an engraver (under the signature of *Wildrake*) who specialised in sporting architecture, publishing a book under that title in 1841.

Thomas Boston (1676-1732) struck chords with rural folk in his preaching of independent Calvinism. In his *Fourfold State* (1720) he discoursed upon human nature as (1) primitively noble (in Eden); (2) entirely depraved (by the Fall); (3) recovery begun through life on Earth, and (4) happiness or misery eternal thereafter.

Opposite: Top *Parish Church, Cockburnspath.* Left *Steps, Allanton.* Bottom left *Cove Harbour.* Right *Polwarth Kirk*

The lands are inclosing and yield very good barley, oats and clover; the banks are planting ... I speak in the present tense; for there is still a mixture of the old negligence left amidst the recent improvements, which look like the works of a new colony in a wretched impoverished country.
Pennant

Lord Kames published *Progress in Flax Husbandry in Scotland* in 1766 *to encourage landholders and farmers to apply (themselves) vigorously to flax-raising.* He also declared (on arable farming): *A Scotch farmer behaves worse than Esau: the latter got a mess of pottage for his birthright; the former surrenders his to weeds without recompense.*

Lord Kames was a connoisseur as well as a thinker: *Whether should a ruin be in the Gothic or Grecian form? In the former I say, because it exhibits the triumph of time over strength, a melancholy but not unpleasant thought. A Grecian ruin suggests the triumph of barbarity over taste, a gloomy and discouraging thought.*
Elements of Criticism, 1762

Right *Anton's Hill*. Below and bottom *Eccles Parish Church*

minister here from 1699 to 1707. **Simprim Old Barn**, 1686, elongated three-storey, with crowstepped gables, originally L-plan. Sadly now engulfed in modern buildings.

Purves Hall, possibly 17th century
Peel tower much altered but still occupied, with replacement Victorian house adjacent.
Belchester, a house of *c*.1800 built around a peel tower core, with Victorian additions.

Anton's Hill, 1836, William Burn
Typical high-quality small-to-medium two-storey house, employing Burn's vocabulary to the full. In the grounds **Wrangham's Well**, marked by inscribed stone well-head.

Stainrigg/Stoneridge, 18th century
Three-storey mansion house with central pediment over four-bay and entrance front. Oddly aligned central top window pair, twin flanking pavilions. **Bughtrig**, early 19th-century Regency house, centre three-storey block with two-storey wings, remodelled both inside and out.

Eccles village has some remains of **St Mary's Cistercian Priory**, 1156, burnt by Hertford, 1545, then laicised to the Hume family. Only two barrel-vaulted cells of the east range and architectural fragments built into later garden walls survive.

Eccles Parish Church, 1774
Large 5 x 3 bay, barn-like kirk, Gothick glazing-patterned sashes in round-headed openings (Hay describes these as *Georgian windows, gradually being invaded by stained glass*) unconvincingly stubby vernacular bell-tower at the east end. Bell dated 1659; additions and internal alterations, 1930.

Birgham

A centre for Border diplomacy in the 12th and 13th centuries: the Treaty of Birgham in 1290 agreed the marriage of the infant Queen Margaret of Scotland to the English Prince Edward. Her death shortly after the Treaty led to the Wars of Independence. **Springhill**, 1816, dower-house of The Hirsel, overlooking the Tweed. Two-storey and basement, ground floor Venetian-windowed, rusticated quoins. T-plan, Victorian wing to rear.

Prince Edward was the first Prince of Wales. The death of the Queen, and the consequent inability of the Scots to decide the succession, allowed Edward I to press his case for overlordship. Had the Maid of Norway survived to marry the son of Edward I, as the Treaty of Birgham identified, the union of the kingdoms would have taken place although each was to be ruled *separately and distinctly*. With her death, with no clear successor to the Scots throne, some 13 claimants came forward.

North elevation, Milne Graden

Milne Graden, 1822, James Gillespie Graham Neoclassical mansion (formerly Kersfield) overlooking the Tweed, that elevation with twin bow-fronts to capitalise on the view, the north front pedimented and porticoed. An ancient site with a D-plan earthwork. The **stables courtyard**, in similar style, is entered by an archway within whose pediment is a doocot.

Kames, 17th century
Two-and-a-half-storey mansion with barrel-shaped corner turrets, centre block crowstep gabled. **Kames stables**, 18th century, U-plan courtyard, harled, painted, rusticated quoins, hipped slated roof.

Kames was the birthplace of Henry Home, Lord Kames (1696-1782), agricultural improver, philosopher and judge. Benjamin Franklin visited here in 1759. Kames had the misfortune to preside over the trial of a chess-playing and drinking companion who had killed in inebriation. The jury returning an unfavourable verdict, Kames followed the death sentence with the wry comment *And that's checkmate to you, Matthew.*

Lord Kames in *The Gentleman Farmer* in *an attempt to improve agriculture by subjecting it to the test of rational principles* (1776) suggested to landowners that they provide for all their tenants *a hearty meal at which discussions of the best methods to be followed should take place, and rewards be given, such as ploughs and harrows of the best construction, to those who have been the most diligent in carrying out improvements.*
Handley

Kames

R G Bolam and Son

Longridge Tower, 1878, J C & C A Buckler
Irregular Tudor mansion in sandstone ashlar.
Porky porte-cochère and plethora of pinnacles.
Now a school with square carbuncular 20th-
century chapel, but bizarrely accompanied by
scatter of suburbia in the grounds, all the more
surprising given the attractive **courtyard
block** just to the north of the main house.

Top *West front, Longridge Tower,
1920.* Above *Longridge Tower.*
Right *Ord House*

On taking the English throne in
1603 James VI proclaimed in all six
Marches *the foul and insolent
outrages lately committed upon the
Border of our realms of England and
Scotland by persons accustomed in
former times to live by rapine and
spoil, preying daily upon our good
and loving subjects, without fear of
God or man, hath given us just
cause to use all means convenient,
both for the relief of our subjects
damnified, and for prevention of the
like mischief hereafter.*

Berwick-upon-Tweed Record Office

Ord House, 18th century
Present appearance of two-and-a-half storey
and basement due to new façade and front
rooms, added 1789, for William Grieve, with
original two-storey linked pavilions. Finely
proportioned five-bay principal elevation with
three-bay pediment. Good Gothick fanlight.
Garden walls to north, north-west, and west
probably contemporary with the 18th-century
developments. Now caravan site headquarters,
regrettable tile roof with heinously ugly
timber-clad farm shed.

East Ord Farmhouse, 1820-30
Two-storey, L-plan with Welsh slate roof, brick
chimneys and sixteen-pane sashes. From south
elevation high garden walls ramp down to a
low front.

Middle Ord, 1788
For J Grey, rear wing added, 1910. Deep-
gabled, two storeys, slated, droved ashlar
sandstone; 19th-century bay windows, glazed
porch and Doric door surround to the front.
Walled garden, 1788, with two-storey square
pyramidal-roofed doocot/summerhouse.

West Ord, c.1700-10
Five x two bays, symmetrical house (each pair
of opposing façades is identical) of painted
ashlar, let down by 20th-century glazing of tall
narrow openings. Impressively near-pyramidal
roof. Built for Elizabeth Ord, mistress of Sir
William Blackett, a coal, lead and shipping
magnate, of Wallington Hall.

Murton Farm, c.1880
Square group of planned farmbuildings
constructed of *block and sneck* with Welsh slate
roof. Gabled carriage arch feature contains
doocot topped by weathervane.

Horncliffe
Literally a by-water, at the furthermost point
of the tidal Tweed. Formerly a low ford
attracting much traffic, thus explaining the
Union Suspension Bridge, 1819-20, Captain
Sir Samuel Brown RN, with advice on tower
and abutment designs from John Rennie.
Timber roadway suspended from pairs of

Above *Middle Ord*. Below and
bottom *Union Suspension Bridge*

Top Cable and bolt bracket, Union Suspension Bridge. Above *Horncliffe House*

wrought-iron chains with elongated bars connected by wrought iron. Brown invented the bar link, used here for the first time, constructing the longest suspension bridge of its day. The technological jump was palpable – providing a structure at a quarter of the anticipated cost of a masonry equivalent. Europe's first and oldest surviving suspension bridge carrying road traffic. Look for the iron inscriptions with their intertwined thistles and roses. By the Tweed here are **fishing shiels**.

Horncliffe House, *c.*1800
Seven-bay, three-storey red sandstone Palladian mansion for William Alder, with concave single-storey linking wings to Venetian-windowed end-pavilions.

Thortonpark Farmhouse, *c.*1830
Two-and-a-half-storey three-bay, double-pile plan house in tooled-and-margined ashlar (an attractive Gothick stair window) under a gabled Welsh slate roof. **Shoreswood Hall**, early 18th century L-plan, two-storey house in dressed stone with red tile and Scotch slate roofs.

Right Morris Hall. Below *Norham Village Cross*

Morris Hall
Core of *c.*1700, clad, with front range *c.*1750 and wings of *c.*1830. Welsh slate gabled roof. Intricate finialed gatepiers, and range of offices.

NORHAM
The North Ham of the monks of Lindisfarne lies low on meadow land in a bend of the Tweed where the river was fordable. One of the most dangerous places in England in times of Border warfare. A triangular village green punctuates the main street of comfortable houses, dominated at its east end by the Castle.
Village Cross, medieval base of six circular steps upon which stands the restored shaft, 1870, of clustered columns and tall pyramidal top surmounted by a salmon weather-vane, a reminder of the Norham salmon fishery.

St Cuthbert's Parish Church

The salmon fisheries *here are very considerable ... they lie on each side the river, and are all private property ... the fishers never failed going as near as possible to their neighbour's limits. One man goes off in a small flat-bottomed boat, square at one end, and taking as large a circuit as his net admits, brings it on shore at the extremity of his boundary where others assist in landing it.*
Pennant, 1769

Richard of Wolveston *was one of the foremost designers of the 12th century* (John Harvey in *English Medieval Architects*), with the Galilee porch at Durham Cathedral and Durham Castle, Constable's Hall surviving evidence of his skills. By mistake he once left his wallet in an inn in Berwick containing a fragment of St Cuthbert's mortcloth: the wallet was thrown in error into the fire, but miraculously refused to take harm.

The Vaudois, or Waldenses, were an oppressed Christian sect of French Dissenters, and Gilly's visits and publications, *inter alia*, produced a subscription for their relief led by the King and the Bishop of Durham. The Revd Gilly was also the author of *Peasantry of the Border: an appeal on their behalf* in which he called on landowners to remedy the peasantry's miserable dwelling conditions.

Norham Castle

St Cuthbert's Parish Church, *c.*1170,
Richard of Wolveston
For Bishop Puiset, Prince Bishop of Durham, probably replacing a pre-Conquest building. East bay of chancel added, *c.*1310. Tower added, 1837. South porch and aisle, 1846, Ignatius Bonomi. North aisle and transepts, 1852, D Gray. Romanesque original of the highest quality well treated by subsequent architects, who are detailed with the church wardens on north aisle wall plaques.

Large, Decorated, tomb recess, *c.*1320, containing the effigy of a knight, a recumbent Revd Gilly, 1855, (*Friend of the Vaudois* by John Graham Lough), reading desk and pulpit mid-17th century (salvaged by Gilly from Durham Cathedral in 1840), an 18th-century organ case, and, in the tower, a fine carved timber Royal Arms of Charles II; 19th-century armorial glass by Wailes, later 19th-century glass by Clayton & Bell.

Norham Castle, from 1121
Ubbanford, a burgh of the Northumbrian kingdom as early as the eighth century, was no doubt accompanied by fortification. Built as a motte-and-bailey for the Bishop of Durham in 1121, dismantled by David I in 1138, it was rebuilt, 1157-70, by Richard of Wolveston for Bishop Hugh Puiset, after Henry II had recaptured Northumberland, when the keep was constructed (remodelled in 1422-5). Mons Meg, the cannon now preserved at Edinburgh Castle, was used by the Scots besieging Norham in 1497, and a last period of defensive rebuilding occurred, 1513-15, for Bishop Ruthal following its successful assault by the Scots in 1513. Despite centuries of disuse from the early

Norham Castle

Day set on Norham's *castled steep*
And Tweed's fair river, broad and
deep,
And Cheviot's mountains lone;
The battled towers, the donjon keep,
The loophole grates, where captives
weep,
The flanking walls that round it
sweep,
In yellow lustre shone.
Sir Walter Scott, *Marmion*

1600s (watch for the **Gothick cottage**, *c*.1800 embracing a south turret), it is still one of the most complete and comprehensible defensive structures on the Border. The keep itself is over 25m high.

Ladykirk & Norham Bridge & Tollhouse, 1885-7, Thomas Codrington & Cuthbert Brereton, engineers
Four broad arches, red sandstone rock-faced with ashlar dressings, apsidal central cutwater with similar projection in parapet, outer cutwaters triangular and broached; built for the Tweed Bridges Trust.

Below Ladykirk and Norham Bridge. Bottom *Twizell Bridge*

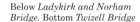

Norham Station, 1851, Benjamin Green
For the now disused Newcastle & Berwick Railway. Tudor-style station-master's house with waiting-room, office, telegraph office, porter's room and store, all Welsh-slated and around two platforms. Coal cell and former lime store now used exclusively as coal depot. Engine shed converted to goods warehouse, 1852.

Twizell Bridge, 15th century
High, single, round, narrow arch of 27m span (longest in Britain until the Causey Arch in 1727), of squared stone, strengthened by five close-set chamfered ribs. Later low flood arches, parapet and dentilled cornice. A significant player at the Battle of Flodden in 1513, enabling the Earl of Surrey to cross his artillery over the Till and pin down the Scots' northern wing. Setting diminished by insensitive road and bridge *improvement* abruptly to the south (see colour p.110).

Twizell Castle, *c*.1771, James Nisbet
A Gothick hall for Sir Francis Blake, whose ruin is convincingly sited, decrepit, and vegetating. The commanding location also offered some genuinely medieval castle

Left *Twizell Bridge and Castle.*
Above *Twizell Castle*

remains (destroyed by Scots, 1496, in support
of Perkin Warbeck) duly incorporated, and the
aged appearance was aided by the long time of
building – almost fifty years, without
occupation (George Wyatt worked here in
1812). Extraordinarily, completed *c.*1830, and
then latterly robbed in the building of
Tillmouth Park.

Tillmouth Park announces itself by means of
its pair of **lodges** & **gateway**, *c.*1810, so
striking in their castellated quatrefoiled
Gothick that the unwary may be tested by the
awkwardness of the main roadline.

Perkin Warbeck claimed to be the
younger of the princes *murdered* in
the Tower of London. He married a
Scotswoman, Catharine Gordon, a
relative of James IV. He was
executed in 1499 following a further
unsuccessful invasion of England.

Tillmouth Park Hotel, 1882,
Charles Barry Jnr
Elizabethan house on site of earlier. Three
ashlar floors, the ground rock-faced and
battered, the roof Westmorland slate. The
interior incorporates many marble fireplaces

Sir Charles Barry, architect of the
Houses of Parliament, had an
illustrious family as well as career.
Charles Barry, 1823-1900, his eldest
son, was an architect as was his
third boy, Edward. Alfred, the
second-born, became Bishop of
Sydney as well as writing his
father's *life*. And his fifth son, John,
was the engineer of Tower Bridge,
being made a baronet in 1897.

Tillmouth Park Hotel

from the earlier house (*c*.1810), several having down-tapering columns with Corinthian capitals. A particular feature of the 1882 house is its original central-heating system, most prominent elements of which are the elaborate cast-iron grilles.

Courtyard Cottages complete with doocot, 1825, garden walls, carriage arch and arbour, *c*.1810, copper-roofed (over an iron frame), yacht-finialed **garden pavilion**, *c*.1900, the Gothick **Dean Burn Bridge**, and the 30m-long **Henlaw Tunnel** (for mushrooms or just a Gothick experience?) in ashlar with iron railings, all of *c*.1810.

Tillmouth Dower House

Felix Kelly, 1914-94, was a country-house topographer, muralist, illustrator and stage designer. His last murals were for the Garden Room at Castle Howard.

Tillmouth House

Opposite the Tillmouth Park Lodges, screened from the road luckily or many more accidents would occur, is the **Tillmouth Dower House**, a five-bay Gothick gem, so completely perfect that it is astonishing to learn that the greater part of its Gothickness reflects the creative skill of Felix Kelly, artist, b. New Zealand, and dates from 1972-7 (for a 20th-century Sir Francis Blake) rather than the *c*.1810 of the original.

Tillmouth House, 1879
Gothic former school and schoolhouse, now private with 13th-century lancets and trefoils, snecked stone with ashlar dressings and Welsh slate roof.

Tiptoe Farmhouse, mid-18th century with early 19th-century additions
Four-bay two-storey house of random rubble below steeply pitched Scotch slate roof with Welsh slate verge courses.

Melkington House

Melkington House, *c.*1800
Earlier core from before 1764. Double-span roof
– the rear span older and more steeply pitched
– in Scotch slate over simple ashlar elevations.
Hilltop location, with contemporary serpentine
ha-ha to the south. Good early 19th-century
offices to the north-east and north-west.

Castle Heaton, late medieval
Two-storey defensible vaulted structure some
21x7m in plan, which suffered at Scots hands at
the same time as the original tower at Twizell.
Welsh slate roof over largely medieval masonry.

St Cuthbert's Chapel, *c.*1800
Gothick restoration (Sir Francis Blake again)
incorporating some medieval masonry, derelict
by the latter part of the 19th century. **St
Cuthbert's Railway Viaduct**, 1849, disused
but still significant in the landscape, its six
arches with brick soffits on high rock-faced
battered rectangular piers.

Cornhill House
Probably incorporates earlier peel tower of
*c.*1400 (barmkin still visible), extended 17th
century and after, nursery wing added and
extended in 19th century. Unsurprisingly,
therefore, an irregular plan, *the ancient cross-
shaped seat of the Collingwoods*. A roughcast
exterior with painted stone surrounds and
irregular openings below steeply sloping Welsh
slate roof with crowstepped gables.

St Helen's Parish Church, Cornhill, 1840,
Ignatius Bonomi
Random rubble incorporating masonry from
church of 1751. Altered 1866 and block and

St Cuthbert was born *c.*635 when
Lauderdale was part of
Northumbria. After his death in
687, his body apparently remained
uncorrupted. It left Lindisfarne in
875, arriving in 995 at Durham via
Chester-le-Street and Ripon. Women
were not allowed to approach his
shrine until the Reformation. His
grave was opened in 1826, when
inside three coffins and five robes of
embroidered silk was found his
complete skeleton.

St Helen's Well was located in
woodland between Cornhill and
Campfield. Cold water baths were
built here, *c.*1750, but were little
used and eventually destroyed,
although the bathing well was still
marked on maps at the turn of the
20th century.

Within the churchyard is the
grave of Percival Stockdale (1736-
1811), author of the *Remonstrance
against Inhumanity to Animals,
particularly against the Savage
Practice of the Bull-baiting.*

Cornhill House

St Helen's Parish Church

Ignatius Bonomi, *the first railway architect,* Surveyor of Bridges for County Durham, designed the first railway bridge in England (at Skerne, by Darlington, 1824). His father Joseph was born in Rome in 1739, coming to work in England for the Adam brothers in 1767, and eventually building up a successful country-house practice of his own: a neoclassicist he could not come to terms with Gothic, mourning *the revival of such absurdities in this country* in a letter to the Earl of Buchan in 1807. The younger Bonomi was more pragmatic, designing well and successfully in both neoclassical and Gothic styles. His brother, Joseph Bonomi Jnr (1796-1878) archaeological illustrator, was curator of Sir John Soane's Museum.

sneck chancel added (probably F R Wilson). Welsh slate roof with gabled bellcote, from whence comes the chime of the clock on the front elevation. Good stone steps incorporated in graveyard wall. Interior largely 1840s, parapet of the west gallery carrying mid-18th-century carved rococo-mantled Collingwood arms.

Collingwood Arms, early 19th century Described by Mackenzie in 1825 as *comfortable and excellent*, this coaching inn is named after Cuthbert Collingwood, the Northumbrian Admiral who *finished* the Battle of Trafalgar. Ashlar with Welsh slate roof, expansively fronted, the frieze over the stone porch carrying the relief letters POST HORSES.

Collingwood Arms

The building of **Smeaton's bridge** was a notable benefit, but at that time, it should be remembered, carts had only just superseded transport on horseback, roads having been improved only to the point that *it requires two days' work of a cart with two horses to carry four bolls of wheat or five of barley from near the west end of the county to the markets of Berwick or Eyemouth. Sometimes they take loads in return which is a saving.*
Alexander Lowe's *Agricultural Report,* 1775

Coldstream Bridge, 1763-6, James Smeaton, for the Tweed Bridges Trust, is seven-arched with arch bands, triple keystones and battered semi-octagonal cutwaters. The main arches are all of the same radius to save on shuttering costs. The spandrels hold large keyed oculi with dark flint infilling. The pilastered parapet has been corbelled out to achieve the widening of the bridge surface in 1960-1 (see colour p.57).

Contemporary with the bridge is **Coldstream Marriage-house,** single-storey random rubble with pantiled roof and inscribed tablet on the

Coldstream Bridge

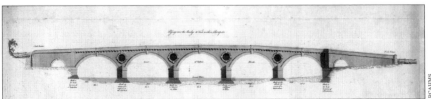

lower extension. After 1754, declaratory marriages were made illegal in England, but until 1856 (when a three-week residence qualification was introduced) it was still possible to become more or less instantly wed here in Scotland. The Marriage-house was where the tolls were exacted until their abandonment in 1826.

COLDSTREAM

Formed at the first major ford above Berwick, crossing at the mouth of the River Leet, Coldstream was the site, just east of the **Market Place**, of a Cistercian Priory, c.1165, occupied by nuns of whom no less than five prioresses in a century came from the Hoppringle family. Nothing of it remains today. *Birnd and destrued the nonery cald Colestreme, so to Fogga (Report of the second Hertford expeditions, 1545).* Market Place is large and open, a surprise to those who have not before been seduced from the town's through route. Most of the buildings, as in many Scots burghs, are superficially unremarkable – in this case the southern range less so – but all contribute to the framing of the civic space. **12** Market Place, **Guards House**, 1865, is inscribed *Headquarters of the Coldstream Guards, 1659*, slated, six-pane sashes, symmetrical, two-storey, rubble building, now a museum, about a pend.

Cameron House, Market Place, c.1800 Pair of three-storey houses in droved ashlar with polished margins, slated roofs with brick stacks. To the rear two-storey workshops with *joiner's workshop* glazing. The three-storey Market Place frontage continues with the **Crown Hotel** (formerly Black Bull), three-bay with six-pane sashes and Scotch-slated roof, then later refacing, in a French Renaissance style, of **Nos 27-28**, with a good pilastered shopfront, and **No 29**, elevation of c.1800.

Coldstream Manse (now Trafalgar House), **Guards Road**, 1830-2, Thomas Hamilton Large, square two-storey classical block of quality, slated piended roof with centrally clustered brick stacks, the whole struggling to maintain its presence shorn of its Tuscan porch. Desperately unsympathetic modern extensions.

Abbey House, Abbey Road, late 18th century Two-storey house with single-storey 19th-century rear extension. Three-bay symmetrical

12 Market Place

Strang

Although both **Thomas Hamilton** (1784-1855) and W H Playfair (1790-1857) were prime movers in the Greek Revival, their consummate neoclassicism was learned from books such as Stuart & Revett's *Antiquities of Athens*, for neither had set foot on Greek soil.

Coldstream Manse

RCAHMS

Above Corn store. *Right* Court House
Lodge

High Street details: Below *Fanlight.*
Bottom *Ironwork*

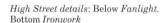

garden front in rubble with ashlar dressings,
Regency porch, 12-pane sashes, slated roof
with brick end stacks. Adjacent is the
Marjoribanks of Lees **burial ground**, later
18th century, enclosure walled in droved ashlar
with rusticated quoins and an inscribed panel
over the entrance.

Corn-store, Church Lane, mid-19th century
T-plan, three-storey slate-roofed block,
comprising two earlier outer blocks infilled to
form the T. Various window openings, usually
slatted lower sections, hoist doors centrally on
the middle block, elevations otherwise rubble
with ashlar dressings.

Court House Lodge, Court House Place,
late 18th century
Symmetrically planned two-bay cube below
pyramidal slated roof with (hopefully temporary)
Victorian rustic bargeboarded slated porch,
unsympathetic glazing and rear extension.

1, 2 & 3 Doocot, late 18th century
Gothick eleven-bay single-storey decoratively
battlemented range with pointed openings and
other contemporary features below slated roofs.

Hope Park, Duns Road, *c.*1830
Two-and-a-half-storey, three-bay classical villa
with projecting centre bay, Tuscan porch, and
single-storey wings, these last with piended
roofs. Within the stable block is built a stone
sarcophagus, conceivably retrieved from the
Coldstream Priory, or perhaps a relic of Flodden.

Ivy Lodge, Duns Road, 1876
One-and-a-half-storey *cottage orné* in brick
with ashlar lintels and cills, lying-pane sashes,

patterned slating to dormers and porch, piended slate roof, deep eaves, triangular lucarne. Later lean-to additions.

High Street (north side) has several ranges of late 18th or early 19th-century two-storey terraces, with fanlights and ironwork, their development presumably resulting from the construction of Smeaton's bridge, for before it the old ford crossed upstream and the road east from there would have been relatively minor.

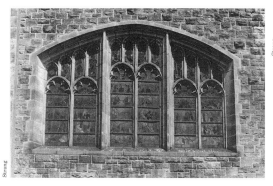

Church Centre (former West UF Church), 1907, George Reavell Jnr
Perpendicular Gothic, transepts and square three-stage tower, all in snecked rubble with ashlar dressings below slate roofs. Stained glass by Percy Bacon & Bros, London, and Ballantine, Edinburgh. A major punctuation given even greater presence by the ball-finialed **War Memorial**.

Top and left *Church Centre*. Above *59 High Street*. Below *Town Hall*

Frontage of continuous quality from **29-69** High Street, a particular feature being **No 59**, *c*.1900, Arts & Crafts infill or refaced three-storey house and timber-arcaded shopfront with blue-glazed brick stallriser and *through* white marble display slab.

Town Hall, High Street, 1862
Formerly **Mechanics' Institute**, provides the stop at the end of the street frontage: classical two-storey, three-bay front, pedimented above four Tuscan pilasters.

High Street south is of lesser interest if consistent of frontage. Its focal point is the **Coldstream Parish Church**, 1795, rebuilt 1906, J M Dick Peddie, incorporating the bell turret and cap of the earlier kirk (modelled on

Above *Coldstream Parish Church.*
Below *Marjoribanks Monument.*
Right *The Lees*

Charles Marjoribanks, first MP for Berwickshire after the 1832 Reform Act, had, if the inscription is to be believed, *high talents, amiable qualities and political principles.*

that of Eccles) in a suitably severe design in snecked rubble with ashlar dressings, its tower being of four stages. Within the kirk the interior is simple early 20th century with 20th-century stained glass.

Bank of Scotland, 88 High Street, late 19th century, probably George Washington Browne Former British Linen Bank, in blousy French Renaissance.

Gazebo, Henderson Park, late 18th century Petite two-storey octagonal structure of rubble, its first floor approached by forestair formerly providing one of the best riverside views in the Borders and a fireplace for colder days, the chimney incorporated in the battlements to maintain the symmetry. What better place to retreat from, or with, one's loved ones?

Marjoribanks Monument, 1832
Doric column topped by statue (Currie of Darnick after the original, by Handyside Ritchie, was struck by lightning in 1873) of Charles Marjoribanks, MP, of The Lees.

Lees Farm, later 18th century
Two-storey extensive farm steading and stable ranges now reduced to U-plan, squared rubble with ashlar quoins, piended slated roofs, and the seemingly ubiquitous vast infill modern prefab shed. Accompanying row of early 19th-century single-storey cottages. Opposite is **The Lees Lodge**, late 18th-century, single-storey, three-bay ashlar ornamented lodge and gatepiers to the Kelso road.

The Lees, *c.*1770 (destroyed 1975)
All but the two-storey, five-bay semicircular ashlar bow from the garden front has vanished. Converted, if that is the correct term, 1980, by Nicholas Groves-Raines, to a **circular house**, conical slated roof with central stack, rendered brick and ashlar margins completing the round with a Doric portico salvaged from the original remains. His subsequent extension, 1988, proved the merit of the original (see colour p.57).

The Lees Stables

The east wall of the stables
carried the kindly thought that *Any
VAGRANTS or BEGGARS passing
through these GATES will be taken
to the CONSTABLES at
COLDSTREAM.*

The Lees Stables, *c.*1770 and later
Two-storey east range with central raised
section, elliptically arched pend and flanking
cart-shed openings. Four-stage tower with
pyramidal roof over pend. Piended slated roofs.
Through the pend are two single-storey, seven-
bay ranges of stables and cottages.

The Lees Temple, later 18th century
Octagonal ashlar gazebo on the bank of the
Tweed, Roman Doric columns on pedestals with
parapet supporting entablature and bellcast
faceted roof. Visible from the Wark/Cornhill road.

The Hirsel, from at least 17th century
The Homes moved to The Hirsel after 1650
when their main residence, Hume Castle, was
razed by Cromwellian forces. The U-plan part
of the house, with square corner towers, one
incorporated in the later wing, must be of the
1670s, even if the southern part incorporated
into it is 18th century: William Adam did work
here for the 8th Earl of Home between 1739-41,
building offices and court walls, and adding a
new wing. Very fine Restoration staircase on
the model of that at Holyroodhouse. Alterations
and additions, 1813-15, William Atkinson, and
(mainly) 1813-18, William Burn, including the
fine central hall. The house at one time had
persiennes (see The Haining). Further
alterations, 1858, David Bryce and
subsequently, James C Walker, although H M
Wardrop & Reid prepared an abortive scheme,

Below *The Lees Temple.* Bottom *The
Hirsel*

*c.*1880. **Lodges**, 1851, William Burn. **Chapel**, *c.*1897, George Henderson. Reductions, 1958-9, Ian G Lindsay (restoring the entrance front, removing the Chapel and Victorian wing, rather on the model of Brechin Castle), have resulted in the present unusually proportioned, characterful building.

The Hirsel offices, *c.*1800, with doocot in low tower are charmingly converted into a Museum of Estate Life (*open to the public*), while the **stable block**, 1900, houses more practical functions. Within the grounds, a fine park **obelisk** to Lord Dunglass, d.1781. The lake was formed from a marsh in 1786 and is now the heart of a bird sanctuary.

Lennel Church, early 18th century, ruined kirk and graveyard: most noticeable for the fact that Alexander Gilkie (*c.*1756-1834), master mason of Coldstream, is buried here.

The following proclamation used to stand in Lennel kirkyard: *Take notice. An armed watch is placed here every night for the protection of this burial ground. And has orders to fire upon any person who may enter at improper hours without permission.*

Above *Lennel Church*. Right *Lennel House*

Lennel House is similar to Paterson's unexecuted plan for Castle Forbes, 1811. He was chief assistant with the Adams' Scottish practice, and after their deaths became the foremost exponent of the Adam castle style.

In the previous house on this site **Robert Burns** had *an extremely flattering reception* when he visited Patrick Brydone in 1787.

Lennel House is also favoured by associations with Rupert Brooke and Beatrix Potter.

Lennel House, *c.*1820, attributed to John Paterson
Approached through an open courtyard, with eastern face framed by a more intimate offices wing, two-storey ashlar classical house on butterfly plan. Beyond, to the east, rosemary-tiled **stable range**, *c.*1910, and Italianate terraced **walled garden**, enjoying fine aspect over the Tweed.

West Learmouth Farmhouse, *c.*1840
Ashlar, L-plan house, single two-storey bay overlooking entrance, with modillioned cornice below shallow-pitched Westmorland slate roof. To the north, the early 19th-century symmetrical E-plan group of **farm buildings** in random rubble with tooled ashlar dressings below Westmorland and Welsh slate roofs.

West Learmouth Farmhouse

Cartsheds, stables, granary, stores, smithy, and in the centres of the yards, turnip stores carrying a doocot and a clock. **VR letter-box**.

West Learmouth Cottages, *c.*1800
Group of farm labourers' cottages (13, now nine) in rubble, slated, with red brick stacks and buff cans, stepping down the hill in pairs, with the steward's at the top. Across the road, an enormous modern agricultural shed, in the farm colour of green, with swept roofs taking their cue from the cottages.

West Learmouth North & East Railway Viaducts, 1849
Rock-faced stone with seven and five high round brick arches respectively, and two broad flat pilasters at each bridge end.

Pressen Farmhouse, from early 18th century (centre three bays); extended and remodelled *c.*1870
Roughcast with ashlar and painted ashlar dressings. Gabled roofs and a good range of farm buildings, stepping down the hill, in the middle of which is the adjacent **Bastle**, *c.*16th-century fortified house, now workshop. Random rubble with dressed quoins, 18x8m in plan, originally two floors, the lower vaulted, now sadly demolished all but for a recess at the west end. Crowstepped gables containing 19th-century roof, outshots to the south.

Wark Castle, early 12th century, rebuilt 1153-6, extended later
Motte-and-bailey castle holding the southern bank of the Tweed, with a huge keep, 75x50m on the motte, now just rubble, barely defining the line of the keep walls below a blanket of trees and scrub. Wark's royal artillery left in

Agricultural workers in the 19th century were housed, even post-Improvement, in primitive conditions. Alexander Somerville, in *The Autobiography of a Working Man* (1848), reflected on his upbringing as one of 8 children in Berwickshire in *one of a row of sheds ... about twelve feet by fourteen, and not so high in the walls as will allow a man to get in without stooping. That place without ceiling or anything beneath the bare tiles of roof; with no floor save the common clay; without a cupboard or recess of any kind; with no grate but the iron bars which the tenants carried to it, built up and took away when they left it; with no partition of any kind save what the beds made; with no window save from small panes at one side.* Employment on the land could be from year to year: Somerville's parents *had a window consisting of one small pane of glass, and when they moved from one house to another in different parts of Berwickshire in different years, they carried this window with them.*

Left *West Learmouth Cottages.*
Below *Pressen Farmhouse.*
Bottom *Pressen Bastle*

Wark was defended against the Scots by the Countess of Salisbury in 1346, and after the Castle was relieved by Edward III the victory celebration was the scene of the famous occasion when the Countess's garter descended to the floor unbidden, the King picking it up and donning it with the words *Honi soit qui mal y pense.*

Parish Church of St Cuthbert

Davies produced many church monuments throughout Northumberland. As a provincial his more testing work was not always well received in the metropolis: in 1844 the *Literary Gazette* described his *Actaeon devoured by his hounds* showing in London in less than glowing terms: *We wish the unfortunate hunter had been entirely devoured, so that we might have been spared the sight of so disgusting a group.*

The Northumbrian kingdom's northern boundary was at one time the Forth/Clyde line. Edinburgh passed into the hands of the Scots *c.*AD960, Lothian in AD975. At the Battle of Carham, *c.*1016 the border was (more or less) defined.

Carham Hall

1633 after five centuries of royal military activity, and the site was left to nature.

Parish Church of St Cuthbert, Carham, 1790, R Hodgson Huntley
Huntley was amateur architect and lord of the manor. Romantic setting in hamlet across bend of the Tweed (Carham is the terminus of the Great Tweed Raft Race). Random rubble, ashlar and Welsh slate roof; *c.*1870, castellated west tower and chancel added and nave windows Gothicised. Original 18th-century box pews within, and on chancel north wall, a monument to Anthony Compton, 1830, by Davies of Newcastle. Eighteenth-century rusticated corniced gatepiers with steep pyramid caps, gates, 1938, wrought iron with arched panels and fleur-de-lis finials.

Carham Hall, *c.*1870
For the Compton family, Tudor mansion, now old folk's home, on older haughland site. Buff sandstone ashlar with pink dressings, stone slate roof. Elegantly spindly, with west five-eighths altered and refronted, *c.*1920, and tree cover for shelter making it an island in the pastoral landscape. Perhaps a rebuilding/remodelling of the Hall described as a *handsome modern building* in 1811, which itself may have been the parsonage house of 1800.

Sprouston Parish Church, 1781
Harled and white-painted, rectangular, four-bay, round-headed main windows (some original crown glass, one fine stained glass, 1922, Douglas Strachan), Welsh-slated, stone

bellcote with ball finial. Repaired 1822, 1845, with alterations and additions, 1912. Strangely mis-scaled **War Memorial**, J S Rhind, with lion atop a rock-faced ashlar monument.

St Anne's Parish Church, Ancroft, from 12th century
West end formed into defensible tower, 13th century, restored 1836, 1870, F R Wilson (nave extended, chancel rebuilt, door and windows replaced), tower restored, 1886. Romanesque, squared stone (18th-century sundial on gable) with Welsh slate roof. Elaborate 19th-century interior with some stained glass (memorial window to Lavers Westlake, 1892). Graveyard contains interesting sandstone early 19th-century tablet to nuns who were accommodated in Haggerston Castle following the French Revolution.

Top *Sprouston Parish Church.*
Above *War Memorial.* Left *St Anne's Parish Church*

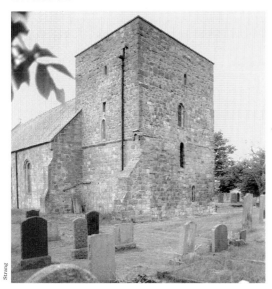

Northmoor Presbyterian Chapel, Ancroft, 1815
Random rubble with dressings, Welsh slate gabled roof, with gable quatrefoil and obelisk finials at each corner. Restored and improved, 1886; now a store.

Duddo Parish Church, 1879, F R Wilson
Snecked stonework with ashlar dressings below a Welsh slate roof, the whole in Decorated Gothic, with the buttressed, bellcote tower modelled upon St Mary's Church, Holy Island.

Strang

Former Church & School, Duddo, 1832,
Ignatius Bonomi
Built at request of the Revd Gilly of Norham,
dedicated to St James the Great, much
influenced by the Norman aspects of Norham
Church (see p.67), that here a single room, lit
by round-headed sash windows framed by roll-
moulded arches and shafts with waterleaf
capitals. Now a house. The L-plan school
building to the rear may well be later, with its
Tudor-arched doorway and sinuous bargeboards.

Duddo House, *c*.1825
Plain, classical, Scotch-slated two-storey ashlar
farmhouse with plinth and 12-pane sashes.
Completely renovated, 1948-9. The large porch
(six Corinthian columns in timber) was brought
from Peddie & Kinnear's University Club in
Princes Street, Edinburgh, in the 1960s.

Strang

Duddo Tower, late 16th or early 17th century
Ruined tower-house of which the south-west
corner and part of the south wall stand to
around 10m. James IV destroyed a tower at
Duddo in 1496 (see Twizell Castle, p.68-9)
though not completely since a fragment with
barmkin was standing in 1541.

ETAL
*The whitewashed cottages, some thatched and
others roofed with slate, together with the Bull
Inn, forms an unpretentious and pleasing group
of 18th-century buildings under the tall trees*
(Pevsner). In truth it is a pretty group, mostly
rebuilt for Lord Joicey when he bought the
estate in 1907, combining work of the 18th,
19th & 20th centuries, the **Black Bull** being
Northumberland's sole thatched inn. The
village street leads down to a ford on the Till –
a bridge here below the Castle was swept away
by floods in the 16th century and never
replaced.

Strang

Strang

Left and above *Etal Castle*

Etal Castle, from 1342
The Manners family had licence to crenellate in support of the Royal Castles guarding the Tweed. Overwhelmed and dismantled, 1497, by Scots. Now small but beautifully formed. The **gatehouse** incorporates a just visible coat of arms above the entrance triple-chamfered arch (with portcullis groove) flanked by projecting three-storey turrets. The **curtain wall** remnant to the south stands to the base of parapet level, with rounded corbels on the inner face as platform supports. The **south-west tower** remains only as a single-storey structure of pointed arches and vaulting. The four-storey **Great Tower** at the north-west corner is now detached from the rest of the ruins, an open shell in whose interior can be seen an arched fireplace, door and window openings.

Adjacent, the former **Presbyterian Church**, 1800, is, at the time of writing, a

Royal agreement was necessary before a castle was constructed – hence the *licence to crenellate* (i.e. fortify).

While the Scots might have seemed to us the obvious foes, danger could also come from nearer home, and the Manners family had a long-running feud with the Herons of nearby Ford. In 1427 John Manners was found accountable for the violent death of William Heron (who himself had attacked Etal with a *gret assaut made in shotyng of arrowes and strykyng with swerdes*). In recompense he had to give the widow a large cash sum **and** pay for 500 masses for Heron's soul.

Opposite: Top *Former Church and School, Duddo*. Middle above *Duddo Tower*. Middle below *Thatched cottages, Etal*. Bottom *Black Bull*

Former Presbyterian Church

Etal Manor

Lord Fitzclarence was one of the Duke of Clarence's illegitimate sons: such behaviour did not prevent the Duke from becoming King William IV in due course. Lady Augusta was a daughter of the Earl of Glasgow, who owned Etal Manor, and the Fitzclarences moved there after their marriage in 1821. The Chapel was built following the death of her husband and only child, in quick succession, in 1854 and 1855.

joiner's workshop, rubble with ashlar dressings below high, steeply pitched gabled Welsh slate roof. The adjacent former manse is earlier and pantiled.

Etal Manor, 1748

For William Carr, on site of 17th-century or earlier house. Originally L-plan, two-storey, 7x7 bays, infill range 1767, rear extension 1888. House with presence, ashlar, plinth and rusticated quoins, pedimented Venetian doorway and 12-pane sashes below hipped Scotch slate roof. To the east a squat sandstone **monument**, *c.*1850, carries inscriptions recording the happy days of two 19th-century occupiers of the estate. The two-storey **stable block** to the north may incorporate stonework taken from Etal Castle. To the south are strikingly tall **double gates**, **corniced gatepiers** and **flanking railings** in ashlar and wrought iron, *c.*1830.

Etal Chapel of the Blessed Virgin Mary, 1858, William Butterfield

For Lady Fitzclarence, as a memorial to her husband who died in India. Decorated, pink sandstone ashlar, with dressings and bands of buff sandstone. High, steeply pitched roof in graded Westmorland slate below tiled ridges, raising expectations of a spectacular interior. Sadly inside the chapel is something of a disappointment, without much in the way of enrichment.

Right and below *Etal Chapel*

FORD

Set in Glendale, Ford is a Gothick planned village on the Till. The estate was unenclosed moorland until the time of George III, at which point Lord Delaval improved by fencing, draining, hedging and building 13 of the grey stone farm groups. In the 1880s Tomlinson thought that Ford's *cosy-looking, homelike cottages, half hidden in foliage and trimmest of gardens ... present a picture of rural peace and retirement* and this description still applies today once the tourists have departed.

Strang

Parish Church of St Michael & All Angels,
Ford, early 13th century

Squared stone, nave (with aisles), Welsh-slated, chancel clay tile roofed, monumental two-tier bellcote. Internally the south arcade is 13th-century, six medieval grave slabs are set into the west end of the nave. Extensively restored, 1852-3, John Dobson. Decorated stone reredos erected to Marchioness of Waterford's memory by subscription of *rich and poor*, 1892, W S Hicks, and 1920 War Memorial in coloured marble and ceramic. Stained glass by William Wailes, Clayton & Bell, James Powell & Sons (1920, behind the War Memorial) and Douglas Hogg, 1972.

The churchyard entrance is a mid-18th-century ensemble of large square rusticated and corniced gate-piers, topped by three square blocks, pyramidal caps and ball finials, with, to the left, a flight of steps into the churchyard and a four-stepped mounting block. The rococo

When **John Dobson** established his architectural practice in Newcastle he modestly considered that, with the exception of Ignatius Bonomi based at Durham, he was *the only professional architect between Edinburgh and York.*
A Memoir of John Dobson, 1885

Left and below *Parish Church of St Michael & All Angels*

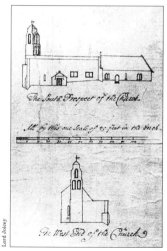

Lord Joicey

Marchioness of Waterford's gravestone and cross

G F Watts considered Louisa Waterford (1814-91) to be one of the greatest artists of her time, as evidenced by her pictures and book illustrations.

The 3m-high **Black family** gravestone, 1829-33, describes the loss of children, in a very forthright fashion;

> *Reader*
> *Let the memory of these*
> *young blossoms cut off in the*
> *morning of life, speak to thee*
> *With this friendly admonition*
> *Be you ready also*
> *For in such an hour as ye think not*
> *The son of man cometh.*

In the earlier 18th century around 60 per cent of the Scottish population died as children.
Rogers, *Social Life in Scotland*

Right *Ford Castle and gateway.*
Below *Ford Castle, 1716*

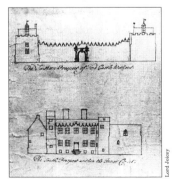

wrought-iron double gates were made by local blacksmiths in 1971.

West of the church is the **Marchioness of Waterford's gravestone** and **cross**, 1891, G F Watts. Two kneeling angels hold a wreath and shield with the Waterford arms, while in front lies an inscribed Celtic cross resting on four low walls. The cross to the Rector, Hastings Neville (author of *A Corner of the North*), and his family, is also of note.

Parson's Tower, medieval
Probably a *vicar's peel*, first mentioned in 1541, of which about 4m remain in squared stone, the walls 2m thick, the ground floor segmentally tunnel-vaulted.

Ford Castle, *c.*14th-century core
Licence to crenellate granted to Sir William Heron in 1338 but castle recorded here in 1287: originally with four corner towers, north range converted to mansion surprisingly prior to 1589. E-plan mansion house, incorporating King James' tower, medieval squared stone and ashlar below stone slate and Westmorland slate gabled roofs. The central portion by David Bryce, from 1862, has intentionally irregular Gothick openings, a stone balcony and large oriel window, both on stone brackets. Now field studies centre.

Flagpole Tower, or Cow Tower, originally south-west corner tower of the quadrilateral Castle. Now linked by 30m of forecourt wall,

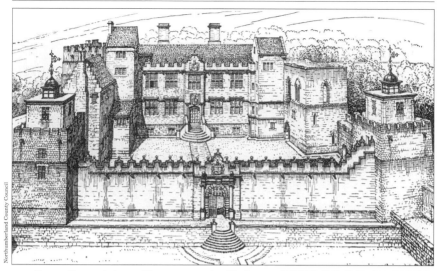

Northumberland County Council

mostly castle curtain walling, parapet added, 1771, James Nisbet. Tower repaired and top floor renewed, 1862, David Bryce. Presently five-storey and basement, Welsh slate roof. **Forecourt walls**, **towers** and **gateways**, 1771, James Nisbet, and 1791-5, Alexander Gilkie, all in Gothick style, those to the south incorporating earlier masonry.

Within the policies of the Castle stand various mid 19th-century structures, e.g. **walled garden**, **terrace walls**, **game larder** and rock-faced **Dene Bridge**. **West Lodge** and **Gateway**, 1866, probably David Bryce: Gothic lodge, with banded purple and blue Welsh slate, incorporates Marchioness of Waterford's monogram, while to the left stand castellated, octagonal gatepiers flanked by arcaded screen walls.

Ford Bridge, 1809, incorporating one arch from a 16th-century bridge, has two broad segmental arches, with arch bands, which share a triangular cutwater.

Earliest part of Ford (estate) village is now 1860 Waterford-inspired, Welsh-slated, hood-moulded cottages. **Jubilee Cottage**, 1887, has a banded slate roof and Royal Doulton ceramic plaque portraying Queen Victoria.

Waterford Fountain, 1860, Sir George Gilbert Scott
Quatrefoil sandstone basin with cable-moulded edge, a marble angel holding the Waterford

Top *Ford Castle*. Middle *Flagpole Tower*. Above *West Lodge and gateway*. Below *Jubilee Cottage*

Lord Joicey

arms standing on the polished granite central Corinthian column from whose base project stone water-spouts. (Now alas a planter.)

Above and right Waterford Fountain.
Below right Lady Waterford Hall.
Bottom Heatherslaw Mill cartshed

The fountain commemorates the Marchioness of Waterford's husband (they met at the Eglinton Tournament in 1842 where she was Queen of Beauty) who died following a hunting accident, with the inscription *with joy shall ye drink out of the well of salvation. Drink ye abundantly, O beloved.*

The hall was decorated, 1861-83, by the Marchioness with Pre-Raphaelite-style biblical paintings, featuring figures of village folk and castle staff, distemper and watercolour on paper on canvas to give a mural effect. Lady Waterford was an amateur of some skill who sought tuition variously from such as Ruskin, Rossetti and Watts. Ruskin was dismissive of her *murals. I expected you would have done something better.*

Lady Waterford Hall, 1860
Former village school, in stone with ashlar dressings, banded Westmorland and Welsh slate roof, octagonal stone flues and decorative (but now mostly incomplete) ridge tiles.

Strang

Heatherslaw Mill, 18th century; extended and remodelled, c.1860
Water-driven corn mill, rubble with dressings below Welsh slate roof. Five-bay granary, c.1808, to rear, now incorporates a café. A double mill with two wooden undershot wheels driving two sets of machinery: the upper mill is in full working order. The corn-drying kiln is rubble-built, with some patching in old brick, and pantile-roofed: attached former stores now gift shop. To the west, a pantiled former cart shed. The bridge across the river (one car at a

Strang

time, please) reminiscent of Meccano, with officious but effective stone lecterns to channel vehicles, on the site of a ford.

Below *Ford Smithy.* Middle and bottom *Advertisements for Ford Smithy*

Strang

Ford Smithy, 1863

Unmistakable with its boarded double-doors within a raised horseshoe-shaped surround. Later informal additions to the village are rosemary-tiled Edwardian (*c.*1909) two-storey gabled semi-detached houses, and the pair of two-storey semi-detached pantiled houses, 1963, with compatible and consistent single-storey post office/café to the north.

Ford Forge, 1779; extended, *c.*1835

Large estate smithy making iron goods, from nails to grates, later used as a commercial spade-making forge.

Encampment Farmhouse, 1780

Ashlar with Welsh slate roof, the lower extension, 1864, to the right in similar style. Garden walls and gatepiers to the front in rubble, with roughly dressed sandstone copes and sandstone ashlar piers. Adjacent farm buildings incorporate 18th-century brick and tile presumably from the Flodden Tile Works to the south, established in 1768.

CROOKHAM

Blue Bell, late 18th century

Former coaching inn, brick (some particularly fine gable detailing), hideous modern glazing, minor additions to rear in stone, the whole pantile-roofed.

FRONT ELEVATION

SMITHS SHOP

PROPOSED TO BE BUILT

AT

FORD

FOR

LADY WATERFORD

FORGE
11 4

SHOEING
STALLS

GROUND PLAN

Lord Joicey

ADVERTISEMENT.

TO be let and entered upon immediately, a compleat Iron Forge, with a Hammer of three hundred Weight, wrought with a large and conftant Supply of Water, together with various Conveniencies, fituated within two Miles of a working Colliery, ten Miles from Berwick, twelve from Kelfo, and fix from Wooler: This Factory is newly built, and well conftructed and contrived for Spade, Saw, or Edge-tool-makers, or for a Smith who could employ feveral Hands, and perform Jobs by Patterns or Orders.

For further Particulars inquire of Mr. Oxley at Heatherflaw.

Berwick-upon-Tweed Borough Council

Crookham Cottage
Combination of three cottages, that to the left late 17th century with formerly thatched, steeply pitched roof over Gothick pointed-arch windows; section to the right, c.1830.

Crookham United Reform Church, 1932, Gray & Patterson
Formerly the Presbyterian church, incorporates a panel commemorating predecessor, 1745, and its rebuilding, 1932, art deco, in stone, cut deliberately off the square, and bellcoted, with a Westmorland slate roof. Beside the church the village pump in cast iron, a fluted column with lion-mask spout, at its base an iron shelf for the buckets.

Crookham Manse, c.1750
Former Presbyterian manse, re-roofed and extended to rear, c.1850, two-storey, five-bay, with rusticated quoins below Welsh slate roof and brick chimneys.

Mardon Farmhouse, c.1840
Rubble with ashlar dressings, two-storey 3x3 bays, hipped Welsh slate roof, ha-ha, fine cart-shed range.

Top *Crookham Cottage*. Above *Crookham United Reform Church*. Right *Mardon Farmhouse*

In 1678 the **Crookham Affray** was the last border incident, involving mounted Scots and English, where men died.

Memorial drinking fountain

BRANXTON
Peaceful village belying its historical significance as site of Battle of Flodden, 1513, where *shivered was fair Scotland's spear and broken was her shield*. **Branxton House**, early 19th century, Welsh slated. Former post office, 1854, attached. **Memorial drinking fountain**, 1910, George Reavell. Ashlar and iron, pilastered and decorated with carved fruits, in memory of William Askew Robertson. **Cement garden**.

Church of St Paul, *c.*1200
Only the chancel arch is medieval: rebuilt,
1849. Romanesque, built of snecked rhyolite
with sandstone dressings, and stone pyramid
roof to the tower.

Flodden Memorial, 1910
Polished granite tapering cross, severe and
uninspiring, given that it is dedicated to the
dead of both nations (9000 Scots, 5000
English). Erected by the Berwickshire
Naturalists Club.

Above *Church of St Paul.*
Left *Flodden Memorial*

The battle of Flodden, a
disastrous defeat for the Scots, has
been described as one of the last
medieval battles, won by footsoldiers
with bills (2.5m long axes with
curved blades), for despite the fact
that James IV brought his culverin,
the *Seven Sisters*, they had no
effective role in the slaughter. The
English bills broke the Scots' 5.5m
spears, and then could pick off the
Scots out of range of their swords. In
the massacre which developed
surprisingly (inasmuch as the
armies were numerically evenly
matched and the Scots initially had
a strong if not impregnable
position), the king, nine earls,
thirteen lords and their supporters
were slaughtered.

Ironically, **James IV's attack** on
England and Henry VIII was in the
face of a papal bull from Pope Julius
II which stated that the Scots king
would be excommunicated if he
invaded England. The attack was
also in breach of the *Treaty of
Perpetual Peace* of 1502, papally
confirmed, although King James had
already, in 1511, written to the Pope
presuming that English unprovoked
violence had set at naught the
Treaty.

Prophetically, in 1498, the **Spanish
Ambassador, Pedro de Ayala**
described King James IV as ... *rash
in warfare; he does not take care of
himself; and he is not a good captain
because he begins to fight before he
has given his orders.*

Marmion's Well
Used by Scott as setting in his epic poem, the
well was reconstructed in late Victorian times,
its inscribed ashlar slab being built for Lady
Waterford who brought posses of guests from
Ford to see it.

Flodden Lodge, 1865, David Bryce
Decorative (Waterford monogram) two-storey
house in stone, with hood-moulded openings
below a gabled crested roof, fleur-de-lis finialed
and banded in green slates. Built for the
Marchioness of Waterford.

Pallinsburn

Pallinsburn takes its name from Paulinus, a bishop from Kent who accomplished the conversion to Christianity of King Edwin of Northumbria in the 7th century, and took to wholesale baptism of Northumbrians in the countryside.

The freestone used in 18th-century buildings was obtained from quarries at Newmills on the Whiteadder just within the bounds of Berwick, and from quarries at Tweedmouth. *Rough Stones sell at these quarries from 8d the double cart load.*
Fuller

John Mackay Wilson (1804-35) became Editor of the *Berwick Advertiser* in 1832 having... *already formed habits of intemperance.* Tales of the Borders were published weekly from 1834, continuing after his death until 1840 under Editor Alexander Leighton.

Pallinsburn, from late 18th century Palatial brick Jacobean, the older material said to be Dutch (unlikely given the existence of local brick and tile works), the wings hipped Scotch-slated roofed, the main block flat concrete thankfully concealed by parapets. Extended mid-19th century, main block remodelled, 1912, top storey removed *c.*1933, which is missed from the garden front but strangely not from the south courtyard. Policy features include matching brick garden pavilions with pedimented fronts and (blank) Venetian windows.

TWEEDMOUTH

Tweedmouth to Spittal is where the majority of traditional industry was to be found in the Berwick area, outwith the town's walls.

Tweedmouth, in particular, was spectacularly industrious when the Scots held the town and the English forces fretted south of the Tweed, and was definitely English, part of North Durham (from the border at Carham to Holy Island, under control of the Bishops of Durham), before it became part of Northumberland in 1844. Tweedmouth's oldest parts are around the end of the Berwick Bridge (and Main Street was, of course, the main road to Newcastle until 1928), where there was a fortified tower in the 16th century.

20-32 West End Road

The former *Tammy Shops* built by Mackay & Blackstock at the same time as they were building the Royal Border Bridge. The *Tammy Shops* were originally stores, stables and workshops, but by 1857 had been converted to dwellings. The *Tammy* or tally shops were places where the railway construction navvies could acquire goods on credit in return for a deduction (with interest) from their wages.

Thatch Inn, c.1886

A tavern of 1535 stood here, but only a louping-stane (mounting block) has survived a fire of 1886 which destroyed interiors which had housed the pay office for workmen building Berwick Bridge.

Tweedmouth House, 4 Main Street, 18th century

Stucco with stone margins, on a raised terrace, Tuscan-columned portico with a Venetian window and pediment over.

46-48 Main Street, early 18th century, mostly pantiled small cottages arranged in a little close on the hillside of the river bank. Opposite is **Tweed Dock**, 1872-7, and former **Toll House**. The Dock railway branch connected along the river front to the main line, marked today only by the stone arch at the foot of **Howick Terrace** and **Falloden Terrace**, red-brick railway houses. **Short's Mill**, Dock Road, is a 19th-century granary, now a flour mill.

The Old Brewery, Tweedmouth, 18th century Stone complex on a sloping site which, with the kiln-projecting pantiled and Welsh-slated roofline, forms a picturesque group.

Church of St Bartholomew, Church Road, 1783, late Georgian gallery. Restored and enlarged, 1841, enlarged (chancel) and Gothicised, 1866, F R Wilson; nave windows, ceiling, tower arch and south porch, 1906. Stained glass window by Kemp. In the graveyard lies John Mackay Wilson, author of *Tales of the Borders*. Tudor half-timbered **Vicarage**, 1888, F R Wilson.

Lifeboat House, Tweedmouth Formerly (from 1901) on the beach, the lifeboat was relocated with its dismantled and

In **1799** there were two tile and brick manufacturers in the vicinity of Berwick, Mr Foster of Cocklaw, three miles west of Berwick, and Mr Selby Morton in Tweedmouth. *Mr Foster's father, who farmed Cocklaw, accidentally discovered this stratum of clay. He then took a lease of the farm, and established a manufacture of tyles and of bricks, which he carried on for 25 years.* His son took over the business in 1787 and employed an average of eight men making between 150,000 – 180,000 tiles per year. Selby Morton, who took over an earlier and unsuccessful business in tile making in 1788, was by the end of the century employing seven men making 170,000 tiles and 200,000 bricks.

The Inn was in the Heslop family for centuries, being entailed (if there were no male heirs it passed to another branch of the family bearing the name). A pre-1886 description mentions *the antiquated-looking windows, the low roof, the great ingle side in the kitchen, and the beautiful Dutch tiles, illustrating scriptural subjects, which lined the fireplace.*

Below *Short's Mill.* Bottom *The Old Brewery*

Lifeboat House

In 1760 one stagecoach, travelling once a month, linked Edinburgh and London: depending on the weather, the journey took 10-15 days.

The post that left Edinburgh on *Saturday 12 November 1725 was never heard of after it quitted Berwick. It was presumed that the rider and his horse had missed the road and strayed into the sea.* Handley

In Fuller's day the **Spa Well** was well known in the Borders as a place to take the waters. In the summer season, many who came to drink were obliged to go home again for want of lodgings. As a result of the increasing popularity, Spittal expanded south toward the Spa Wall and beyond. Many of the houses took in lodgers, most from the Border towns but some from further afield. Ambitious Spittalers saw the village becoming a thriving holiday resort, building the Promenade in 1892 in the hope of encouraging business.

Below *Spittal Pavilion.*
Right *Promenade shelter*

reassembled house in the 1930s, when this great reinforced concrete ramp was built, no doubt as a benefit of the technical expertise put into the 1928 road bridge.

Beyond the former Co-op building, 1937, now Cochrane's Showroom, on the East Ord Industrial Estate the **Berwick Ambulance Station** stands out, even in buff brick, with shallow-pitched corrugated metal roof with oversailing eaves detail picked out in green. Tweedmouth Industrial Estate across the road has the brash **Allan Bros** office block, yellow brick, banded base-courses, oversailing eaves, deeply recessed openings utilising the company's window products: the accompanying open warehouse is brutally diagonal-boarded like some gigantic advertising hoarding.

SPITTAL
For many years just a fishing village and isolated site of the medieval leper hospital of St Bartholomew, Spittal's **Spa Well** attracted some 18th-century visitors to take the waters; and in the 19th century sea-bathing increased its popularity. Any curative benefits would have

been countered by the effects of the Victorian gas works, chemical works and fertiliser factories, but the economy clearly benefited from the growth of tourism, and the **Promenade** was created in 1892-4, following a major local fundraising effort to make Spittal the Blackpool of Northumberland. The **Venetian Pavilion** began as a corrugated iron building, c.1930, for the Forte family, and it was so successful that it was enlarged and improved, with its classical colonnade later that decade.

Askew Crescent, 1928, George Reavell Arts & Crafts-influenced, semi-detached and flatted *buts-and-bens*, the gift of W H Askew of Ladykirk House and still let today by the Askew Housing Trust.

SCREMERSTON
Sub-rural colliery village typical of the larger Northumbrian pit-villages in size and appearance: pit now closed. **Parish Church**, 1842-3, Bonomi & Cory: Early English, stone with ashlar dressings and Welsh slate roof. The west tower's clasping buttresses support a broach spire with two tiers of lucarnes.

Scremerston Town Farm, 1820-30 L-plan, two-storey, five-bay house in ashlar with Scotch slated hipped roof, its improvement accompanied by the construction of sixteen workers' cottages, each complete with cowhouse, pigsty and privy. **The Cottage**, Scremerston Hill, early 18th century, steeply-pitched Westmorland slate roofs over dressed stone house and outbuildings. At **Scremerston Old Mine**, the colliery pumping-**Engine House**, 1840, for the Commissioners of Greenwich Hospital is now a roofless shell. **Water Tower**, 1840, Thomas Forster, engineer, three storeys of rock-faced stone with an iron water tank on top.

Inlandpasture, 1820-30 Elegantly proportioned two-storey, three-bay farmhouse rebuilt, like the Town Farm, for the Commissioners of Greenwich Hospital who had gained the estates of the Earl of Derwentwater, executed as a Jacobite in 1715. Hipped Welsh-slated roof and lower service wings to rear. Contemporary low garden wall ramps down to form a ha-ha in front of the house.

Just east of Oxford, an early 19th-century **limekiln** (now standing sentinel to a

Top *Tile framing of plaque, Askew Crescent.* Above *Scremerston Town Farm*

The formerly unenclosed moorland to the south of Spittal was where, in the reign of Charles II, **Grizel Cochrane** robbed the English mail carrier of her father's death warrant (John Cochrane of Ochiltree), he languishing in Edinburgh's Tolbooth.

In Scotland estates forfeited after the '15 and '45 risings were controlled by a Board of Commissioners (Lord Kames was one) until 1784 (when the lands reverted to original owners or heirs) over which period significant investments in improvement, and their returns, were made.

Inlandpasture

Oxford limekiln

Strang

municipal tip) three large segmental arches giving access to the kiln furnace. Adjacent quarry pit is water filled.

Strang

Above *Chinese lion, Cheswick House*. Right *Cheswick House*

Cheswick House, 1859-62, F R Wilson
High Victorian Gothic country house for William Crossman in ashlar and Welsh slate, the service wing rock-faced stone. Vertical emphasis in the gabled roofs and tall chimneystacks is accompanied by trefoil, quatrefoil and even sexfoil decorative punctuation. Framing the front door stand two 19th-century Chinese lions on plinths, the beasts being imported from China in the 1870s. Additional features of interest include the **East Lodge & stable block**, both 1862, F R Wilson, the **main gates**, **gatepiers & lodge**, 1887, and late 19th-century brick-lined walled garden with its terracotta urns.

Strang

East House, *c.*1810-15
Rendered with ashlar dressings and rusticated quoins. Concave hipped Welsh slate roof. To the south-east gatepiers and screen walls of *c.*1810. **Farm cottages**, *c.*1820, are unusually fine

(despite conversion from eight into five in the 1940s) and complete with railings, the eighth at the foot of the L retaining its original fenestration. East House also has a range of **offices** dating from 1808, altered 1879, and a pair of 1816, pantiled **field hemels** (cattle shelters) to the south-east.

Cheswick Cottage, c.1820

Two-storey, L-plan house with ashlar dressings and quoins. Welsh slate gabled roof. To the north a fine range of early 19th-century offices, two-storey centre block with single-storey L-plan wings, the whole Scotch slated.

Top *East House farm cottages.*
Above *East House farm range.*
Left *Ladythorne House*

Ladythorne House, 1721

Two-storey five-bay Scotch-slated house built for Robert Wilkes in brick with ashlar dressings and rusticated quoins. A former 17th-century house south-east of Cheswick Old School is now a store with a corrugated-iron roof. Its interest is now almost entirely archaeological, with features such as the chamfered 17th-century door surrounds, blacksmith-type windows and a small fire window. **Cocklaw Dunes Nature Reserve** boasts a dramatically sited triple-arched **limekiln**, in whin with sandstone arches. **Cheswick Shiel**, 18th-century origins, is a salmon fishermen's shelter at the shore, a small whitewashed rubble, pantiled cabin.

Broomhouse Farmhouse, mid-18th century

Two-storey brick house with ashlar dressings and Welsh slate roof. 1857, porch altered and right bay extended to the front. **Bridge Mill**, mid-18th-century corn mill and miller's house. Ashlar, rusticated quoins, L-plan, two-storey and attic. To the rear 18th-century former **byre**, **stable** and **forge**, now garage and store, random rubble with dressings and Scotch slate gabled roof.

A Scottish Act of Parliament in 1456 included *Item, it is ordainit that al maneir of man that has landis or gudis be redy horsit and geirit eftir the faculté of his landis and gudis for the defens of the Realm at the comaundement of (the King) ... And that al maneir of men betuix sextie and sextene be redy on thair best wyse to cum to the Bordouris for the defens of the land quhen ony wittering [ie information] cumis of the incuming of ane greit Inglis host.*

Lady Gadsden

The Castle Club THEATRE BAR

Strang

Haggerston Castle: Top *South front, 1930*. Above *Tower*. Right *Stables*

Haggerston Castle, rebuilt 1889-93, R Norman Shaw
For Thomas Leyland, the new owner. Home of the Haggerstons, the castle (all but the main tower) was burnt down in 1618, and the remains incorporated in a new building which was not completed. Extensive alterations and repairs, 1805; 1903 rebuilding, J B Dunn, after a fire. In 1933 all but the rotunda and tower were demolished, contents and fabric being widely dispersed. The baroque **rotunda** (former entrance to the castle) is a single tall storey, its doorway pedimented and with a Gibbsian surround, each window carrying triple keystones and an oculus over. The twelve-storey **tower** is an ashlar, L-plan water tower and belvedere. **Haggerston Castle stables**, 1908, possibly J B Dunn, a square of four ranges, the carriage arch tall, rusticated and pedimented and the courtyard interior particularly fine and complete.

Strang

Italian Garden, *c.*1910
Stone and brick with house and arbour Westmorland-slated, and a fine pair of rococo wrought-iron gates. Within the garden a

contemporary fountain – now, alas, a planter – and a cruciform stone and brick pergola. In 1933 the garden was described as having a *shelter of classic design, a stone-built tea-house, Roman rose pergola and lily pond.* To the south, a late 19th-century **animal shelter**, probably an antelope shelter (Leyland set up a private zoo at Haggerston and there are other, less significant animal shelters), timber-framed, vertical boarding and Welsh slate gabled roof with ornamental cresting.

Chapel House, 1930

Chapel House (Priest House), late 18th century
Former RC chapel and priest's house, ashlar with pantile and concrete tile roof. To the left the house with its Gothick window: to the right the chapel with its contemporary lean-to two-storey vestry to the front. To the west a 17th-century roofless, circular **doocot** in random rubble with brick nesting boxes.

Aidan was the founder of the Northumbrian Church, having been summoned by King Oswald to become Bishop of Northumbria. From Lindisfarne he made successful missionary journeys to the mainland, in the face of the ravages of Penda, the heathen ruler of Mercia.

St John the Baptist's Parish Church, Lowick, rebuilt 1794 by Henry Penny Selby Morton (so inscribed over the doorway), Gothicised in the 1830s, chancel and vestry added 1887, F R Wilson.

Below *Priory Church and Castle.* Bottom *Monastery and Castle, 1728*

HOLY ISLAND
Known also as Lindisfarne, Holy Island is the cradle of early Christianity in the north-east. Priory established by St Aidan (who arrived from Iona in 635), St Cuthbert and St Wilfred on relatively secure (until the Vikings sacked it in 793 and forced the abandonment of cathedral and monastery in 875), certainly contemplative, site reached by tidal causeway or boat. Holy Island village served the Priory, now fishing and tourism drive the local economy, watch for upturned boats as stores. Post-Viking rebuilt,

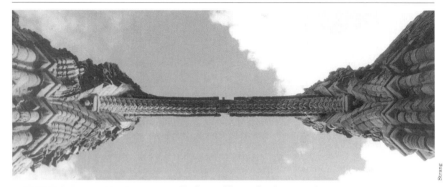

The Governor of Lindisfarne Castle in 1635 was *Captain Rugg, who is as famous for his generous and free entertainment of strangers as for his great bottle nose, which is the largest I have seen. There are neat, warm and convenient rooms in this little fort* (Sir William Brereton). Rugg had considerable difficulty paying his bills, for at one time he was owed 16 months' back pay, and petitioned King Charles I in verse: Rugg later delivered the Castle into Parliament's hands.

Priory Church, from 11th century, 13th-century monastic buildings, ruined since Henry VIII struck. Rebuilt/restored 1855-6 and early 20th century. **Visitor Centre**, Bain Swan, English Heritage, Christian and pagan incisings. *English Heritage; guidebook available*

Abbey Church of St Mary, 13th century, but possibly with an earlier shell. 18th-century buttressed bellcote, small north *porch*, early 19th century, built as mortuary for victims of the deep. Restoration, 1860, F R Wilson, stained-glass window, 1883, by Mayer of Munich. The National Nature Reserve is topped by **Lindisfarne Castle**, 1539-40, for Henry VIII, garrisoned until 1819, coastguard use in 19th century, interior derelict until converted to private house, 1903, Edwin Lutyens, for Edward Hudson, owner of *Country Life* magazine. Lutyens' first (and best?) *castle house* (colour p.109). **Walled garden**, 1906-12, Lutyens & Gertrude Jekyll. *National Trust; guidebook available*. Spectacular views and coastline to south includes Bamburgh Castle and Farne Islands. Note also the bank of limekilns (in the 1860s, a Dundee firm was established here, using local limestone and Scottish coal) and upturned cobles now fishermen's stores, but in the 19th century frequently used as housing.

Berwick-upon-Tweed Borough Museum and Art Gallery

KELSO

The most architectural of all Border burghs, its irresistible combination of open landscape setting on the banks of the River Tweed, ruined abbey, spired skyline and Continental Square suggest a pleasantly unmilitary history. The truth is somewhat different, given the proximity to Roxburgh Castle, Kelso playing second fiddle while Roxburgh Castle and Burgh thrived, and thereafter, as the Abbey grew, taking its share of sackings too. *Town trail and guidebook available*

Prospect of the town of Kelso

The Square has its **Bull Ring** subtly delineated in the centre of the grand sett-covered space (conceivably an ecclesiastical garden in medieval times): the ring used for tethering bulls during cattle markets. A waste that such a splendid space does not now hold markets like that of Berwick's Marygate, or at least accommodate the present Kelso Sunday market (held near the racecourse).

Opposite: Top *Priory Church.* Middle *Lindisfarne Castle.* Bottom left *Priory Church.* Bottom right *Lindisfarne Castle and stores*

¹ **Town Hall**, 1816
Tetrastyle Ionic edifice with piazza basement and a cupola replacing, thanks to public subscription, the old thatched tolbooth. Infill of the ground-floor arcade and other remodelling works. Infill, 1904-6, J D Swanston & Syme of Kirkcaldy, of the ground-floor arcade and other remodelling works give an Edwardian baroque character without tampering overmuch with the original form. Four blocked Ionic columns, town crest, pediment, octagonal belfry (clock of 1841) leaded bellcast roof topped by a weathercock.

Below *The Square and Town Hall, 1880s.* Bottom *Blair's, Jewellers*

RCAHMS

² **Blair's**, Jewellers, *c.*1750
Four-storey five-bay gracefully aged, the *Queen Mum* of Kelso, Venetian windows and lugged surrounds, a pilastered 19th-century shopfront (with original shutters) and pronouncedly bellcast slated roof with brick stacks.

Strang

Top *Detail, Royal Bank of Scotland.*
Above *Hogarth's Mill.* Right *Cross
Keys*

3 Royal Bank of Scotland, 1934
Banker's Georgian introduction of red brick
and rosemary tile, in contrast to the vast
majority of the Square's elevations in stone or
painted render.

The west and north elevations of the Square
are characterised by three-storey blocks of
c.1800 or later, with good shopfronts (often
pilastered and large brick stacks (quite
possibly original) with buff cans, providing a
lively and important skyline above slated roofs
and a choice collection of traditional dormers.
A variety of wynds slip westwards down to the
River Tweed.

At the south-west end of the Square, the
4 former **Ednam House stables**, Oven Wynd,
*c.*1761, presumably James Nisbet, two-storey
U-plan in coursed rubble with rusticated
quoins and piended corrugated-iron roof.

5 Hogarth's Mill, Peat Wynd,
early 19th century
Island block of three-storey mill buildings with
offices, now passed by service access to Mill and
supermarket. At the river's edge of **Duns Wynd**
the masonry remainder of the medieval monks'
water-mill can be seen. **Lombardi's** steeply
pitched roof is redolent of thatched days.

6 Cross Keys, 1761
Coaching inn for James Dickson,
reconstructed with Italianate front and added
top floor, 1880. Four-storey seven-bay front
(the central bay a depressing pend arcade)
rusticated quoins, architraves, balustraded
parapet with ball and spike finials. Through
the pend were the Cross Keys' extensive
stables, now all regrettably razed. Here too

7 the **Red Lion**, 1905, Edwardian pub whose contextualism puts more recent adjacent developments to shame.

Further round the Square, the north-east corner provides a glimpse through *the Dardanelles* to the former **Trinity North Church & Church Hall**, 1885-6, John Starforth. UP Church, replacing church of 1788. First Pointed Gothic, rubble, southern four-stage angle-buttressed tower with lanceted belfry, hall to the north across the axis of the main kirk.

5-7 Bridge Street, 18th century
Two-storey seven-bay house, built over *c.*1700 vaulted cellar, raised to three-storey and shop-fronted (probably in two stages) in Victorian times. Rusticated quoins, moulded architraves and centre Venetian window. **No 9**, early 19th century, two-and-a-half-storey five-bay house with later shopfront, the first building lit by gas in Scotland, in 1818. (The town gas company was established in 1831.)

Above *Former Trinity North Church.*
Left *Ednam House, pre-1951*

The Dardanelles is a narrow wynd, a local parallel to the strait joining the Aegean Sea and the Sea of Marmara.

In 1804 there was a celebrated false alarm that Napoleon had invaded. 500 volunteers turned out at St Boswells, John Younger the village shoemaker among them. At Kelso Bridge there was a barricade against the French, and the seat of his corduroy trousers was terminally ripped in its scaling. *So in we must march through the Kelso causeway to join the assembling force in the Cross Keys' big ballroom – my shirt all the while doing, of its own free will, the kindly office of a Highlandman's kilt very sympathetically. No matter for the colour of kilts in such a night as this, and such a ballroom surely!*

10 **Ednam House Hotel**, Bridge Street, 1761, James Nisbet
Two-and-a-half-storey-and-basement, seven-bay front, projecting the central three bays of the garden elevation as a semi-octagon. Outstanding interiors, the better for their public accessibility. The doors, for example, are made of hardwoods from Havana, replete with original brass locks, handles and hinges. Plasterwork by Thomas Perritt and Joseph Rose (Sen). Mid-19th-century screen walls to left and right, hotel additions, 1932, south wing, and 1937, north wing, hideous 1955 western extension which, at a stroke, reduced the character of the ensemble on the banks of

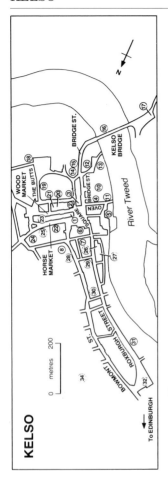

the Tweed to that of a seaside boarding house. Nisbet's first recorded work, and *one of the most elegant private mansions Nisbet ever designed*. And so it should have been, since he apparently cribbed much of the plans and elevations from Issac Ware's *Complete Body of Architecture*, where also can be seen the drawing room ceiling design of Apollo's chariot pursuing Aurora across a cloudy sky, with the four elements represented in the corners. Built as Havana House for James Dickson who had made his fortune in the New World, having left Kelso under a cloud himself after an act of vandalism.

[11] Of two late-18th-century **Gothick garden houses** here, the lower was swept away by the 1948 floods. The survivor, converted to a house in 1948, features slim clustered Gothic shafts and quatrefoils below a piended slated roof (see colour p.163). The hotel's present main entrance constructed, 1928-9, over the site of the Tron (public weigh-beam). Original main entrance off Abbey Court.

Right *Garden Houses, Ednam House.* Below *Detail, Bridge Street*

Queen's Head, Bridge Street, late 18th century
Three-and-a-half-storey four-bay former coaching inn, with rusticated quoins and attractive engaged Tuscan porch. **Spread Eagle Hotel**, Bridge Street, 1809, to Abbey Row. Bridge Street elevation more formal, with the bar window a masterpiece of etching.

21-31 Bridge Street, *c.*1870
Fine sequence of flats over shopfronts, much of the latter in cast iron. Opposite, a fine piece of street frontage culminates in **46** Bridge Street/**1 Abbey Row**, 1873, a confident three-storey end block undaunted by the presence of its 600-year older neighbour.

6 Abbey Court, mid 18th century
Three-and-a-half-storey (slated roof with
catslide dormers) carries Kelso's only firemark.

[12] **No 8, Turret House**, 1678, two-storey four-bay, with a massive round forestair (probably a
later addition) corbelled into a square plan at
attic level (*National Trust for Scotland*).
Contains the **Kelso Museum**, an essential
stop for the visitor, even if only to examine old
maps of the area. The old bridge access can still
be followed some way out of Abbey Court down
towards the river. A particular feature to watch
for is the stone gutter detailing on the old
causeway, which might, of course, pre-date
any bridge at this location.

[13] **St Andrew's Episcopal Church**, 1868-9,
Sir Robert Rowand Anderson
Geometric Gothic, bull-faced coursed rubble
with buff freestone dressings. Understated
spire – conical on a drum turret – not as
originally designed but very successful. Interior
very fine, with sculptured reredos (scenes from
the life of St Andrew), stencilled decoration in
the chancel, rich scissor-beam roof structure,
and splendid stained glass including some
20th-century by Douglas Strachan and an east
window designed by Anderson himself,
executed by Burlison & Grylls of London.
Within the restricted churchyard are
memorials from the earlier church, and the
whole is clasped by the terraces of Ednam
House, whose old gates and gatepiers dominate
a splendid sea of cobbles.

[14] **Kelso Abbey**, from 1128
*One of the most spectacular achievements of
Romanesque architecture in Scotland.* Originally
established 1113, near Selkirk, then moved here
to a more hospitable, if vulnerable, site within
the Tweed's lazy curve. In fullest extent the
largest of all the Border abbeys, with both
eastern and western transepts, now the
smallest, for only the western transept, tower
and two bays of the south arcade of the nave
remain. A bloody history, including 1523 vaults
demolished, roofs removed, set on fire. Partly
destroyed 1545, burnt 1547. Part (now
demolished) used as parish church 1649-1771, a
thatched roof covering part of the transept. 1805
ruins cleared of unsightly additions. Thoroughly
repaired, 1866, for Duke of Roxburghe (see
colour p.161). *Historic Scotland. Open to the
public; guidebook available*

Top *Turret House.* Above *St
Andrew's Episcopal Church*

When Hertford's troops attacked
Kelso Abbey in 1545 they *devised
thereuppon with the Italion fortifier
that ys here, Archam, and the
master mason of Berwik.*

Detail, Kelso Abbey

War Memorial

John Rennie, 1761-1821, was a millwright who left Scotland seeking work, and found it with James Watt, who wanted to utilise steam power for milling as well as the more conventional pumping. But the power of the steam engine required iron, rather than the traditional wooden, milltrain wheels and gears. Rennie was so successful, inventing the steam governor which ensured a steady power delivery to the milltrains, that Watt made him sign away any possibility of making steam engines, and Rennie then turned to civil rather than mechanical engineering.

Below *Kelso Bridge and Toll-House.*
Right *Springwood Park Gateway*

15 Dukes of Roxburghe Memorial Cloister, 1933-4, Reginald Fairlie
Built off the Abbey, two sides of a Romanesque cloister, L-plan, two-bay-by-four, incorporating a 13th-century doorway. Just to the south the **War Memorial**, 1921, Sir Robert Lorimer, mercat cross type, with niche on pedestal housing Pilkington Jackson statue of St George with broken lance, expiring (Teutonic?) dragon and (token) saltire on his shield.

16 Kelso Bridge & Toll-House, 1800-3, John Rennie
Level carriageway supported on five elliptical arches, the piers built off rounded cutwaters which carry paired engaged Doric columns. At the west end cast-iron lamps salvaged from Rennie's London Bridge on its demolition in the 1930s. Kelso was his first major bridge, replacing that of 1754 (swept away in 1797). Sir William Fairbairn, Kelsonian (1789-1874), the mechanical engineer, worked here as a 14-year-old, being almost crippled by a falling stone. The Toll-House stands one-storey to the carriageway, three-storey to the river.

17 Springwood Park Gateway, 1822, James Gillespie Graham
Classical archway, coupled Tuscan columns, flanking screen walls punctuated by square pyramidally capped terminal piers. On the axis of Rennie's bridge, it served as the access to **Springwood Park House**, 1756, altered 1820s, James Gillespie Graham, enlarged 1850-3, Brown & Wardrop, demolished 1954.

Springwood Park Mausoleum, 1822, James Gillespie Graham
More (neo)classicism, with the demolition of

the house remaindering this temple too. A significant element in the view from Roxburgh Castle (although seen against a backcloth of caravans some day, hopefully, to go the way of all flesh).

1-8 Maxwellheugh Terrace, 1859-64, attributed to Lady Douglas of Springwood, one-and-a-half-storey picturesque double cottages in rubble, some ashlar decoration, gingerbread gables, bargeboards and finials.

18 **Waverley Lodge**, The Knowes, mid-19th century
Incorporates the cottage where Walter Scott stayed with his aunt in 1783: and carries not only a bust of Sir Walter but also a sculpture of his dog Maida over the side gate lintel.

Top *Springwood Park Mausoleum.*
Above *Maxwellheugh Terrace.*
Left *Kelso Parish Church*

19 **Kelso Parish Church**, 1771-3, James Nisbet
Presumably at that time within the abbey structure, the parish church was the subject of a condition report in 1770 by James Brown. Nisbet designed a new octagonal church, two-storey, coursed rubble (probably harled, which coat has been lost over the years) with droved dressings, hood-mouldings over windows, Gothick astragals, pyramidal slated roof with octagonal central lantern; most pleasant, well-lit interior. Flat ceiling introduced, 1823, for acoustic reasons, William Elliot of Kelso. Italianate timber belfry added over north porch, 1833.

The earlier 19th-century frontages of **Woodmarket** from the Square are checked back 20 at **Nos 21-23** (Barclay's Bank), *c*.1850, an

Kelso Bridge
In 1854 the toll-keeper paid £715 for 6 months of toll concessions. In the same year *A mob ... took advantage of the Queen's birthday which was celebrated at the end of May and 'after committing many wrong acts' set off from the Market Place for the bridge, carrying a pole topped with a sack full of shavings and other fire-lighting material. They did not succeed in firing the toll-gate because, in their enthusiasm, they inadvertently threw their incendiary device over the rails but they tore the large gate from its hinges and threw it over the bridge ...*
Gordon

The present church of Kelso is a misshapen pile, having the peculiarity of being, without exception, the ugliest and least suitable in architecture of all the Parish Churches in Scotland – and that is saying a good deal – but it is an excellent model for a circus.

Woodmarket: Right *Nos 21-23.*
Below *No 25.* Middle *Corn Exchange.* Bottom *Nos 22-24*

Italianate former seedsmen's & nurserymen's business, principally two-storey, three-bay, punctuated by classical gardening motifs, flowers and fruits. **No 25** (formerly Bank of Scotland), 1860, John Burnet Sen, Greek Revival two-storey five-bay front grandly delineating its entrance by a projecting porch and a pair of cast-iron tripod lamps on pedestals.

21 **Corn Exchange**, Woodmarket, 1855, David Cousin
Built by public subscription: Cotswold Tudor frontage complete with oriel windows: within, a superb hammer-beam roof and musicians' gallery indicating that in better days the building doubled up for business (there was a weekly corn market with 71 business stands) and social events.

22 **22-24** Woodmarket, probably late 18th century
Two-and-a-half-storey four-bay front, balustraded wallhead with central open-pedimented gable, 19th-century pilastered shopfront (originally a pair). **32-34**, mid 19th-century three-storey four-bay pair of houses with continuous pilastered shopfront.

23 **Woodmarket redevelopment**, 1974-9, J & F Johnston
Colourful if somewhat artless, particularly when related to the remaining older townscape around. At one time it was suggested that the entire block from the Town Hall to Coalmarket be demolished! Unfortunately the traditional building lines were not adhered to in this

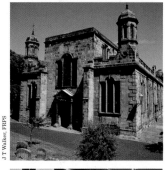

Top *View from Spittal to Berwick.*
Middle *Holy Trinity Church,*
Berwick. Above *Cowe's of Bridge*
Street. Above left *Chandlery,*
Berwick. Left *The Ship Room,*
Lindisfarne Castle

109

Top *Twizel Bridge*. Above *Quay Walls with Custom House*. Above right *Interior, Cowe's of Bridge Street*. Right *Interior, Holy Trinity Church*

110

Top left *Berwick from Tower House, Tweedmouth*. Top *Roofscape, Bridge Street*. Middle *Granary, Dewar's Lane*. Above *Salmon fishing from Spittal*. Left *Lions House, Berwick*

111

Above *Lions Gardens Allotments,
Ravensdowne*. Right *Brewer's Arms,
Castlegate*. Below *Aerial view of
Berwick*

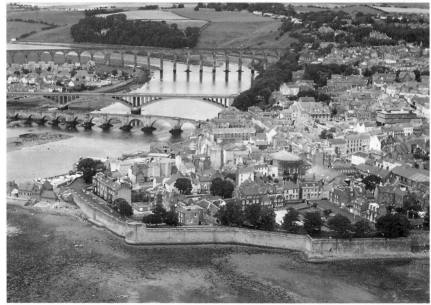

infilling exercise leaving Coalmarket particularly baggy and shapeless. Its previously best building the **Waggon Inn**, once the finest completely Edwardian town building in the Borders, has a bizarre extension (more like a residential caravan than a piece of building) glued across its frontage.

Shedden Park was given to the town in 1851, in memory of the donor's nephew, Robert Shedden, who died, 1849, searching for Sir John Franklin's expedition. Its **triumphal arch entrance gateway**, 1852, erected by public subscription as grateful thanks. Look for the classical **Keeper's Lodge**, c.1852, rectangular building in ashlar, an inscribed parapet raised over the door with an armorial panel, piended roof with central stack.

Above Waggon Inn. Left Shedden Park Gateway

Sir John Franklin (1786-1847) was the youngest of 12 children. After he was lost in 1845, seeking the North-west Passage (from the Atlantic to the Pacific, north of Canada), between 1848 and 1854 some 15 expeditions were sent to find him.

Rosebank, Shedden Park Road, early 19th century
Remodelling of 18th-century house which once (briefly) belonged to Sir Walter Scott. Two-storey three-bay front to the Tweed, piended slated roof. Later 19th-century **lodge** & **gatepiers**. In the walled garden, **new house**, 1985, Forgan & Stewart, self-contained slated pyramid-roofed residence oriented to the river and at arm's length from the original so that its brick does not jar.

Woodside House Hotel, c.1800
Two-and-a-half-storey-and-basement, 3x2 bay with advanced pedimented centre bay and pilastered doorpiece, piended slated roof with pair of central rendered stacks.

Edenside, Edenside Road, late 18th century
Two-and-a-half-storey-and-basement three-bay classical villa, doorpiece of attached Tuscan columns. Flanking screen walls. Contemporary **stable range**.

Edenside

Broomlands House

Broomlands House, 1719
Attributed to William Adam but likelier to be
James Smith (published in *Vitruvius Scoticus*
but never claimed as his by Adam), altered and
extended mid 19th century. Two-storey-and-
basement five-bay west front has mid 19th-
century pedimented doorpiece and symmetrical
bay windows to ground and basement, the
house also being deepened from two- to five-bay
at this time. Piended, platformed slated roof.

Above *Broomlands Primary School.*
Below *Roxy Cinema.* Bottom *Former
Post Office*

Broomlands Primary School, 1980,
Borders Regional Council
Cheerful glass and metal structure making the
most of its sylvan setting by views out and
reflections.

24 **Roxy Cinema**, Horsemarket, 1793
Built as a church (latterly East United
Presbyterian), remodelled 1877 – lancet windows
still at the sides, and malt-kiln roof – refronted
in the 20th century when turned into a cinema.

25 Former **Post Office**, Horsemarket, 1910,
W T Oldrieve
Neo-Georgian, polished ashlar, highly
modelled, steep bellcast roof. Nearby,
insensitive infill (now Menzies) sadly replaced
the Kelso Theatre. Better to avert one's eyes
across to **Nos 1-3** Horsemarket, mid-18th-
century, three-storey, four-bay, mid-19th-
century, pilastered shopfronts, chimney gable
over central bays, slated roof.

Roxburgh Street was the principal route linking Easter and Wester Kelso (Wester Kelso was in the present-day grounds of Floors Castle). **Nos 13-19**, 1987, Forgan & Stewart, pastiche housing of little imagination and less originality which holds the building line of Roxburgh Street (well) and Jamieson's Entry (adequately). **Nos 18-24**, early 19th century, three-storey seven-bay block with ground-floor pilastered shopfront range, polished ashlar elevation, piended slated roof with brick stacks.

26 **Presto Supermarket**, Roxburgh Street, 1984, Comprehensive Design
Inexplicable waste of the best riverside prospect in the Borders (the view is available on Chalkheugh Terrace and is recommended) but at least the street frontage has two floors and some articulation. Concrete blockwork shows why stone is making a comeback.

27 **Roxburgh House**, 48 Roxburgh Street, late 18th century
Square, formal classical villa with piended bellcast slated roof around grouped brick stack: coachhouse and stable wings flank its forecourt.

Above *Roxburgh House*. Left *Public Library*

28 **Public Library**, Union Street, 1905-6, Peddie & Washington Browne
Scottish Renaissance, large Jacobean windows, Westmorland-slated roof with carved decorated pedimented dormers, wrought-iron entrance-way and pilastered doorway with sculptured panel over. Good interior, high, well-lit space conducive to learning.

29 **Ragged School**, 51 Roxburgh Street, 18th century
One-and-a-half-storey, harled, slated roof with moulded skewputts, with its cobbled lane, sits gable-on to the street.

Kelso North Church

Strang

At the Disruption, in 1843, Horatius Bonar was the Minister of **Kelso North Parish Church**, and he with his Kirk Session broke away. A legal battle ensued and the Free Church lost, and thus had to build a new church for themselves.

Frederick T Pilkington was a Lincolnshireman, with an architect and Methodist father: he studied mathematics at Edinburgh University and became an architect. Arguably his most famous building, the Barclay Church in Edinburgh (see *Edinburgh* in this series), was described by Professor Blackie in 1888 in *The Builder* as *The most disorderly building in the city ... it looked like a congregation of elephants, rhinoceroses and hippopotamuses, with their snouts in a manger and their posteriors turned to the golf players on the [Bruntsfield] links*. Thomas Pilkington, father of Frederick, retired to Kelso where he carried out a number of architectural jobs.

30 **Kelso North Church**, 1864-6, F T Pilkington & Bell
Formerly St John's, built as Free Church; starting point English Decorated Gothic. *The* Kelso landmark, its pinnacled spire made more powerful by its springing from such a compactly bundled main building (around the triangular auditorium as in the Barclay Church, Edinburgh), with its sculptural stonework and deep plinth.

31 **Walton Hall**, Roxburgh Street, 1820
Built as a fishing lodge for John Ballantyne, Sir Walter Scott's publisher. Behind tall rubble wall with gated entrances, single-storey square-plan house, Ionic-colonnaded recessed porch, piended slated roof with octagonal central lantern and fish weathervane, linked stable range.

32 **Floors Castle Lodges & Gates**, 1929, Reginald Fairlie
Two-storey rubble lodges with bellcast slated pavilion roofs and central square stacks, linked by wrought iron screens and gates to tall urn-topped square ashlar gatepiers. The gates were designed to be opened and closed electrically. Can it really be essential to mar this vista with opening signs?

Edenside Group Practice Surgery (now
Health Centre), Inch Road, 1967,
Peter Womersley
Exquisitely contemporary, maybe even leaning
to timeless, all the more surprising given its
use of traditional materials, white render, glass
and slate. Extended to Womersley's plans,
1980, Aitken & Turnbull (see colour p.162).

Sheltered Housing, Inch Road, 1988,
Aitken & Turnbull
Sensitive composition in facing brick, thus not
competing with its Womersley near-neighbour.

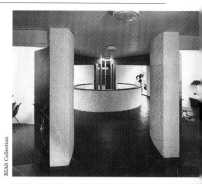

Top and above *Edenside Group
Practice Surgery*. Left *Kelso High
School*

34 **Kelso High School**, 1936, Reid & Forbes
Principal block with (typical Reid & Forbes)
entrance tower, Mayan art deco details, wings
to each side. Science block, also with tower,
curved glass corner. Finely laid out and
detailed, inside and out, although its setting
has not always been fully considered when
accretions have been proposed. Nonetheless,
the hall, c.1960, is in its own way a period
piece, and at least the main block's metal
glazing has been replaced sensitively.

Reid & Forbes first came to
prominence in 1928, winning a
competition for Leith Academy,
proposing *inter alia* a roof garden
(above the hall), where pupils
might be introduced to sunshine
and fresh air.

Kelso Racestand

Kelso Racestand, 1822
Racecourse formed on a morass, the stand being
a model of that at Doncaster. In 1788 John Carr
of York (who designed at Doncaster, York and
possibly Richmond) produced plans which may
have been the basis for the 1822 building. In the
distance, **Thomson's Monument**, Ferneyhill,
1819-20, neoclassical obelisk in memory of James
Thomson, poet and Borderer.

Yetholm was formerly the principal settlement of Scottish gypsies, and it is easy to see how the peace and quiet of the area could be aspects attractive to the travellers. The last Queen of the gypsies, Esther Faa Blythe, died in 1883. She described Yetholm as *sae mingle-mangle that ane micht think it was either built on a dark nicht or sawn on a windy ane*. Formerly many buildings here were thatched. Now this is more the exception than the rule, but with a vigorous imagination the visitor can still savour Yetholm's closeness to its origins.

YETHOLM

Village lying in two parts across the Bowmont Water, both largely composed of unassuming buildings grouped around green spaces just dominant over tarmac. The simpler **Town Yetholm** is the lower and younger, with **Kirk Yetholm**, ranged around a square, marked by the church tower on the skyline to the south.

Yetholm Parish Church, 1835-6, Robert Brown

Till lately, the oldest thatched church in Scotland was standing in this Parish (Pigot's Directory, 1837). Gloomy Gothic style, whin rubble with sandstone dressings (designs were also submitted by John & Thomas Smith and Walter Elliot); minor addition, *c*.1900, interior altered, *c*.1935, and then, *c*.1980, Duncan Cameron Associates, still no lightness of touch.

The Cross Keys, originally an inn, two-storey three-bay harled, with painted stone dressings, slated roof with rolled skews. Sundial on corner. **Hillview**, 18th century, three-storey harled building with plain gables and slated roof.

Cherrytrees

Strang

Cherrytrees, *c*.1800

A thing of beauty; two-storey main block, seven-bay symmetry, centre pedimented, single-storey flanking wings, all in ashlar with rusticated quoins. Hipped slated roof restrained by parapet urns. Good early 19th-century **steading** with square clock-tower two-stage doocot, slated pyramidal spire, vaulted lambing shed, 1838. In walled garden, five-bay Gothick **hothouse**, originally flanked by lean-to glasshouses. T-plan classical **gate lodge**, wrought-iron gates, square ashlar piers with whin quadrant walls.

Cherrytrees gave its name to the Revd Williamson, later of St Cuthbert's, Edinburgh, who as a persecuted Presbyterian was chased here by dragoons. The quick thinking of the lady of the house found *Cherrytrees Davie*, boots and all, successfully concealed in her (presumably also chaste) daughter's bed. The compromised maiden became the first of CD's seven wives, or so it is said.

The gardens and plantations about Cherrytrees showed that the Estate had fallen into the hands of a man of good taste and skill in ornamental landscape gardening. Groome

MOREBATTLE

Small, irregular but charming village set in the coils of the Kale Water. **Morebattle Parish Church**, 1757, repaired 1840 (recast and additions 1899 and 1903): rectangular round-headed windows, lofts and bellcote. Early stained glass by Douglas Strachan. Former **Morebattle U F Church**, 1866, F T Pilkington, suffering visibly in its new garage workshop use.

Corbet Tower, 1575
Datestone may be a refugee from Whitton or Grubet but a tower on this site was burnt by English, 1544. Restored from ruins, c.1820, the tower is small (5x7m in plan) and vertical, some three-storeys to its crowstepped gables, a garden feature of the florid Victorian house which now takes its name.

Old Belford House, late 17th century
Two-storey T-plan house (now in agricultural use) within the farm of Belford. Harled rubble with a steep roof (now clad with corrugated iron) and surviving crowstepped gable.

Top *Former Morebattle U F Church.*
Above *Morebattle Joiner's Workshop*

Hownam Church, c.1600
Extensive repairs, 1844 and later, render origins virtually indecipherable save the early round-headed doorway. Harled, two-storey T-plan, early 19th-century manse by the churchyard. Good memorials and gravestones.

In the 18th century a 13th-century church was taken down and replaced by a barn, on the sole ground that to build the said barn would cost £17 less than the repair to their ancient shrine.
Alison

Hownam Church, 1890

In Hownam Parish The great decrease of inhabitants within the last 40 years is evidently occasioned by the too general practice of letting the land in great farms.
Old Statistical Account

Hownam Kirk
Considering the ruined condition of the bridge above the Kirk, which is now rendered very unfit for passengers, especially for such as attend the ordinances, therefore to remove the said Inconveniency the Session thinks it proper that people according to their severall Abilities may give in their collections against next Lord's Day which shall be gathered at the church doors for repairing the said bridge that those that attend the ordinances may both come to and go from the same with all possible Conveniency.
Kirk Session Records, 1738

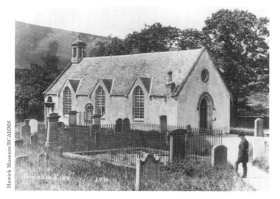

Linton Parish Church, from 12th century
Altered in 1616, 1774, 1813, porch of 1857 (housing finely lettered marble memorial tablet, 18th century, to the Reads/Turnbulls) and (finally) in a restorative frame, 1912 by P MacGregor Chalmers. Romanesque, nave

Linton Parish Church

The Linton worm (or dragon) was said to have been defeated by Sir John Somerville, knighted by William the Lion because of his feats of beast slaying. The weathered tympanum to the untutored eye would appear to confirm the worm-slaying. To the expert, though, the beastly target is a brace of bears.

Linton Tower, the Somervilles' base, stood by the church until its demolition by the forces of Henry VIII.

We shall give them such a buffet upon their Borders as shall make them to repent it, seeing that the corn is now in the houses and stacks the which they should live by, by the whole year, shall be so destroyed that they shall be the more easier to meddle with hereafter.
Duke of Suffolk to the English Privy Council, 2/9/1543

and chancel plan. Exquisite stained glass, four windows, 1936 (Douglas Strachan?). Incorporated in the south wall is a semicircular stone tympanum apparently depicting the alleged slaying (by an ancestor of the Somervilles) of a giant serpent or worm in the vicinity. The church sits on a knoll which suggests ancient use, whether for religious purpose or not.

Linton Mill, 1779
Standing on a tributary of the Kale Water, battered walls, slated roof with ventilator, complete with barn and single-storey mill house.

Cessford Castle, from mid-15th century
Massive (4m-thick walls) L-shaped tower, main portion three-storey, wing four-storey, all to common wall-head height, two storeys above now fallen. Surrounded by stone and earth rampart and ditch. Attacked by English 1519 and 1523. Burnt by English 1543 and 1544. Traditional stronghold of the Kers until 1650 when the family vacated and subsequent emphasis was placed upon the Roxburghe titles.

Eckford Church, 1771
Fragments of 1668 and aisle (burial vault, laird's loft over) of 1724. Alterations, 1848, John & Thomas Smith. Interior revamped, 1898, and porch added. Jougs (from 1718), mort bell and 19th-century castellated red sandstone **watch-house**. Many fine 17th-century gravestones.

Cessford Castle was the home of the Kers of Cessford. Sir Robert (*Habbie*) Ker was made warden of the Scottish Middle Marches, and Lord Roxburghe, in 1616, from hence the Dukes of Roxburghe eventually take their title.

Cessford Castle

Left *Kalemouth Suspension Bridge.*
Below *Marlfield House.* Bottom
Crailing Kirk

Kalemouth Suspension Bridge, *c.*1830,
Captain Samuel Brown, engineer
Fifty-four metres long, 5m wide. Twin stone
pylons at each end, wooden deck and railings
suspended by iron rods fixed to the centres of
chain links. Tolls presumably paid at
Kalemouth Cottage, now *improved.*

Marlfield House, *c.*17th century,
possibly William Adam
Formal three-storey five-bay main block with
corner towers, flanking pavilions linked by
curved screen walls. Repairs and alterations,
*c.*1754, George Paterson (probably the father of
John Paterson). Reconstructed, 1891, J M Dick
Peddie. **Stables block**, 18th-century two-
storey range.

Crailing Kirk, *c.*1775
Early 19th-century aisle, alterations and
additions, 1892 and 1907, P MacGregor
Chalmers. Crailing was where David
Calderwood, Kirk historian, ministered in
the 17th century.

Failure to make the most of a
promising subject is the last charge
that can be brought against David
Calderwood (1575-1650). His
Historie of the Kirk of Scotland
(published posthumously in 1678) is
a sort of left-wing rival to that of the
right-wing Archbishop Spottiswoode
... He certainly did valuable work in
popularising the left-wing point of
view, for Spottiswoode's calm and
judicial sobriety had small appeal
beside Calderwood's edifying detail
of executions and scandals in high
life (including his loving
descriptions of opponents' death-
beds – the Marquis of Hamilton had
blisters of *six divers colours.*

Crailing House, 1803, William Elliot
Finely proportioned Regency elegance for
W Paton, two-storey-and-basement, 1-3-1 bay,
centre section giant order pilastered and
pedimented. Altered, 1952, Reginald Fairlie.
Stables centre block topped by cupola, wings
ending in pavilions.

Monteviot House created from farmhouse of
1740, very good with symmetrical wings (on site
of medieval Hospice of Ancrum, Spittal) *c.*1830,
Edward Blore, but only about 50% of his heavily
battlemented and chimneyed scheme completed.
Attempted reordering, 1960, Schomberg Scott.
Seat of Marquis of Lothian. **Stables court**,
*c.*1830, attributed to Edward Blore. **Doocot**,
circular, rubble, lower half perhaps *c.*1600,
upper Victorian. Gardens redesigned, 1961-8,
Percy Cane of London, landscape architect.

Edward Blore (1787-1879) was the
son of Thomas Blore, the
topographer. The architect's
commissions here probably reflected
his contemporary work on
Buckingham Palace, and thus his
social credentials, rather more than
his earlier work for Sir Walter Scott
(see Abbotsford).

In **1632** the Earl of Ancrum (incidentally a fine poet who was given John Donne's manuscripts when the latter went abroad) wrote to his son, the Earl of Lothian, with advice on the improvement of Newbattle, by Dalkeith: ... *the Tower, which to begin with I would have you (keep) for your present use ... to make the room under the hall your ordinar eating room: not weakening the walls there, by striking out new windows, but taking away partitions, that all the three lights as there are may meet in the centre, and so yield light, being only glazed and kept as they are, strong in the outside, **because the world may change again** ... you must always remember never to weaken the tower, but leave it as strong as you can, to keep in a mister (i.e. a crisis) for a sure staying house, with the iron gate before and ... all the iron windows kept in it.*

Old Ancrum Bridge

In **1641** the Earl of Lothian, part of the Covenant Army at Newcastle, wrote to his father, *I must trouble your lordship to desir that I may have two nightcaps and two pair of slippers, one grass green, the other sky colour, with gold or silver or gold and silver lace upon them.*

Old Parish Church

Woodland Centre, Harestanes, 1877
Home Farm converted to visitor centre and craft workshops, 1979-80, Alistair M Smith, in a most forward-looking, robustly detailed effort of interpretation and diversification. Now **Regional Countryside Centre**.

Old Ancrum Bridge, c.1782, possibly William Elliot or Alexander Stevens
Funded by a levy on the Heritors, red sandstone three-arch bridge, its cutwaters expressed above as pedestrian refuges.

ANCRUM
Triangular village layout around the tree-lined green and the (almost on its original site) **Market Cross**, late 16th-century (Ancrum was made a burgh of barony in 1490), intact but for its head, 3.5m shaft set in 1m square leaf-patterned socket stone. **War Memorial** in red sandstone competes with the cross. Houses surrounding the green are principally 19th-century, although there are some 18th-century ones probably thatched originally.

Old Parish Church, 1762
Aisle of 1756 at the east end of the kirk remains roofless and ruinous in spite of repairs, 1832. Hog-backed gravestone, 10th- to 12th-century, within the churchyard, the top of the stone ridged, the sloping sides representing a tile or shingle pattern, and with *gable ends*.

Ancrum House, core 1558, destroyed by fire 1873, rebuilt and burnt again 1885, rebuilt in Scots Baronial thereafter, James Maitland Wardrop, finally demolished 1970, leaving only its attractive Deer Park landscape setting.

Kirklands, c.1830, Edward Blore; rebuilt and additions, 1907-8, Sir Robert Lorimer

Tudor-style – oriel windows, mullioned and transomed hood-moulded windows, and tall clustered chimneys – two-and-a-half-storey mansion in stugged ashlar. Lattice-windowed **gate-lodge** of similar style, date and (probably) architect.

Peniel Heugh (Waterloo Monument), 1817-24, Archibald Elliot
William Burn's design, begun 1815, collapsed, 1816, in the course of construction – as an estate worker brought the news to his feudal lord *Yon muckle stane has fallen!* Greatest man-made feature of the central Borders, providing literally breath-taking views (spot the good sequence of hill-forts, one on the site of the Monument itself, from early Iron Age to pre-Roman in the vicinity) from the timber cap-house (added 1867), and still impressive panoramas from ground level. Presently closed to preserve the public as well as the remains of this notable landmark (see colour p.162).

Monteath Mausoleum, Peddie & Kinnear, in a domed Byzantine style complete with lions (could it have been an unsuccessful entry in the Scottish Albert Memorial competition?) which accommodates Sir Thomas Monteath Douglas of Stonebyres, Lanarkshire, d.1868.

JEDBURGH
Akin to the Old Town of Edinburgh in plan, a long uphill street terminating in a castle, **Jedburgh** was a place of importance even before the Charter of 1165 by William the Lion. Even allowing for a little *puff*, it must have warranted a considerable part of the description by the Earl of Surrey in 1523 to Cardinal Wolsey that *There was two times more houses*

Kirklands

The Battle of Ancrum Moor
occurred in 1545, when the English army, having completed their raiding were on their way south, only to be caught and defeated by the Earl of Angus (whose ancestors' tombs the invaders had defiled in Melrose) and the Laird of Buccleuch. Lillyard's Monument, just off the A68, marks the place where a Scots Boadicea met a heroic end.

Fair Maiden Lillyard lies under this stane,
Little was her stature, but great was her fame;
Upon the English louns she laid many thumps,
And when her legs were smitten off, she fought upon her stumps.

A certain McGonagall ring to the verse, but while it is conceivable that there was such a woman at the battle, the name of Lilliard or Lilliot was identified with the place long before.

Monteath Mausoleum

The castle was the location of the wedding-feast of King Alexander III in 1285, when a ghostly apparition warned of the King's impending death (a cliff-top fall from his horse in the following year). Because of the strength of position and strategic importance (and, it must be said, because of frequency of enemy occupation) of the castle, it was demolished – by the Scots – in 1409.

Sir Robert Rowand Anderson (1834-1921) trained with John Lessels and Sir George Gilbert Scott. He worked for the Royal Engineers from 1860, and in his own right from 1868. His years of practice were characterised by the breadth as well as the depth of his scholarship: a veritable colossus, he also established the School of Applied Arts, the National Art Survey and, by spirited revival, the Royal Incorporation of Architects in Scotland, to whom he left his Edinburgh townhouse and contents.

Below *Jedburgh Abbey*. Bottom *Jedburgh Abbey and Visitor Centre*

therein than in Berwick, and well builded, with many honest and fair houses therein, sufficient to have lodged a thousand horsemen in garrison, and six good towers therein. So of course he burnt it. Nor was it sufficient to quarrel only with the English. During the Civil War, 1569-72, when Jedburgh supported the King's party, Ker of Ferniehirst supported the Queen. The Queen's Herald proclaimed from the Market Cross, and the Provost commanded him down, and *caused him to eat his letters, and thereafter loosed down his points, and gave him his wages on his bare buttocks with a bridle, threatening him that if he ever came again he should lose his life.* In response Ker of Ferniehirst promptly hanged ten citizens and burnt the burgh's winter provisions.

Jedburgh Abbey, 1150-1225
Astonishingly complete given its vulnerable location, grand arcaded structure with square crossing-tower and wheel-window within the west gable. The 1642 Report by John Mylne on the dangerous state of fabric of the Abbey Church was not implemented, fortunately, since part of his recommendations involved the reduction in height of the nave arcades. Restoration, 1875, Sir R Rowand Anderson, encompassing remedial works (part of the nave had been used as the parish church) and reconstruction of south doorway. Further restoration, 1923. **Marquis of Lothian Memorial**, Reginald Fairlie. In guardianship since 1913. *Historic Scotland; open to the public, guidebook available*

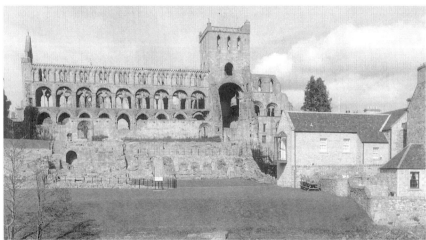

Visitor Centre, 1982-7,
Historic Buildings & Monuments
Award-winning conversion and addition to
form shop, museum and viewpoint,
accompanying a major archaeological
excavation. SDA Regeneration of Scotland
Award, 1987; RIBA Award, 1988. **War
Memorial**, 1921, James B Dunn.

Parish Church, 1873, Thomas Wyatt
One of only two Scottish works (the other was
Dunmore Chapel near Airth) by this member of
the Wyatt architectural dynasty, RIBA
President, and RIBA Gold Medallist in 1879.
Rock-faced ashlar, graded Westmorland slate
roof, good stained glass. Additions, 1888,
Hippolyte J Blanc.

Above *Parish Church*. Left *Public
Hall*

The Wyatt family produced many
architects, notably James Wyatt
(who built Fonthill Abbey for
William Beckford) and Sir Mathew
Digby Wyatt, Slade Professor of Fine
Arts at Cambridge and Secretary to
the Royal Commissioners for the
1851 (Crystal Palace) Great
Exhibition.

Public Hall, 1901, James P Alison
Buff sandstone with French roofline and
detailing showing influences of Kelso's
municipal building.

Jedburgh Abbey was a community
of Augustinian Canons, established
by King David I. They lived
according to a rule but were not
cloistered monks, and could go out
to serve neighbouring churches.

Jubilee Fountain

National Tourist Information Centre, 1975,
Morris & Steedman
Something of a missed opportunity, an artificial
stone-clad, lead flat-roofed shoebox whose best
feature is blandness, unassertively plugging on
to the Town Hall.

Jubilee Fountain, 1889, George Bell
Ornamental Gothic column with clustered
shafts, topped by unicorn holding heraldic
shield. Cast-iron lamp brackets with modern
fittings, but no sign of water, unfortunately.

County Hall, 1812
Ashlar façades with flat Doric pilasters, a strong
and positive *stop* at the end of Castlegate.

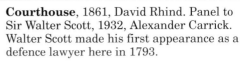

Courthouse, 1861, David Rhind. Panel to Sir Walter Scott, 1932, Alexander Carrick. Walter Scott made his first appearance as a defence lawyer here in 1793.

Newgate, 1756, steeple dated 1761; finished 1791
Replaced the Tolbooth/Town House on its site to the south-west of Market Place. Gatehouse surmounted by a 36m-high steeple containing three bells, one of which is pre-Reformation, likely from the Abbey.

Castlegate has a long and absorbing range of vernacular houses (all thatched in Thomas Girtin's painting of 1800) on both sides of the street, notably one gable projecting end-on in more historic fashion, its plan form now this building's most historic external element, following its *improvement*. **Library**, 1900, George Washington Browne, Scots 16th century. **Nos 7/11**, 17th century, Prince Charlie's House (Prince Charlie stayed there *en route* to the abortive invasion of England in 1745). Wall-mounted elaborate sundial at **Blackhills Close**. **7-10 Market Place**, from 17th century, altered 18th century, is three-storey with crowstepped gables. This entire area was part of a far-sighted programme of repair and (much) rebuilding by the Scottish Special Housing Association in the 1970s, retaining and reinvigorating the fabric and appearance of this part of the historic burgh, in marked contrast to many others, Selkirk, for instance. Saltire Award, 1977; Civic Trust Award, 1978.

Castle Gaol, 1820-3, Archibald Elliot Designed according to *Reformatory*

Above Newgate Steeple. Below Library, Castlegate. Right Prince Charlie's House, 7/11 Castlegate

J Dewar/RCAHMS

Imprisonment principles of John Howard (penal reformer), on the site of the old castle on which, in 1819, only the town gallows were still standing. Museum both of correction and of the locality. *Open to the public; guidebook available*

Glenburn Hall, early 19th century, William Elliot
Geometric mini-mansion, two-storey and whin-faced basement, hipped slated roof, three-bay in ashlar with strongly balustraded parapet and ball finials. **Lodge** and ball-finialed gatepiers contemporary, classical.

RCAHMS

Top and above *Castle Gaol*.
Left *Glenburn Hall*

Strang

Canongate
Principal route was across the River Jed at the Canongate Bridge, and so this street frontage was memorable once upon a time, with fine 18th-century and earlier buildings. The bypass in 1974 wrecked the street (and the bottom end of the High Street too) but would have increased the attractiveness of Jedburgh to residents and visitors had it not been accompanied by peripheral commercial development to the north. Subsequent

Sir Walter Scott's maiden case at Jedburgh's Sheriff Court was one where he successfully defended a poacher: *You're a lucky scoundrel,* Scott whispered on hearing the verdict, to be met with *I'm just of your mind, and I'll send you a mankin* (a hare) *the morn, man.*

When the prison reformer John Howard visited Scotland in 1779 he found there most of the failings of the English prisons: neglect, dirt, ill-health, overcrowding, bad design and ventilation. Scotland's only advantages over England were that there was less extortion of fees from prisoners and – because, Howard suggested, poor Scotsmen were morally superior to poor Englishmen – a smaller proportion of the population was locked up.
MacIvor

I'd rather lie in the belly o' a Whale, Than spend a nicht in Jethart Gaol.

Sir David Brewster (1781-1868) was born in Jedburgh: physicist and academic, inventor of the kaleidoscope in 1816, Principal of Edinburgh University from 1859.

Canongate development has been at best damage limitation. **Housing**, 1985, by Duncan Cameron Associates, for example, being a palely colourful response to the Market Square.

Canongate Bridge, 16th century
Three segmented arches, almost sculpted with its cutwaters battered back into refuges at carriageway level. Gateway on centre section removed late 18th century. **Piper's House**, 1 Duck Row, 1604, upgraded and remodelled, 1896.

Spread Eagle Hotel, High Street, early 19th century
Traditional painted stucco front with pilastered doorpiece carrying a cast-iron frieze. Behind the street frontage, up Jewellers' Wynd, lies the **Observantine Friary**, archaeological site, from whence Adam Abel wrote his *Wheel of Time*, or world history, in the 16th century. **Royal Bank of Scotland** (formerly British Linen Bank), High Street, is a two-storey three-bay house set back from the street, Tuscan-pilastered porch and single-storey wing to the west. The house of Sir Walter Scott's companion, Sheriff Shortreed, complete with its *louping-on-stane*.

Sheriff Shortreed accompanied the bold Walter Scott on his ballad-hunting forays into Liddesdale, where they collected and set down (not without occasional resistance) what had previously been an oral history and art form.

Mary Queen of Scots House, Queen Street, late 16th century
Bastel-house, T-plan, vaulted ground floor, now museum (interior display 1986, Page & Park) with wall paintings by John Boyd Brent. Queen Mary's temporary residence in 1566. Never slated in its life (the whole of Jedburgh was thatched in 1817) until 1980 when the Victorian rosemary tiles were replaced. Early photographs exist of its pre-tile thatch, and the roof form would certainly show off a thatched covering to best advantage.

Trinity Church, High Street, 1746
Reconstruction of 1818: severely classical, portico set between flanking projections. Stained glass *Adoration of Shepherds and Magi*, 1902, by Benson. **Grammar School**, 1884, Hardy & Wight, Edinburgh; extensions 1926 & 1935, Reid & Forbes.

St John's Episcopal Church, 1844, J Hayward
Gothic, graded Westmorland slate above buff sandstone masonry with ashlar dressings. Oak **lych gate** with rosemary-tiled open roof. **Brae**

Mary Queen of Scots House

Strang

128

House, its rectory, unconvincingly classical set into the brae. **St John's Episcopal School**, 1844, William Butterfield, enlarged 1854 & 1934. Gothic, two-storey, rubble with steeply pitched slated roof.

Bongate Mill, mid 19th century; demolished 1986 Four-storey eight-bay mill building, a particularly sad loss to the townscape in view of its ornamental finialed gable, pedimented bellcote and weathervane. **St Mary's RC Church** (and priest's house), 1937, Reginald Fairlie. Simple, traditional and economic use of materials.

Above *St John's Episcopal Church.* Left *Bongate Mill, 1964.* Below left *Hartrigge*

William Butterfield (1814-1900) was the architect of Keble College, Oxford.

John Ainslie (1745-1828) was born in Jedburgh, began work as a surveyor/engraver on English county surveys, but most of his work as a cartographer was carried out in Scotland, on counties or estates: he produced new maps of Scotland in 1782 and 1789.

Hartrigge, 1854, David Bryce (demolished) Scottish Baronial apart from its stables, this house was one of Bryce's most powerful compositions, with additions, 1938, and alterations by Reginald Fairlie.

Oxnam Parish Church, 1738 T-plan with bellcote, alterations and additions

Right *Oxnam Parish Church.*
Above *Tombstone detail*

An inventory of results and booty
taken south between July/Nov. 1544
totals as follows:

Towns, towers, steads,	
barmkins, parish churches,	
bastel houses burnt	*192*
Scots slain	*403*
Prisoners taken	*816*
Nolt	*10,386*
Sheep	*12,492*
Nags and geldings	*1,296*
Goats	*200*
Bolls of corn, (usually fired	
where it lay)	*850*
Inside gear, etc.	

Ferniehirst Castle

James VI & I's close favourite
Robert Ker was a younger son of
Ferniehirst.

In the 1540s Jean de Beaugue was
a young French staff officer with
Monsieur d'Esse, commanding
French forces in Scotland against
the English. He was part of the
Franco-Scots force at the siege of
Ferniehirst, its English tenant being
refused an honourable withdrawal
because of his brutal regime. The
Englishman slid out when the
courtyard's defences were breached
and surrendered to French officers,
but he was recognised and
decapitated on the spot by a Scot
whose wife and daughters he had
raped.

1880. White-painted, open landscape
dominating, set baldly as it is within the graveyard. **Watchhouse**, jougs & *louping-on-stane.*

Hunthill
Possible 16th-century tower core, but heavily
disguised with early 19th-century three-and-a-
half-storey rubble east façade with screen
walls. Entrance (west) front contains doorway
dated 1850 and crowstepped porch dated 1955.

Ferniehirst Castle, from late 15th century
Origins as the seat of the Lothian branch of the
Kerr family, known here as Ker. Rebuilt, 1598.
Fascinating plan, especially main Renaissance
block with study tower. Disused in the 18th
century, re-roofed and repaired c.1830, major
restoration (part only) c.1890, 50 years a youth
hostel until 1985. Repair, 1988, freeish
restoration and alterations, including an
uncomfortably thatched kitchen wing, Simpson
& Brown, painted frieze David Wilkinson. **Ker
Chapel**, 17th century, probably a mortuary
chapel, re-roofed 1938, restrained conversion
and repair, 1988, Simpson & Brown.

Glendouglas, c.1805
Two-storey-and-basement three-bay ashlar
house with pediment and pilastered doorpiece
with fanlight, slated roof. Extensive
contemporary **stables range** to the rear.

Mossburnford House, early 19th century
Present house, two-storey, Venetian ground-floor
windows about a central doorway, all below a
hipped slated roof. A long-occupied site: *Here is
an ancient baronial fort, strong in the walls,
erected to suit the state of things in the time of
the border feuds, and continuing to be inhabited
till about the middle of the [18th] century.*

Edgerston, from *c*.1720
Palladian mansion, three-storey-and-basement,
main block entrance front with centre
pedimented feature and flanking pavilions,
bowed projecting centre bay to garden front,
1834-5 battlemented tower addition. **Edgerston
Doocot**, late 18th century, octagonal plan,
rubble with ashlar dressings, circular window,
pyramidal slated roof with finial.

Mervinslaw, 16th century
Two-and-a-half-storey peel-tower intact but for
its roof, the best example of a peel-house
(according to the RCAHMS Inventory a peel-
house, unique to this part of Scotland, built of
coursed rubble set in clay, is less substantial
than a bastel-house or a tower) of which there
are a number – **Kilnsike**, **Northbank** and
Slacks Tower – within a short distance.

Overton Tower, late 16th century
Similar in layout to peel-towers, but more
substantial, being built of rubble and lime
mortar, and having fireplaces.

Carter Bar
Bleak, buildingless and weatherswept national
boundary marked variously by 20th-century
standing stone, musical beggars and mobile
shops. But at least one can raise one's eyes to
the Eildon Hills on the northern skyline.

Retreating from the Border, one finds a collection
of towers, houses and hamlets, some just
remains, as the **Southdean Parish Church** in
old kirkyard, 1690 and later, with some medieval
fragments excavated and stabilised, 1910.

Top and above *Edgerston*

Rutherford of Edgerston was a
descendant of Robert de Rutherford,
killed in battle against the Moors in
Spain along with the Black Douglas
(and Bruce's heart).

Southdean Parish Church

131

Top *Chesters Church.* Above *Hobkirk Church*

Dame Magdalen (Nicholson) Elliot, widow of the first Baronet of Stobs, borrowed *40 Punds Scots* for her share in the expenses of *Hobkirk bigin*, the building of the heather-thatched Hobkirk Church of 1690-2.

James Thomson, the Romantic poet, was a son of the Manse. Born in Ednam, he moved to Southdean as a child, where his Calvinist father (a superstitious man) died in the course of an exorcism at Wolflee.

Greenriver

Chesters Church, 1876
Early English, simple rectangular plan in red sandstone with Westmorland slate roof, stained glass by Ballantine & Son, one window by J H Baguley of Newcastle.

Chesters House, 1787-90, William Elliot
Two-storey centre-pedimented block with connected pavilions on either side. Elliot was *a local man with up-to-date ideas so that the spreading pediment is supported by rustic pilasters, while a bold Doric porch marks an easy transition between indoors and outdoors.*

Hobkirk Church, 1869
Restored, 1914. Great square tower with pyramidal roof, incorporating Romanesque fragments from the chancel arch of the old kirk of 1692 (this kirk had a belfry, 1741, was barely *heather thackit* in 1758, then slated 1777 and demolished, 1869). At that time the church had an earth floor, a foot below churchyard level, and a low roof which made it impossible to stand upright in the galleries. **Manse** of 1770.

Wolflee, 1862, David Bryce, destroyed by fire 1977
This Scottish Baronial creation was itself formed from a new house of 1825-7, John & Thomas Smith, which preserved only a single vault of the earlier building, 17th century at least, which had been extensively rebuilt in 1698. Wolflee housed Dame Magdalen Nicholson, whose *account-book* has survived to rival Grizell Baillie's at Mellerstain (see p.168).

Greenriver (formerly Hobsburn), *c.*1770
Three-storey T-plan house, harled and painted, steeply pitched piended slated roof. Renamed by James Chisholme (owner, 1793-1802) after his Jamaican plantation.

Weens House, *c.*1775, for William Oliver
Old house demolished, 1774, a doorway being
built into the north-west wall of the kitchen
garden. Red sandstone mansion, three-storey
five-bay main block with pilastered main
doorpiece and lower flanking wings. Fine 18th-
century wrought-iron gates and ashlar
gatepiers carrying urns and heraldic figures.

Bedrule Church, from 1804
Rebuilt 1877, enlarged 1914, T Leadbetter.
Excellent stained-glass windows, 1922, by
Douglas Strachan. Two fragments of hogbacked
gravestones within, and some 17th-century
gravestones without.

Wells House, 1906, Leadbetter & Fairley
New house on old site retaining the 18th-
century wrought-iron gates. Armorial
pediment, *c.*1690, showing the then owners'
family tree, is now in Hawick Museum.

Lanton Tower, 16th century
Tower embedded in progressively extended two-
and three-storey house. Thoughtfully pared
back and recast, 1989, Philip Mercer. **Old
Manor Inn**, Lanton, early 18th century, two-
storey house of good proportion though
somewhat shorn, through over-restoration, of
much feeling of genuine antiquity.

Knowesouth, *c.*1870
Large Elizabethan villa built for William O
Rutherford. Floridly bargeboarded, on site
of earlier mansion house. **Knowesouth
Doocot**, 18th century, double lectern (883 nests
per chamber) with 900mm-thick walls,
crowstepped gables and massive slates.

Towerburn, 1914, Leadbetter, Fairley & Reid
Sprawling baronial mansion, now flatted.

Top *Lanton Tower*. Above *Knowesouth
Doocot*

Fatlips Castle, 16th century
Four-storey 9x8m tower with machicolated
parapet walk and crowstepped caphouse,
perched on the Minto Crags, a picturesque
set-piece. Restored, 1857, and then 1897-8,
Sir Robert Lorimer. Dilapidated but Scheduled
Monument in sore need of protection, at the
least from further decay. One of the pleasures
of a visit here used to be, according to
Chambers, *that every gentleman, by indefeasible
privilege, kisses one of the ladies on entering the
ruin*. The more bookish explanation for its

Right *Fatlips Castle.*
Below *Leyden Monument*

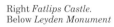

James Augustus Henry Murray
(1837-1915) was born in Denholm
and became schoolmaster in
Hawick. In 1873 he published
*Dialects of the Southern Counties of
Scotland*, and from 1879 began
editing the *New English Dictionary*,
completed and published in 1928
after his death.

name is in honour of its first builders, the
Turnbulls, who were renowned for the fullness
of their pucker (see colour p.164).

Denholm Village
Pleasant place laid out in 18th century for
stocking weaving around a village green,
originally thatched houses with cobbled aprons,
the birthplace of John Scott, botanist (1836-80)
and Sir James Murray (1837-1915) of the *OED*.
Also birthplace of Dr John Leyden (1775-1811)
at **Leyden Cottage**, thatched and harled one-
and-a-half-storey. **Leyden Monument**, 1861,
Hector H Orrock, sculpted by Handyside
Ritchie, a Swinton stone Gothic spire set on
two tiers of red Aberdeen granite columns with
foliated capitals, all set within railings.

Westgate Hall, Denholm, 17th century
Two-and-a-half-storey robust rubble building,
lintel dated 1663, whose form is similar to that
of Old Alton House, by East Boonraw, north of
Hawick, ruins of which are dated 1675.

Westside Mill, late 18th century
Three-storey, rubble, with slated roof. Upper
floors with small square windows each lighting
a stocking-machine. The mill represents an
interim stage between cottage industry and the
full-blown factory production of the Hawick
mills. Unfortunately its conversion to a
dwelling has diminished its authenticity
somewhat.

Sir Gilbert Elliot of Minto is credited with the introduction of the *German flute* to Scotland.

Minto

Charming estate village laid out for the Earl of Minto by W H Playfair who also designed many of the houses and the Gothic **Minto Church**, 1830-1, interior revamped, 1934.

Left *Westside Mill*. Below *Stairwell, Minto House*. Bottom *Minto House*

Minto House, *c.*1738-43, William Adam; demolished
Incorporated an earlier 16th-century tower, rebuilt 1809-14, Archibald Elliot, following the unusual V-plan of the original. Alterations, 1837, William Playfair, and later James Maitland Wardrop. Terraced gardens, Sir Robert Lorimer. Reports of its demolition in 1973 greatly exaggerated – still standing but derelict and unprotected, 1991, as talk of possible *export* to Japan continued. Set on fire, 1992, and much demolished as a result for the owner, the Earl of Minto.

Hassendeanburn (Hassendean = Hazeldean)
This was the first and largest nursery and
seeds business in the kingdom. *The banks of
the Teviot are, in the neighbourhood of Hawick,
ornamented in no small degree, by the extensive
nurseries of Messrs Dickson & Company,
established here, under the auspices of the same
firm, or at least the same family, considerably
upwards of a century ago.* (Pigot, 1827)
Hassendean Old Kirk, in 1659, had its fabric
removed to Wilton. At the Restoration it was
returned for re-erection, but both kirk and
graveyard were destroyed by *ice-flood* in 1796.

HAWICK

Glasgow in miniature, according to Chambers,
and surely the only town in the Scottish
Borders with a truly urban feel. One of the
most land-locked settlements in Scotland
(69km to the nearest sea), built around the
junction of the Teviot and the Slitrig. A close-
knit community, maybe as a response to its
sufferings as a frontier settlement – such a
condition which could lead the *inhabitants* to
burn the town (presumably its thatch, in the
street) to prevent occupation and more damage
by the Earl of Surrey in 1570 – a cyclical
prosperity over the last 200 years has been
built on first the stocking, then fine underwear
and lately the twin-set.

¹ **St Mary's Church**, St Mary's Place,
from 12th century
There has long been a church on this site. *From
St Mary's Church Sir Alexander Ramsay of
Dalhousie, a noble and patriotic knight, while
holding a court of justice, was dragged by*

HAWICK

0 metres 150

To SELKIRK

To CARLISLE

ALBERT BRIDGE

River Teviot

HIGH STREET

BUCCLEUCH STREET

HOWEGATE

DRUMLANRIG SQUARE

TOWER DYKESIDE

SLITRIG CRESCENT

Slitrig Water

N

*Grey traditions gather round
Church, and tower, and town
Passive in the Druid Mound
Centuries look down.
Still the hum of busy life
Rises from her streets,
Still in fond, unending strife,
Teviot, Slitrig meets.*
R S Craig, *A Border Town*

St Mary's Church

*Douglas to Hermitage Castle and in the
dungeon there was starved to death.* The
antique appearance slightly misleads, the
shape with its outstanding bellcast-roofed
tower dates from rebuilding in 1764, of which
little more than the tower survived a major fire
in 1880 (rebuilt 1883 Wardrop & Reid) by
which time it had passed the mantle (1844) of
parish church to the larger specimen in
Buccleuch Street. Churchyard sadly
landscaped and tidied up, 1973. The **Old
Manse**, 1765, L-plan two-storey harled house,
its main front to the garden having a projecting
pedimented bay.

2 A single jamb at the top of **Drumlanrig Square**
is all that remains of the old **West Port**. Note
the inscription to the provost who was
instrumental in clearing away the ancient core of
buildings, the auld **Mid Row**, to form the square

Mid Row, pre-1884

3 and gardens, 1884. **Memorial Fountain**, 1910,
J P Alison, consists of fountain and clock
constructed courtesy of the Will of William
Brown of Alloa, a Teri (native of Hawick).

4 **Drumlanrig Hospital**, *c*.1856, formerly the
Combination Poorhouse serving 11 parishes,
whin with red sandstone dressings, a long
block with central features, to the front a
classical doorway and fanlight, to the rear a
central pediment, gable carved stone (Hawick
coat of arms) from Buccleuch Memorial, 1887,
demolished 1971, sculpted by Thomas Beattie.

5 Further up is the **Motte**, a truncated cone,
12th-century origins, with a ditch barely
perceptible at its foot. Excavated, 1912
(sections across the ditch, not the Motte itself),
finds included a coin of Henry II (1154-89).

There is still standing a few
venerable structures, which are not
only interesting from their antiquity
but which whilst occupied as
ordinary dwelling-houses, have
evidently been constructed as places
of security and defence amid the
troubles of a warlike age. These
ancient tenements are built on
arches of rough whinstone, whilst
the walls are of massive thickness,
almost defying injury from fire, and
capable of being stoutly defended,
and though they certainly present a
somewhat rugged exterior, they seem
internally to have been planned with
no small degree of ingenuity.
New Statistical Account

6 **St Margaret's Dominican Convent**, 1912,
Reginald Fairlie
Last building of red sandstone from the
Denholm quarries. **Chapel**, 1914, and **Home
for Aged and Sick** in the grounds, 1934.

Corn Mill

7 **Corn Mill**, **Mill Path** and **Mill House**,
Slitrig Crescent, *c*.1805
A period piece; the mill, three-storey in whin
with red sandstone dressings, the house two
storeys with pilastered doorpiece and
entablature. **Slitrig Crescent**, a burgh
extension of *c*.1800, two-storey terraced
whinstone houses in the main, only a few
of which have retained original details.

Above and right *St Cuthbert's Episcopal*. Below *Corn Exchange*. Bottom *Tower Mill*

George Gilbert Scott, 1811-78, Gothic revivalist, *built or restored 26 cathedrals, 9 abbey and 2 priory churches, 1 minster, 474 churches, 26 schools, 5 almshouses, 23 parsonages, 57 monumental works, 10 college chapels and 16 colleges, 27 public buildings, 42 mansions, etc.*

8 **St Cuthbert's Episcopal Church**, 1858, Sir George Gilbert Scott
Early Decorated, chunky and self-sufficient. Contains fine glass, notably memorial window, 1889, to the Duke of Buccleuch (showing the Duke handing a model of the building to the Bishop of Glasgow) who had paid for site, building and endowment. Reredos, J Oldrid Scott, 1905, chancel screen, Sir Robert Lorimer. To the south-west the former **rectory**.

9 **Corn Exchange**, 1865, J T Rochead
Completed despite its foundation arch over the Slitrig collapsing in 1864 during construction. Little used as an exchange, acquired as a movie house in 1910. In 1994, a shell after a fire. The actual exchange was a delightfully open segmental arched structure. A corner tower over 20m high was part of the original design. Rochead, whose Wallace Monument near Stirling is a *tour de force*, also designed St Andrew's Free Church, 1870, in North Bridge Street, with a spire 32m high, demolished 1959.

10 **Drumlanrig Bridge**, 1776, widened 1900, crosses the Slitrig by a pair of segmental arches with a cast-iron balustrade.

11 **Tower Mill**, Elliot's, Towerknowe, early 19th century
Three-and-a-half-storey double-roofed plan in whin with sandstone dressings: built over the Slitrig Water off a wide flat-arched bridge, possibly the Auld Brig of 1741. Contains a massive wheel in the basement towards the High Street. On one corner is the stump of a brick chimney; it also carries a richly varied pattern of openings and glazing, reflecting developing industrial processes and technology.

12 Towerknowe, 1852, John Dick Peddie
Former National Bank, latterly Royal Bank of
Scotland. Terminal block of great character,
mostly Italianate, sumptuously crafted interior
fittings by Scott Morton & Co (not all have
survived the transition from bank to bistro,
unfortunately) from an upgrading, *c*.1930.

Above *Tower Mill*. Left *Towerknowe*

Sir Thomas Wharton to Henry
VIII, recommended to him Douglas
of Drumlanrig, an otherwise sound
chap whom circumstances had
forced beyond the jurisdiction of
Scots law: *His offence was very little,
being only accused as accessory at a
murder.*

13 Tower Hotel, from 15th century
Strong dark three- and four-storey frontages of
whinstone dominating the chicane leading to
Newcastleton. Originally the site of the
residence of the Douglases of Drumlanrig,
apparently surrounded by a deep moat drawn
from the River Slitrig. The Earl of Surrey's *visit*
to the town in 1570 left only the tower unburnt.
Occupied in later years by Anne, Duchess of
Buccleuch and wife of the Duke of Monmouth.
From the 17th century, part of it was used as a
prison of the barony, this becoming a wine
cellar on the conversion to a coaching inn,
c.1773. Stage-coaching ended 1862 with the
coming of the railway. Imaginative conversion
and part-peeling, Gray Marshall from 1990 for
the Scottish Historic Buildings Trust.

In Hawick in 1621 three locals
*have from January to November
worn hagbuts and pistolets, have
shot and slain great numbers of
their neighbours' proper doves, and
use the same for revenge upon all
persons against whom they bear
quarrel.* This was in spite of the law
of 1567 which protected pigeons and
doocots from destruction: a first
offence meant 40 days' gaol, a
second one a hand to be amputated,
and a third was a capital offence.

Allies could be more of a burden
than enemies: Froissart, in the 14th
century, described a Scot's view of
the French that *They will very soon
eat up and destroy all we have in
this country, and will do us more
harm, if we allow them to remain
amongst us, than the English could
in battle. If the English do burn our
homes, what consequence is it for us?
We can rebuild them cheap enough,
for we only require three days to do
so, provided we have five or six poles
and boughs to cover them.*
Annette Hope, *A Caledonian Feast*

Tower Hotel Project

Howegate

Alexander Orrock was the parish minister in the late 18th century. In his will in 1771 he left funds for a school, dwellinghouse, and a salary for a schoolmaster to provide free education for poor children.

James Wilson (1805-60), born in Hawick, founded *The Economist*.

Hawick Old Parish Church

[14] **Howegate** follows the medieval line of the street, constituent buildings of no great architectural interest except in their contribution to the whole; 19th-century and earlier, subject of successful revival (sneak into the backlands to the south), 1978 and later, Aitken & Turnbull. Civic Trust Awards, 1982 & 1986, Borders Regional Council Architectural Award for Conservation, 1984.

[15] **Sandbed**, formerly an enclosed space used for markets/fairs. In 1815 when **Buccleuch Street** was laid out the market moved to Towerknowe. Pressures of traffic and Philistines inspired the demolition of a particularly fine townscape feature here, the island block at **3 & 4** Sandbed, leaving a less striking open space, and **Orrock Place**. The **Ewe & Lamb**, Orrock Place, c.1960 (known locally as the Monkeys) is a not-unattractive-if-you-care-for-the-period ground-floor pub with housing over. **Chisholme Antiques**, Orrock Place, occupies 1825 United Parish & Grammar School with its pedimented doorpiece and multi-paned high-silled windows (those to the left subsequently insensitively altered). Possibly John & Thomas Smith (see schools at Bowden & St Boswells). In 1860 the school moved again to Buccleuch Street.

2 Buccleuch Street, c.1800
Vernacular three-storey end block formerly the Burns Inn, which once housed Robert *Lurgie* Wilson, the writer of the first history of [16] Hawick in 1825; restored, 1992. **Nos 8-22**, c.1820, comprise two-and three-storey terraced units some with good details (elegant fanlight of **No 10**) principally built of whin with [17] sandstone dressings and quoins. **St George's West Church**, St George's Lane, 1844, Andrew Thomson & John Smith; rebuilt 1913-16, J P Alison. First Pointed Gothic, with lancet windows. Stained glass, 1930 & 1935, Lilian J Pocock.

Hawick Old Parish Church, William Burn, demolished 1992; and **Church Hall**, Buccleuch Street, 1844
Romanesque, with an Italianate belfry. Financed by the Duke of Buccleuch on condition that he was given St Mary's Church. Hall built, 1885; stained glass, 1896, Ballantine & Gardiner.

18 Bank of Scotland, 7 High Street, 1863,
David Cousin
Formerly British Linen Bank, worthy
Venetian, complete with first-floor balcony.
Similar to that in Selkirk.

19 Border Club, 9 High Street, after 1902,
J P Alison
Rakishly slim piece of confident red sandstone
infill, splayed bays over the ground-floor shop.
20 Topping wallhead gable. **Trustee Savings
Bank**, 11 High Street (built as Hawick Savings
Bank), 1915, also by Alison, is classical, three-
storey five-bay ashlar front, ground floor
rusticated, elsewhere appropriately rich
details. Interior work by Scott Morton & Co.

7 & 9 High Street

The soprano, **Dame Isobel Baillie**,
1895-1983, was born in Hawick, a
baker's daughter. Her first job was
in the piano-roll department of a
music shop: one of the greatest
singers of oratorio, she gave over
1,000 performances of Handel's
Messiah.

Left *Trustee Savings Bank*.
Below *William Beck's Stocking Shop*

21 William Beck's Stocking Shop, 21 High
Street, c.1800
Transitional building set at the back of the rig
and across it, a building which links the
cottage industry with the satanic mills, its
square and regularly positioned windows each
lighting a work station for a stocking-weaver
(or should it be knitter?). Converted, 1991, to
housing by Dennis Rodwell, for the National
Trust for Scotland under its Little Houses
Improvement Scheme.

22 Sundial, 25 High Street, 1683, was found built
into one of the grates of this three-storey,
superficially Victorian, house. Today it carries
the inscription *Tak tent o' time ere time be tint*

William Beck was an employer
who would not participate in a
manufacturers' lock-out in 1805.
His grateful workforce subscribed to
present him with a silver cup, and
this can be seen in the Wilton Lodge
Museum.

141

[23] on a panel. **Royal Bank of Scotland**, 33-35 High Street, *c.*1870, built as National Bank of Scotland, classical three-storey, seven-bay stucco front (modern marble ground-floor [24] facing) topped by balustraded parapet. **Nos 65-67**, built as Co-operative Society Store, 1885, possibly Joseph Blaikie; civic three-storey building, decorative stone frontage topped by part-mansard roof with iron railings, round-headed dormers with acroteria.

[25] **No 12**, former Royal Bank of Scotland, 1859, Peddie & Kinnear, is another Italianate Bank.

[26] **Nos 24-26**, late 18th century, three-and-a-half-storey pleasantly scaled block of harled and [27] painted whinstone. **Nos 30-32**, Victorian, three-and-a-half-storey ornamental block defining the junction with Cross Wynd by the confident projection of a bowed corner.

Hawick, 1514
Nearly all the men of Hawick fell at Flodden in 1513, with Douglas of Drumlanrig. Following their army's victory, English raiding parties were emboldened, until 1514 when the youths of the town (the callants) came to manhood by boldly riding out to rout the marauders at Hornshole, 3km east of the town. The respite, though welcome, was temporary.

Lord Dacre, Warden of the English Marches (soon after Flodden), to Henry VIII: *In the next (moon) light, I shall, God willing, perform the said raid, and in the meantime shall cause small raids to be made, which shall be as great annoyance to the Scots as a great raid should be, and thus shall your money be employed to the best I can and to the greatest hurt and destruction of the Scots ...*

[29] ***The Horse***, 1514
Memorial intended to celebrate the 400th anniversary of the successful return of Hawick callants from a skirmish, 1514, at Hornshole, sculptor William F Beattie (d.1918), completed by his father, Thomas Beattie, by 1921. Behind *The Horse* fine townscape, 1894, James P Alison, three-storey gushet block, red sandstone with Westmorland slate, carrying details of

The Horse

architect, client, builder and provost on the dormerheads, and an earlier advert now **Prudential**, as the balcony balustrade. **Weensland Mill**, Weensland Road, mid- to late-19th-century woollen mill with extensive multi-storey ranges, one topped by an ornamental bellcote to ensure good timekeeping.

28 **Town Hall**, 1885, James C Walker
Built at a cost of £15,000 after a competition in 1883, a dominant clock-tower and little further architecture. On the site of the Town House of 1781, demolished 1884, which itself had replaced the Tolbooth (1694) and thatched gaol here. The **Mercat Cross** stood in front of the Tolbooth until 1762. This location makes more sense when one realises that **Cross Wynd** was the main road south (to Carter Bar) until the 1830s, and **Walter's Wynd** the route to the ford across the Teviot (first bridged in 1741). The stocks were removed, c.1800.

North Bridge Street, 1899-1900, J P Alison
Lively art nouveau red sandstone. Look for the house and studio, **Nos 43-45**, with its interesting letter box and mosaic work. **Library**, North Bridge Street, 1904, J Nicholl Scott (solid and satisfying corner block, despite the obvious need for glazing), following competition won (!) by Adshead & Sloper of London in 1901. Sculpture by John Birnie Rhind.

Across the **North Bridge**, 1832, John & Thomas Smith, past the slim-slabbed concrete **shelter** of 1959, stands the red-roofed **Leisure Centre**, 1983, Faulkner-Brown, Hendy, Stonor of Newcastle. On the site of the old railway station (the be-scrolled **Station Hotel** is opposite), with the bulk of the swimming-pool block set into the slope, its colour-matched blockwork and cheerful accessories creating a strong and colourful building whose maintenance could be better. Extension for

Top *Prudential.* Above *Town Hall, 1781.* Left *North Bridge Street*

In 1676, following *the most insolent degree of all insolent degrees of insolence and contempt done against the bailies* Adam Brown was fined £20 Scots and had *to lie in stocks during the bailies will and pleasure.*

Leisure Centre

bowling rink not designed to the original architects' high specification and noticeably so.

Burnhead, late 16th century
Three-storey tower-house construction with ashlar dressings, incorporated into modern (19th century) house with parapet walls and first-floor barrel-vaulted rooms.

Wilton UP Church, Commercial Road, 1894, J P Alison & J Chalmers
Referred to as the Iron Kirk, because the original UP preaching station on the site was a prefabricated iron structure brought from Rothesay in 1889. This model, with its elegant flèche, is a beautiful composition of volumes, the more necessary because of the sloping and confined site.

Top and middle *Wilton Church.*
Above *Wilton Church halls*

Wilton Church, 1860-2, J T Emmett
Emmett was the architect of Glasgow's Blythswood Parish Church and designed Wilton Church after competition with Brown & Wardrop, Notman & Rochead. Nave and arcade of Caen stone. Renovated, 1908, and enlarged J P Alison. War Memorial windows, 1924, by Lilian J Pocock. Swanky red-glazed **church halls**, 1987, with spiralling brick chimneys.

Wilton Mills, Commercial Road, mid-19th century
Three-storey ranges on the bank of the Teviot. Elaborate lade system, part of which is still accessible, via the council yard, to the pushy

visitor. Rusticated stonework, subtly proportioned fenestration of earlier block, 1867, later 1877, with cupola-topped clock-tower presiding glumly over a river view including yet another undistinguished supermarket's backside. Charming **Teviot Crescent**, 1832, built as skilled workers' housing, and **Health Centre**, 1989, Scott & McIntosh, the product of a limited architectural competition, yet sadly not slated.

Dangerfield Mill (William Watson's), Commercial Road, 1872-3
Three-and-two-thirds-storey, 11x4 bay with original machinery, notably the lineshaft driving system and Platt spinning mules of 1872. The oldest substantial group of spinning machines in working order (if not production) in a Borders mill.

Wilton Lodge (Langlands until 1790), dated 1859
Earlier core, two-and-a-half-storey, whin with ashlar dressings, pedimented and gabled, porch with flanking bays. Acquired for municipal park, 1889. **Local History Museum** since 1910. To the rear unremarkable exhibition gallery, c.1960, Aitken & Turnbull. Burgh coat of arms from the Corn Exchange salvaged and built into the wall behind the **War Memorial**, 1921, James B Dunn. 6.5m **Cenotaph** of Doddington stone, bronze statue *Spirit of Youth Triumphing over Evil*, Alexander Leslie.

Pringle of Whytbank was visiting Lord Napier at Wilton Lodge on the occasion of the Napoleonic false alarm of 1804. His butler, having announced the meal thus, *My Lord, supper is on the table, and the beacon's blazing,* Lord Napier responded, *Whytbank, if the beacon's blazing, little supper may suffice. The sooner we ride … the better.*

Wilton Lodge, 1889

Hawick Museum/RCAHMS

Patriotic (Boer War) Memorial, 1903,
J Nicholl Scott & A Lorne Campbell, sculpture
by Birnie Rhind.

On the skyline above Buccleuch Street the
Cottage Hospital, 1884, John McLachlan,
built by public subscription, its gables kitted
out with what appears to be stethoscopes as
their curved downpipes conjoin.

Bucklands Doocot, *c*.1800
Square tower, coursed rubble with ashlar
dressings and rat-moulding, slate roof bearing
weathervane.

Right and below *Cavers House*

Andrew Rodger made a
winnowing machine or fanners in
1737 and thereafter sold them in the
area. Before that time separating
grain from chaff had been by use of
the wind, either by way of *through*
barn doors, or riddling on a breezy
hilltop, and the fanners attracted
religious objections that they were
supplanting God's creations.

Cavers House, from *c*.1500
Five-storey tower-house, probably with 13th-
century castle remnants, altered 17th century,
converted 1750 to classical mansion house and
much extended, 1885-7, Scottish Baronial, as
part of a remodelling (when it was dated 1200!)
by Peddie & Kinnear. 1953, part-demolished
and deroofed (a number of mansions were thus
humiliated to avoid their owners paying rates).
A Douglas mansion which formerly housed the
Douglas pennon and the gauntlets of *Proud
Percy* from the Battle of Otterburn, it should be
noted that Cavers was burnt in 1542 by Lord
Dacre *with the help of Sir Walter Scott of
Branxholm*. All was not blood and fire, though:
on the Cavers Estate, Andrew Rodger, a
farmer, made the first Scots winnowing
machine from a description of a Dutch model.

Cavers Old Church, dated 1662
Kirk (now hall) with some Romanesque medieval
masonry built in. Like Roxburgh, Cavers was an

important town in days of yore, demolished by the English in 1596. The present **Cavers Church** dates from 1822, interior remodelled, 1928.

Kirkton Parish Church, 1841
Simple slated three-bay kirk and belfry, with some inserted panels from the previous model. Conversion (guts and stuff), 1906, probably J P Alison. Stable and byre converted to church use, 1933.

Henlawshiel Obelisk, 1895
Dr John Leyden spent his childhood here from 1776, and the granite obelisk commemorates that fact.

John Leyden (1775-1811), poet and orientalist, was a gifted linguist, knowing 34 different languages or dialects.

Orchard, *c*.1800
Georgian house, initially all harled, two-storey-and-basement with much original plasterwork. 19th-century alterations. Orchard **stables** have a pedimented frontage with an inserted armorial panel incorporating rose and (Douglas) heart. **Old Orchard**, restored early 19th-century cottages, harled and limewashed, centre block piended slate roof, lower wings.

Below *Stobs Castle*. Bottom *Woodfoot entrance archway*

Strang

Stobs Castle, 1792-3, Robert Adam, completed posthumously
Adam castle-style mini-mansion (Victorian additions and alterations) with single-storey wings, stable courtyard range and Gothick single-arch bridge approach. Last of the Adam castles, not built precisely to his designs, but with some fine interior spaces, if not Adam decoration. **Woodfoot** entrance archway, late 18th-century, Doric-columned, apparently

Strang

flanked by single-storey pavilions only one of which was built as such, the other purely two-dimensional. Adjacent, the single-arch **Woodfoot Bridge**, 1815, carrying the main road and the name of Elliot of Stobs who funded it.

Shankend Viaduct

Shankend Viaduct, pre-1866
Striding structure of 15 tall arches whose landscape impact is far more formidable than its shabby close-up appearance. Redundant, 1963. **Station Cottages**, Shankend, dourly twin-gabled group of cottages and station which, with the **signal box**, piended-roofed, brick and timber two-storey structure, await the Landmark Trust or similar worthy organisation or benefactor to revive them.

Hermitage Castle, from 14th century
Built by Comyn, Earl of Menteith, a dour ruin whose stability is assured by Victorian restorations funded by the Duke of Buccleuch and 20th-century maintenance by the state. Its present-day isolation in a wild setting is belied by its extensive fortified outworks now reduced

Hermitage Castle

to tight landscape rolls which justify careful inspection. An English agent reported in 1560 that Hermitage was an *old house, not strong, but evill to be winn by the strait ground about the same*. Its main development sequence is 14th-century start (?1360), large 13x22m keep in existence by 1388, small square towers added (for fire cover), *c*.1400, and oblong wing and wooden hoarding superstructure, *c*.1500 (see colour p.164). *Historic Scotland; open to the public; guidebook available*

400m to the west is **Hermitage Castle Chapel**, excavated 1926, by HM Office of Works, a *c*.14th-century site of footings and tombstones.

Thorlieshope, late 17th century
Ruined oblong two-storey-and-attic house, lintel dated 1682.

Castleton Church (presumably Castleton was once a settlement clinging around Liddel Castle on the east bank of the Liddel Water), 1808, altered 1885, complete with its own **school** & **hearse house**. No doubt the hearse would have been required to take the corpse to the kirkyard some distance to the north.

Hermitage Water Bridge, 1832,
John & Thomas Smith
Two-arch road bridge (for the Duke of Buccleuch) in the setting of which can be found some of the most elegant stone dykes.

NEWCASTLETON
Laid out in 1793 to the plan of Mr Keir of Whithaugh for the 3rd Duke of Buccleuch as a handloom-weaving village, the plan is a handsome sequence of hierarchical spaces and gridded streets and lanes far more sophisticated than can be appreciated by merely driving through it. Few if any buildings of note, even Peddie & Kinnear's bank of 1895 is more remarkable for its indifference to the village's simple sturdiness, and the Newcastleton Church, 1782, spire (no longer in existence) 1835, probably Archibald Scott, 1891 recast with additions, is no more than an afterthought on the road south.

Liddelbank, 1793, possibly William Elliot
Mansion sometime called Bellsbank for William Oliver, who as Sheriff had

Tales of Hermitage are colourful – usually bloody. The last of the English Soulis family which held it was reputed a black magician and met therefore a spectacular end being boiled alive in a cauldron at Nine-Stane-Rig a mile away. Here too Sir Alexander Ramsay was starved to death by his one-time companion-in-arms Sir William Douglas, the Knight of Liddesdale. Here, also, the Earl of Bothwell, whose family had exchanged for Hermitage Bothwell Castle in Clydesdale, received on his sick-bed Mary Queen of Scots in 1566 after her epic ride from Jedburgh, a journey which in turn almost killed her.

Below and middle Castleton school and hearse house. Bottom Shop sign, Newcastleton

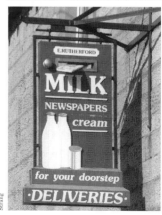

Liddelbank

Liddelbank ... *a handsome modern mansion adorned with two circular projecting bows in the front, with a door case in the centre, finished in the Tuscan Order, and highly ornamented by spacious wings on each extremity, this elegant villa terminates the county and parish ...* W Scott, *The Border Exploits*, 1812

Henry, 3rd Duke of Buccleuch, 1746-1812, who established Newcastleton, was a great agricultural improver. The 5th Duke, Walter Francis, 1806-84, carried on the family tradition by founding Granton.

In 1529 the Armstrongs, no friends of the English either, had claimed the burning of some 52 parish churches in Scotland. James V summarily hanged Johnnie Armstrong and 48 colleagues in an effort to bring the rule of law to the Borders. He failed, and indeed made his country more vulnerable to English incursions.

In 1600 Sir John Carmichael of Carmichael, warden of the Middle Marches, was murdered by a group of Armstrongs on his way home from a football match.

Henry Scott Riddell, 1798-1870, was another shepherd's son, born at Elves, Dumfriesshire. He was minister at Teviothead from 1831.

Branxholme Castle

enthusiastically promoted road improvements. One-room-deep plan set to take advantage of the views (over the Liddel Water) and the sun. Central three-storey, twin-bow-fronted block, pair of two-storey two-bay wings, currently under restoration, 1994. **Dinlabyre Aisle**, 1749, magnificent early Georgian roofless, three-bay burial enclosure of the Olivers of Dinlabyre and Liddelbank.

Teviothead (Caerlanrig) Church, 1856, Mr Cowan, Clerk of Works to Duke of Buccleuch Early English, replacing the church of 1799 which was converted to a school on the new kirk's completion. In the churchyard, the **Johnnie Armstrong Memorial**, 1897, commemorates the hanging of the reiver by James V in 1530.

Colterscleuch Monument 1874
A 13m-high cairn on Dryden Knowes in memory of the poet, the Revd Henry Scott Riddell, who lived in the adjacent Teviothead Cottage.

Branxholme Castle, from 15th century
Burnt by the Earl of Northumberland in 1532, Branxholme Tower (the site of much activity in Scott's *Lay of the Last Minstrel*) in 1570 was demolished by the Scots to prevent its occupation, and then razed by the English under Surrey. Consequently little or no 15th- or early 16th-century work remains, unless well absorbed into the structure constructed, 1571-6, by Sir Walter Scott and his wife Margaret Douglas. Flanking enfilading rectangular towers project from a pair of opposite corners of a long rectangular three-storey range, but the stronger (known as *Nebsie*) is presumably either a survivor of the earlier building or built off its footings. An unusual feature of the 1570s work is a Tudor doorway. **Tentyfoot** is a strengthening tower of the enceinte, the walled (but now incomplete) castle courtyard. Later alterations and additions include work, 1836, by William Burn for the Duke of Buccleuch.

RCAHMS

Goldielands Tower, 1789

Archy Armstrong was the very successful court jester of both King James VI & I, and Charles I. Somewhat ironically he needed to fall back on his considerable savings when, in 1637, King Charles fired him for insolence to Archbishop Laud.

Goldielands Tower, late 16th century
Spare oblong 10x7m, five-storey ruinous tower, whin rubble with ashlar dressings, in commanding position above the Teviot, with barmkin if Grose's view of 1789 bears interpretation. Walter Scott of Goldielands helped rescue Kinmont Willie from Carlisle Castle in 1596, and his (Walter's) tombstone is now in Hawick Museum via St Mary's Church. Goldielands' last laird, according to *base tradition* (Groome) was hung for *march-treason* over its entrance gate.

The reiver, **Kinmont Willie**, was snatched in breach of a truce and imprisoned in Carlisle Castle from whence he was equally quickly liberated by 200 of his compatriots led by Scott of Goldielands.

Snout Youth Hostel, Roberton
Former Free Church, 1843, renovated 1909, in Arts & Crafts manner. **Roberton New Parish Church**, 1863, David Rhind, *a good Gothic building* (Groome). The **Parish Hall**, *c*.1922, J P Alison.

Harden, from *c*.1630
Extended 1680 – characteristic steep roof, thick walls and dormers – restored and north additions, 1864. **Sundial**, 17th-century, from Dryburgh House. Previous house here (demolished 1590) was home of Wat of Harden, whose wife, the *Flower of Yarrow*, subtly served him up a set of spurs when the larder was low. Set in a secluded valley of the Borthwick Water, with a deep dell adjacent where no doubt English beef was concealed in wilder times. A farmhouse from the 18th century while the Scotts of Harden's seat was at Mertoun. Additions, 1913, when they moved back.

Below *Roberton New Parish Church.*
Bottom *Harden*

Strang

Strang

Borthwick Mains Symbol Stone
Pillar with Pictish incised fish outline.
Borthwickshiels, probably 18th-century core but extended, recast, restored. Pedimented

***High over Borthwick's** mountain flood*
His wood-embosom'd mansion stood;
In the dark glen, so deep below,
The herds of plunder'd England low

Scott, *Lay of the Last Minstrel*

Above *Borthwick Brae.*
Right *Chisholme*

garden front and raised terrace. **Borthwick Brae**, *c*.1800, three-storey five-bay house in harled rubble, flanking wings with Palladian windows.

Chisholme, mid 18th century
Three-and-a-half-storey-and-basement with Palladian windows flanking porch. Additions and reconstruction, 1909, J Jerdan & Son.

Craik Outdoor Education Centre, 1980, Borders Region Architects
In the *helicopter architecture* tradition of Visitor Centres such as that at Ben Lawers, a self-sufficient object found in the landscape.

Stirches
Originally a square tower dated 1503 with courtyard wall protecting offices. Upper storeys demolished, 1686, when the house was given its south front. More recently alterations and additions, 1900, by J P Alison. Since 1926 **RC Home for Ladies**, St Andrew's Convent.

Ashkirk
Country retreat of the Bishops of Glasgow, although their palace was last visible as a ruin in the 18th century. **Ashkirk Church**, rebuilt 1790, James Trotter, oak panelling from the old Minto Church (demolished 1831) possibly the Laird's Pew. Interior recast, 1893 and 1962, J Wilson Patterson. **Ashkirk Graveyard**, 17th century (dated 1646), burial enclosure of Corse-Scotts of Synton, rebuilt 1887. Tombstone of a gypsy boy hanged at Todrig for stealing a duck.

Below *Ashkirk Church.*
Bottom *Todrig*

Todrig, 17th century
Still remote tower house in 19th-century farmhouse clothes (from 1862), a rectangular three-storey four-bay house of halves, vertically split by a chimneyhead and subtle changes of proportion and levels.

Riddell

Expansive nine-bay three-storey house burnt down to a shell, 1943, following a fire which was only partly extinguished. Various attendant buildings which survive, particularly the **stables**, **deer larder**, **park bridges I & II** (in the 18th century an owner of Riddell completely changed the route of the river in order to obtain a picturesque landscape, bankrupting himself in the process). **General's Tower**, 1885, on a medieval motte enclosed by a rectangular bailey, a hollow observation tower with a vertiginous spiral staircase in one corner, corbelled parapet and caphouse, constructed by local builder, Herbertson of Galashiels, for Major-General John Sprot.

Riddell

Lilliesleaf

Formerly many of the village roofs were thatched, but today Lilliesleaf has lost much of the close-knit charm which led Groome to describe it as *among the prettiest of the Border villages*, and requires some thoughtful remedial surgery and even sensitive infill. East of the village is **Lilliesleaf Church**, 1771, extended 1883 (the addition of nave and bell-tower transformed the church, 1910). Good stained glass, 1966, W Wilson. Medieval font.

Linthill

Sophisticated three-bay two-storey central block with Venetian ground-floor windows, balustraded parapet, and fine plasterwork. **Alerig**, 1936, Leslie Graham (Thomson) MacDougall, smallish house (originally Newhall), with unusual double-height living space and concept akin to some of Sir Robert Lorimer's more domestic work.

Top *Tombstone detail, Lilliesleaf churchyard.* Above *Cavers Carre Doocot*

Cavers Carre, *c.*1800

Square, forbidding block, two-storey-and-basement, rubble with ashlar dressings and re-used pediments from an earlier house. **Cavers Carre Doocot**, 1532, but datestone and much else probably fake and 19th-century, completing a 17th-century form – rectangular plan lectern doocot with stone nesting boxes.

Midlem Village has an antique, rectangular layout the origins of which may well lie in the Anglo-Saxon *Middle-Ham*. At one time a centre of linen manufacture, Midlem is now a peaceful collection (including a former **Secession**

Top *Old smithy, Midlem*. Middle
Bowden Church gates. Above
Bowden Church. Right *Maxpoffle*

A painted board below the loft
encourages
*Behold the axe Lyes at the Tree's
Root
To hew doune these that Brings not
forth good fruit
And when theyre Cut The Lord into
his Ire
Wil them Destroy and Cast into the
Fire.*

Church) around the sloping village green with
the old smithy in the middle.

Whitmuir Hall, 1892
Carries (salvaged?) datestones of 1250 and
1775, and touches of Norman Shaw in its half-
timbered second floor and multiplicity of gables.

Holydean
Originally castle with a *c*.5000m² courtyard
enclosed by 5m-high walls (demolished *c*.1750),
now only a single vaulted undercroft, the
bakehouse, of this Ker stronghold survives,
built into the farm group.

Bowden Church, from 1128
Wealth of architectural history. Part of the
north wall possibly 15th-century, east end from
1644, cross aisle from 1661, west gable and
doorway at west end of north wall, 17th
century, In 1793 *old, long, narrow and in need
of repair*, restored, 1909, P MacGregor
Chalmers. **Laird's loft**, 1661 (originally set in
the archway leading to the cross aisle), with
shield and crest of the (Cavers) Ker family.
Externally sundial, 1666, good 18th- and 19th-
century gravestones, and fine entrance gates,
1890. **Bowden Manse**, two-storey harled and
painted three-bay house to the west of the kirk.

Maxpoffle, late Victorian
Red sandstone house to an excitingly
asymmetric design with its slim single round
tower feature.
Enjoying the south-facing slope, which
terminates upon the Eildon Hills, is **Bowden
Village**, birthplace of Thomas Aird (1802-76),
author of *The Devil's Dream*. **Bowden Mercat
Cross**, late 16th century, much mutilated, has
been *restored* as a war memorial. **Well**, stone-
enclosed and slated, 1861, with cobbled
surround. **Bowden School**, 1831, John Smith,

converted to house and post office, 1987,
Dennis G Rodwell for the National Trust for
Scotland, lowering the window openings
originally designed to capture the maximum of
light and the attention of the scholars. Behind,
Bowden Smithy, an earlier conversion by the
Trust under its Little Houses Improvement
Scheme.

Bowden Village Hall, 1896, Mr Wallace
Built by local subscription (local farmers gave
free haulage). *Mr Wallace* was the son of a well-
known village family, who won an RIBA
competition for the best design of a provincial
bank, but died at an early age. **Becketsfield**,
Leslie Graham Macdougall, for A D Hutcheson,
steeply pitched Westmorland-slated roofs
which demonstrate the potency of copper salts
(from the roof) to keep the slates below clear of
lichen. **Bothendene**, 1901, two-storey whin
rubble house with red sandstone dressings.

NEWTOWN ST BOSWELLS

Newtown is not so new, being identified on the
1654 Blaeu map of Lauderdale, and indeed a
mill here on the Bowden Burn was where the
tenant farmers associated with Melrose Abbey
brought their grain. An agricultural service
centre, in 1749 Newtown was about 15 houses
strong, but the railway (and thus the mart)
transformed it from 1845, the station location
here rumoured to have been deflected from St
Boswells' Green because of the antipathy of the
Buccleuch Hunt.

Top *Bowden Village Hall.*
Above *Bothendene*

At **St Boswells Fair** in 1849 a
young shepherd was killed by a
railway navvy in the *Great Riot*. The
police having failed to arrest their
suspect (who escaped) at the
navvies' encampment, dragoons
were called, and took into custody
another on the sole evidence of
bloodstained clothing: this latter
unfortunate, almost certainly
innocent, was hung.

Regional Headquarters

RIAS Collection

Competition-winning scheme for
Roxburgh County Offices

Regional Headquarters, 1966-8,
Peter Womersley
Dominates the village by virtue of its squat
cathedral-like scale and utter disregard for its
neighbours. A 1960 competition-winning
scheme, only partly implemented. The main
building has such strength of purpose that its
grey board-marked concrete (initially the
building was to be stone-clad) and extensive
glazing triumph over the original Roxburgh
County buildings, the less than sympathetic but
fortunately minor alterations, and the
cardboard shoe-box offices which attempt to
infill towards the traditionalist art deco neo-
Egyptian **Newtown School**, 1930s, Reid &
Forbes. The Womersley building, the first
completed in-situ lightweight concrete structure
in Scotland, uncomfortable to look at (or work
in) by day, has a light, almost theatrical quality
when internally illuminated at night. Its self-
sufficiency has been under-scored by the
completion of the **Regional Offices
Extension**, 1989, Borders Regional Council
Property Services Department. The original
scheme had a Council Chamber/ Committee
rooms node at the southern end of the site,
linked to the main office by a western
extension, which framed a high-level concourse:
presumably that extension's detailing was not
to have been so inconsistent with Phase 1.

RCAHMS

Railway Hotel

Station Buildings, Melbourne Place
Fine conglomeration of Victorian sandstone,
freely extending the **Railway Hotel** into a
street frontage as rich and accomplished as
could be the pride of any Scots burgh.

Tweedside Road has a more domestic
character, bolstering up the finely proportioned
(Georgian?) **Newtown House**, now part of a
terrace, and leading down the burn to the site
of the Parish Church of 1771. This was

demolished when the present **Newtown Parish Church**, 1868, was built on the southern approach to the village. **Baillie Hall**, 1886, like the kirk, has a well-detailed exterior. The **Toll House** (d.1989) was swept away by road improvers who thought not enough of their heritage.

East towards the Tweed and Dryburgh beyond lies the white-towered building of the **White Fathers**, who in 1935 established a (religious) house in a converted barn. Dismantling and relocating Wauchope House, 1877, Peddie & Kinnear, an English Gothic house, their complex developed, operated latterly by Strathclyde Regional Council as an educational centre, now industrial seed-bed. **The Holmes**, c.1914, T G Leadbetter: introverted design making relatively little use of its commanding position overlooking the Tweed. Adjacent, a cheerful little red sandstone stable group.

Reputedly the largest village green in Scotland (not perhaps a country noted for its village greens), that of **St Boswells** is a 40-acre common, the site of the annual horse fair, whose former attractions were the reasons given by James Hogg the Ettrick Shepherd in turning down an invitation to meet King George in London. Today's horses are found beneath the bonnets of the travellers' cars, or reflections, in the richly chromed caravans, of activities around the **Kennels of the Buccleuch Hunt**. The pink sandstone kennels block to the left, with its pedimented gable, is early 19th century. That to the right is later, another courtyard group with classical undertones, this time in buff.

The range of speculative red sandstone villas at the **Croft** date from the 1870s. At the village end of this group stands their predecessor, the **Village School** (now offices) and well-proportioned, sober **Schoolhouse**, 1836, John & Thomas Smith. South of the main road stands a small group of single-storey post-war **Scottish Veterans' Garden City Association** houses. Adjacent is **Greenside Park**, part-refurbishment, part-conversion of village chip-shop, 1984, Dennis Rodwell, through the National Trust for Scotland's Little Houses Improvement Scheme. **St Boswells Village Hall**, 1892, (dated on the weathervane) has fine-cast light brackets and

RCAHMS

Clapperton Studios

Top *Newtown Parish Church.*
Above *The Holmes*

Below *Kennels of the Buccleuch Hunt.* Bottom *Schoolhouse*

Strang

Strang

attendant red telephone kiosk, 1935, Sir Giles Gilbert Scott. **St Boswells Parish Church**, enlarged 1835, John & Thomas Smith. Stained glass by Ballantine, and (slightly overscaled) Liz Rowley, 1988. Became Parish Church in 1952 on the demise of St Boswells Church (at Benrig towards Maxton), which was demolished to a still-interpretable ground level, part of the operational graveyard.

Braeheads House, *c.*1908, F William Deas
This contribution to the village roofscape marks the genius of both architect and client. Deas (a pupil of Sir R Rowand Anderson, 1890-6) was known as one of the finest one-off house designers of his time, and although one might criticise Braeheads as being largely external show in the traditional Scots elements of slate, stone, and crowstepping (the interior is more comfortable than grand), it responds admirably to the genius loci of a complex and challenging skyline site.

Right *Braeheads House*.
Below *Lessudden House*

Lessudden House
Organically developed house with origins at least as old as 1680 when acquired by the Scotts of Raeburn. Remodelled, 1685; added to in the 18th century; reduced, 1780; improvements, 19th century. Probably as useful an example of the development of the Scots house as any in the Borders, with interior (and detailed) evidence of great architectural skill, somewhat let down by the buttresses (if that is not too great a contradiction in terms). A cylindrical **doocot**, and the Scotts' **Burial Aisle**, 1686, complete the ensemble. Two **sundials**, 1706 and 1739, are built into garden walls.

Mertoun Bridge, 1839-41, James Slight
Built in timber with stone piers and

abutments, the five segmental masonry arches were added later, carrying the main road across the Tweed. The old **Toll-house** adds to the composition, as does **Mertoun Mill**, just upstream.

Maxton Church, mid 18th century
Rectangular kirk with portions of 17th-century work, conceivably the round-headed west doorway on the south elevation could be a century or two earlier, renovated in 1812 and 1866. It carries a Burgerhuys bell of 1609. **Maxton Cross**, restored 1861, stands on the former village green.

Top *Maxton Church*. Above and left *Littledean Tower*

Littledean Tower, 16th century
On what must be one of the best sites in the Borders, overlooking the Tweed (where Duns Scotus may have been born *c*.1265), an earlier rectangular block of four storeys is dominated by an immense medieval D-plan tower extension.

Muirhouselaw, an exceptional range of farm buildings, 1889, with farmhouse, walled garden, and exquisite late-Victorian row of farm workers' cottages. **Fairnington House**, further to the south, is a large late 17th-century house incorporating earlier fragments.

Fairnington House

Rutherford Lodge, principally *c*.1925
Probably an old fishing lodge, extended and refaced into a square three-bay plan, with hipped slated roofs, Alison & Hobkirk.

Makerstoun, from 1590
White three-storey seven-bay block overlooking Tweed, antique-seeming mound to the south. House built here on footings of one destroyed by Hertford's invasion of 1545: Alexander McGill commented in 1714 *the north-west end being very Crazy is to be taken down*. Not crazy enough, apparently, for it was not until 1725 when William Adam carried out an improved version of the McGill scheme, possibly while building at

Makerstoun

Within Roxburgh kirkyard is a gravestone (with Gemmels' knapsack and dog) to Andrew Gemmels (1687-1793), soldier and subsequently wandering beggar, the *Edie Ochiltree* in Scott's *The Antiquary*.

Below *Roxburgh Church*. Bottom and right *Roxburgh Viaduct*

Floors. Later developments, principally 1828, attributed Archibald Elliot II, produced a not unattractive red sandstone castellated block. A fire in 1970 led to the building being peeled, part-deconstructed, and the whole harled, 1973-4, Ian Lindsay & Partners, in their interpretation of the Adam scheme of 1725.

Makerstoun Church, 1808
Ashlar red sandstone main front, the rest harled, rectangular plan with diminutive tower with bellcote, and Gothick windows. Notable array of 1808 original fittings ranging from pulpit, pews, and laird's loft to collection-ladles.

Roxburgh Village
Scattered collection (several cottages thatched into the 1950s when the last local thatcher died) around **Roxburgh Church**, repaired 1828, additions 1865, which along with a pair of cubical sundials on the exterior contains painted heraldic panels and a bell of 1705, and, in the graveyard, the (roofless) **burial-vault** of the Kers of Chatto. Stained glass, 1947, W Wilson. Just downhill the charmingly hood-moulded **rural school**. An effective stop to the village is the **Roxburgh Viaduct**, 1847,

Top *Melrose Abbey* . Above *Detail, Kelso Abbey.* Top right *Detail, Melrose Abbey.* Middle right *Reiver, stained glass, Hawick Library.* Right *Stained glass, Lilliesleaf Parish Church*

RIAS Collection

Borders Regional Council

RIAS Collection

Borders Regional Council

Borders Regional Council

Top *Dryburgh Abbey*. Middle *Peniel Heugh*. Above *Sheep stell, Liddesdale*. Top right *Floors Castle*. Right *Edenside Surgery, Kelso*. Middle right *Aerial view, Kelso*. Far right *Garden House, Ednam House Hotel*

162

Top *Thirlestane Castle*. Middle
Hermitage Castle. Above *Tweedbank*.
Top right *Fatlips Castle*. Right *Chapter
House, Dryburgh Abbey*

John Miller, which crosses the Teviot just upstream of the old ferry-station and the vestigial remains of the 16th-century Wallace's Tower. The curved plan of the viaduct would be impressive enough: the wrought-iron lenticular truss footbridge incorporated into the design at bank level makes this structure more exciting and sophisticated than any provincial railway line has any right to expect. Unfortunately the railway closed in 1964 and the approach bridge, which linked the station (now house) to the viaduct, has been demolished.

A castellated **gazebo** or – perhaps more likely – **eyecatcher**, a small Gothick structure to enliven the view from Floors – c.1800, stands at Daniel's Den, just north of the Maxton/Kelso road, looking across the Tweed.

In the 13th century, old Roxburgh's strategic significance, at the confluence of Tweed and Teviot, was considerable, with its castle *a most important fort, a royal residence, a centre of strife, an eyesore to every great party who had not possession of it, and at once the political glory and the social bane of Teviotdale*. The royal burgh's links with **Roxburgh Castle** (aka Marchmount) were too direct for its survival, and nothing at all remains above ground. The Castle itself was razed by the Scots in 1460, after more than a century of English occupation, in spite of the death of James II, during the siege, through an exploding cannon. The hilltop, with its odd clumps of masonry, is all that remains to punctuate the historic landscape.

Teviot Bridge, 1795, William Elliot
Possibly the brother of Archibald and James Elliot from Ancrum, William was certainly the builder, although the designer of this elegant bridge could well have been Alexander Stevens, who submitted a design and price (£1000) first in 1784, updating it to £1230 in 1788. The principal features of the bridge are engaged Doric columns, as previously used by Robert Mylne at Blackfriars Bridge, London, 1760-9, Harrison at Lancaster's Skerton Bridge, 1783-8, and subsequently by Rennie downstream at Kelso, 1800-3, and at Waterloo, 1811-7. Like the majority of bridge structures it is best viewed from river level where one can appreciate its fine proportions.

The skyline of **Kelso,** and its river frontage, good and ill, is memorable from this west bank. But the long view north to **Floors Castle** across the Tweed is something very special indeed.

Teviot Bridge

Old Roxburgh was, with Edinburgh, Stirling and Berwick, one of the four Royal Burghs and, as such, established many burgh standards and practices. When Berwick was English, and Roxburgh decayed, Lanark and Linlithgow replaced them in 1369. Edinburgh held the national standard measure of length (ell), Linlithgow the measure of grain (firlot), Stirling the liquid measure (jug or pint stoup, which was equal to three imperial pints) and Lanark the weights (first stone and then, from 1567, brass or lead).

There are three caves by the River Tweed near Roxburgh. One was used to hide horses in 1745 when the Jacobites passed through: another has been a doocot, with square nesting boxes cut into the side of the cave.

Floors Castle

William Adam's energy, success and contacts as an architect builder laid the foundation for his sons' achievements: *I took a little time to consider a brickwork belonging to Mr Adam ... who had at that time under his own care near to twenty general projects – Barley Mills, Timber Mills, Coal Works, Salt Pans, Marble Works, Highways, Farms, houses of his own a-building and houses belonging to others not a few!*
Sir John Clerk of Penicuik, 1728

Nor will the very face of the country appear the same, except it be that the River Tweed may, perhaps, run in the same channel: But the land before, lying open and wild, he will find enclos'd, cultivated and improv'd, rows, and even woods of trees covering the champaign country, and the house surrounded with large grown vistas, and well planted, such as were never seen there before.
Daniel Defoe, 1723

Playfair took his aesthetic and functional responsibilities seriously. He never married and told Cockerell that he was *too busy to woo ... Through his concern for good building, these (landscape design) effects are created in surprisingly solid materials which have nothing in common with the often gimcrack short cuts in stucco and flimsy materials deployed by southern Picturesque architects like Nash. The result of his recasting of the severe early 18th-century Classicism at Floors Castle into an extravaganza on the theme of Heriot's Hospital, which holds its own against the Poussinesque landscape of the Tweed Valley, seems oppressive to southern critics unused to the splendour of Scottish masonry.*
Ian Gow

Newton Don

RCAHMS

Floors Castle (Fleurs in the 18th century), 1721-6, William Adam
Previously attributed to Sir John Vanbrugh, but almost certainly Adam's first major if somewhat severe design. He also laid out much of the 18th-century landscape setting, making the most of such distant features as Kelso Abbey, Roxburgh Castle, and the Cheviots beyond. Building material was taken from Cessford Castle. Such building activity might not have been expected from the 1st Duke of Roxburghe, who declared on his Grand Tour in 1701 *The more fine houses and the more fine gardens I see, the more I am determin'd neither to build nor make gardens.* The result was not to everyone's taste: *The whole is built of rough stone, but with window cases of hewn stone. It is strange so large a house should not afford one good room* (Pococke). The present external appearance, whose *impossibly romantic additions and alterations (1837-45 William H Playfair) created its sugary skyline*, was the response of the 21-year-old 6th Duke to his *miserable house in one of the finest situations in Scotland.* The fullest effect can be obtained from the air – but the more conventional visitor can obtain a passing good impression by viewing the model of 1851, created by a Castle chef in *matchsticks and icing sugar*, below stairs in the basement. Many of the interiors were completely remodelled in the early 20th century by the American Duchess May (wife of 8th Duke). Floors became Greystoke during the making of the Tarzan film of the same name (see colour p.162).

Newton Don, 1817-20, Robert Smirke
Three-storey severe neoclassical exercise which applied the architect's geometrical

RCAHMS

preoccupations to (at least part of) an earlier building for which Robert Adam prepared plans in the 18th century. Later alterations included major staircase revisions in order to accommodate the Beaton Panels, now removed to museum conditions in Edinburgh, and a striking nickel-chrome and glass *shower douche spray* cabinet.

Smirke presumably also responsible for the **East Lodge**. Much of landscape setting also dates from *c*.1800. Balfour family acquired Newton Don in 1847 bringing with them from Balgonie in Fife an ornamental gate-arch, 1779, topped by a unicorn. Other landscape features include a **lion sundial**, castellated **electricity generation house** on the River Eden, a **Chinese Bridge**, and a **rustic summerhouse**. A fine **stables complex** pedimented and clock-towered, stands adjacent to the house.

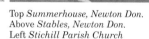

Top *Summerhouse, Newton Don.*
Above *Stables, Newton Don.*
Left *Stichill Parish Church*

Stichill Parish Church, *c*.1770

Some later reconstruction (around 1869, the date over the doorway to the kirkyard). Burgerhuys bell, 1632. Armorial panels *c*.17th-century, inserted in east gable, presumably those of the Pringles whose burial enclosure, 1783, is built on to it: later, polished granite enclosures in the churchyard to the Bairds and the Deuchars, all three families owners of the Stichill Estate in that order.

Set back from the road, **Baird Memorial cottages**, 1894, a fine range of harled and rosemary-tiled, half-timbered gabled, Venetian-windowed single-storey cottages in the vein of those at Foulden, the westernmost being the former post office, and carrying the inscriptions *telegraph office* and *parcel office*.

The magnificent rusticated gatepiers mark the entrance to the demolished **Stichill House**,

Extracts from the *Diary of George Ridpath, minister of Stichel 1755-61* indicates the interest which the 18th-century mind took in architecture: *Read some of Wolff's Elem. Arch. Civ., being led to it by Sir H. Wotton's work; Read chiefly in Wolff's Architecture; Read some of Ware's Palladio, and looked to the cuts which are very beautiful.*

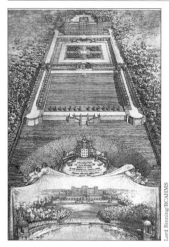

1866, James Maitland Wardrop, *a large and splendid edifice of 1866, whose tower, 100 feet high, commands a magnificent view of the country for 30 miles round* (Groome). One of Wardrop's best houses, with a Dunrobin-type entrance tower.

Right *Stichill House.* Above *Design for new garden, 1911, Sir Reginald Blomfield, at Mellerstain*

Lady Grizell Baillie's household books reveal *inter alia* that she had only one indoor manservant, who had his livery supplied but not his collars. She seemed unlucky with staff despite, or possibly because of, her scrupulous book-keeping: in one year she went through eight cooks.

Below *Hundy Mundy.*
Bottom *Thatched cottage*

Mellerstain House (originally Whitesyde), wings 1725-38, William Adam; main block, 1770-8, Robert Adam

At first there was only one pavilion. Then the family lived in the east wing with the west being converted to accommodate the servants. The servants' wing had part of the floor lowered to give greater height and obtain two intersolls *which I Judge a great Conveniency for sertts lodgeing*, while the 5ft (1650mm) from the kitchen floor to window sill *is so much better that it prevents those in the Kitchen and Scullerie from Looking into the Gardens* (William Adam to George Baillie, 1726). Lady Grizell Baillie was the author of a famous *household book*.

William Adam laid out the formal designed landscape, with two main axes crossing perpendicularly north of the house, and had the River Eden canalised and dammed to create a cascade. The north/south axis terminates on his **Hundy Mundy**, a square-turreted Gothick archway with deliberately smaller than normal openings in the stonework to accentuate the distance of over a mile from the house.

On his return from the Grand Tour in Europe suitably *imbued with classical taste* George Baillie (the younger) employed Robert Adam to design and build the long-missing central block. Superficially spare early Adam *Castle style* links his father's wings but also houses exceptionally refined neoclassical interiors of 1770-9, particularly in ceilings and friezes of drawing room, library and music room. *Open to the public*

Policies include **lodges**, neoclassical **mausoleum**, *c.*1770, to Grizell Baillie, and the

thatched cottage. Italianate **formal gardens** from 1909, Sir Reginald Blomfield, only part-completed sequence towards the canal, but in such a compatible style and form that it contributes to the earlier landscape structure. Of course one would have expected little else from Blomfield, given his eminence as architect, garden historian, and the author of *The Formal Garden in England* in 1892. He also produced the baroque main door on the entrance front, in order to bring the main block into an improved relationship with Adam père's wings.

Smailholm Village
Like an old hedgerow with gaps and a variety of species, the village straggles in clumps along a ridge. **Smailholm House** at the east end, a sheltered early 18th-century laird's house complete with crowstepping, carved skews and harled stonework. Amongst a variety of rural buildings **Smailholm farm**, early 19th century, was originally a posting-inn, standing at the roadside opposite **Smailholm Church**, from 13th century, rebuilt 1632, last rebuilt 1820. A simple kirk with laird's loft and memorial window, 1907, to Sir Walter Scott.

Smailholm (Sandyknowe) Tower,
early 16th century
Rectangular five-storey 17m-high tower prominently located, seen and seeing to the south and east. Its profile is allegedly such *as to be a guiding-mark to mariners off Berwick* (Chambers). Guardianship Monument, restored to more than a stable shell (with archaeological excavation of barmkin), 1980s, Scottish Development Department Ancient Monuments Division. Houses fascinating figure models (Anne Carrick) from Scots history and literature. A strange halfway restoration which is neither domestic nor institutional: its technical quality cannot be faulted.

Mertoun House, from 1703, Sir William Bruce
The Scotts of Harden acquired the estate *c*.1680, at a time when its focus was Old Mertoun House, 1677, the two-storey, harled and crowstepped building which still stands (housing the head gardener) in the present walled garden. Bruce employed Tobias Bachop as master mason, according to William Adam, but the building may conceivably be by Sir Roger Pratt. The three-storey pedimented *Harden House* saw Sir Walter Scott, a relative

Sir Walter Scott spent some of his fragile childhood staying with his grandparents at Sandyknowe Farm. From there, within stone's-throw of Smailholm Tower, he could hardly fail to be receptive to the history and traditions of the Borders. Those who have grappled with Scott's writings will not be surprised to learn that when Dr Duncan, the Parish Minister, visited the family at Sandyknowe he ruefully reported thus on the young Scott's ballad-spouting: *One may as well speak in the mouth of a cannon as where that child is!* Scott got his own back by featuring both Minister and Manse in *St Ronan's Well*.

Below *Smailholm Church*.
Middle *Smailholm Tower*.
Bottom *Mertoun House*

W G Scott/RCAHMS

Edinburgh Public Libraries/RCAHMS

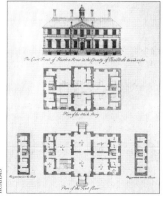

RCAHMS

Mertoun House doocot

On Friday 4 Nov. 1544 700 men *rode into Scotland upon the water of Tweide to a town called Dryburgh with an abbey in the same, which was a pretty town and well buylded; and they burnte the same town and abbey, saving the churche, with a great substance of corne and gote very much spoylage and insicht geir and brought away an hundredth nolte, sixty nagges, a hundreth sheep ... and they tarried so long at the said burnynge and spoylage that it was Satterday at eight of the cloke at nycht or they come home.*

of the family and frequent visitor to Mertoun, write *The Eve of St John* here in 1799, and the house had changed little then. Alterations in 1843, by William Burn, included the construction of a south wing, but this was not balanced until 1913-16 (the Scott family having sold up in 1912 to return to their original home of Harden south of Hawick) when Gibson & Gordon added another pavilion to the north, the two additions somewhat overwhelming the Bruce original. In a major scheme of subtraction, 1953-6, Ian G Lindsay, the house was reduced to its original proportions.

In the south-east corner of the walled garden stands the **doocot**, a circular beehive type with domed roof, dated 1576 over the doorway. The 18th-century single-span **Mertoun Bridge** lies within the policies, as does the picturesque **Mertoun Parish Church**, which dates from 1658 with a bell dated 1762, renovations in 1820 and enlargement in 1898. The old churchyard, with the burial vault of the Scotts of Harden, lies towards the eastern boundary of the policies.

Dryburgh Abbey, from 1150
Built by Order of Premonstratensians (also known as White Canons) who came from Alnwick, the Abbey ruins today stand in the most secluded and serene landscape, on a horseshoe bend of the Tweed, the whole seeming purpose-made for the contemplative life. The Abbey stood by a town of the same name, linked to Melrose and Jedburgh via fords, and was on the itinerary of any self-respecting English raid (see colour pp.162/4).

Within the **Chapter-house** traces remain of the earliest (12th-century) painted ceiling in Scotland. The relatively good state of

Right and below *Dryburgh Abbey*

preservation of the domestic buildings can be put down to their being lived in for more than a century after the Reformation. Robbing of dressed stonework was otherwise common – and the restoration in 1894 at Dryburgh of the east processional doorway (previously *salvaged* to Newton Don) was exceptional. By that time to religious veneration had been added the cult of personality as folk flocked to the grave of Sir Walter Scott. Grave of Field Marshal The Earl Haig has more gloomy significance. *Historic Scotland. Open to the public; guidebook available*

Dryburgh Abbey House, enlarged and rebuilt (possibly after fire), 1877, Peddie & Kinnear Solid, four-square, red sandstone block set on the green and pleasant haugh. The 19th-century Gothick stable-block (John & Thomas Smith?) is surmounted by the (Erskine?) motif of a bludgeoning arm. The cylindrical **doocot**, 1828, and inscribed DE, presumably David Erskine, Earl of Buchan, who carried out policy improvements, with the assistance of John Smith in several cases, almost to the point of eccentricity: the **Temple of the Muses**, topped by a bust of James Thomson, author of *The Seasons*, is a circular, columned gazebo standing on a mound overlooking the **suspension bridge** also originally designed, 1817, by Smith, blown down but successfully re-erected, 1818 (and in turn blown down in 1850 and itself replaced). Conceivably the same architect could have been responsible for the Gothic-arched **Orchard Gate**, and **Stirling Tower** (originally pantiled), similarly battlemented.

Top *Temple of the Muses*. Above *Doocot, Dryburgh Abbey House*

David Steurt Erskine, Earl of Buchan, founder of the Society of Antiquaries of Scotland in 1780, bought the Abbey in 1786 and was responsible for its preservation with certain *improvements* of his own.

Dryburgh Abbey Hotel

Dryburgh Abbey Hotel, 1892-4, Henry F Kerr A late-classical design, *c*.1800, known as Mantle House, virtually rebuilt after a fire, in distinctively pink baronial. Earlier staircase survives.

Top *Wallace Statue, c.1870.*
Above *Bemersyde*

Wallace Statue, 1814, John Smith
Formidable landmark in red sandstone. A
hidden treasure, this image of the Guardian of
Scotland (to which position he was elected in
the Borders at the Kirk o' the Forest in Selkirk)
towers some 7m high, complete with saltire
shield and double-handed sword, above the
public footpath. The Earl of Buchan had
apparently wished for a statue of Burns, but on
seeing the quarried stone it was readily agreed
that only a martial figure could do justice to
the medium. Surprisingly the statue was
originally painted white: its present weathered
state has a natural grandeur and romance
well-suited to its subject. Repairs by Bob
Heath/Graciela Glenn Ainsworth, 1991,
following Saltire Society Appeal. The adjacent
urn carries appropriately patriotic lines.

Bemersyde, *c.*1535
Originally built to protect the Monks' Ford which
lay virtually equidistant between Dryburgh Abbey
and Old Melrose Abbey. Sacked in 1545, and
rebuilt in 1581, it was added to in 1690 (with
stone *salvaged* from Dryburgh Abbey), 1761 (the
west wing), and 1796 (the east wing). Further
alterations in 1841 and 1859 (the replacement of
the west wing) were followed by alterations J P
Alison & Hobkirk of Hawick, 1923. A fashionable
reduction and remodelling 1959-61, Ian G Lindsay
and Partners, removed the (servants') wing to the
north and modified that to the west, restoring, as
it should be, more of the dominant character of the
great tower. The stables, arch and wall are 18th-
century, and the octagonal sundial *c.*1690.

Gladswood, early 19th century
Single-storey pavilion house, possibly by
Alexander Nasmyth, with ornamental cast-iron
gateway (piers topped by gledhawks), and
adjacent Rustick gateway/viewpoint topped by
five stone finials. Nearby **Old Gladswood
House**, 1703, a simple rectangular, harled and
crowstepped building, survives as a barn.

Redpath Village has an air of genuine
antiquity derived more from its plan-form –
topped and tailed by farm buildings at either
end of the straggly south-facing main (and
only) street – than any of its buildings. The
Latin-tagged **village hall** (formerly the
school?) may be from the Smiths of Darnick.
Few, if any, of its 20th-century additions could
be said to respect the village's simple charms.

RCAHMS

Cowdenknowes

Rambling house which in the 16th century consisted of a tower and mansion, 1574, and a smaller tower, connected by curtain walls defining a courtyard. The courtyard now gardens, the smaller tower in ruins, the ensemble is completed by a later linking wing which adds little to the composition.

Clapperton Studios

Top *Cowdenknowes.*
Above *Drygrange House*

Across the River Leader stands the statuesque red baronial **Drygrange House**, 1887-9, Peddie & Kinnear for Edward Sprott, additions and alterations, 1910, J M Dick Peddie, extended in red brick in its role as seminary (St Andrew's College) in the 1950s/early 1960s. In the grounds of this L-plan house stands a remarkable pantiled **summer-house**, *c.*1904, which incorporates Roman stonework from the pit in the principia at Newstead with other salvaged fragments. Good **stables** and steading, 1889-90, Peddie & Kinnear, H-plan, Jacobethan, with central ogival-roofed clock tower. Interesting **south lodge**, 1905, James Speirs in 17th-century Scots style.

Leaderfoot

Known irreverently as *Tripontium*, the site of the historic river crossing now boasts no fewer than three bridges. **Drygrange Bridge**, 1779-80, Alexander Stevens, must be the most appealing, not the least for its 31m central span, exceptional for its date, and incised plaque on the northern end. A victim of dreadful pointing at least once in its lifespan, its credentials for this bridge museum are otherwise impeccable – Stevens was a prolific and skilful architect-engineer who ended his days in Lancaster (after a varied Scottish career) developing the Lune Aqueduct.

Drygrange Bridge

BoTBMAG

Drygrange Railway Viaduct, 1981

The viaduct was a major engineering work worthy of amusing even Queen Victoria, but Lady John Scott of Spottiswoode (author of Annie Laurie) had no confidence in its solidity, and planned her trips accordingly.

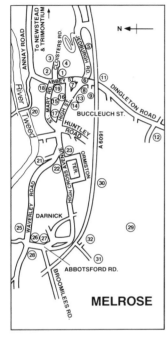

Trimontium's name is, of course, taken from the three Eildon Hills which dominate the Tweed valley here, just to the south of Melrose.

Market Square, Melrose, 1830, from a painting by Thomas H Shepherd

Drygrange Railway ('Leaderfoot') Viaduct, 1865, Charles Jopp & Messrs Wylie & Peddie
Built for the Berwickshire Railway, it takes a more mechanistic approach which succeeds by its very disdain for the valley crossing, the 19 tall red sandstone 13m span arches (up to 37m above water level) striding busily if now redundantly towards Duns and Reston (the line closed in 1948 due to flood damage on other bridges). *Historic Scotland Guardianship Monument*

Road bridge, 1971-73, Sir Alexander Gibb and Partners
As utilitarian in its own way as the Victorian structure. Time will tell if its box girder construction will prove as robust as its fellow exhibits.

Trimontium Monument 1928
Finely lettered stone erected by the Edinburgh Border Counties Association to mark the site and withdrawal of Roman occupations from what was arguably their most important fort in Scotland.

MELROSE
Partly the character of an antique dingy place, with narrow thoroughfares and ancient houses, and partly the appearance of a modern, spruce, aspiring seat of population, with elegant and airy edifices (Imperial Gazetteer). Famed for

the production of Melrose land-linen, this industry died out in the late 18th century and the woollen trade did not expand here. As a result the town has little or no truck with trade, being primarily residential.

Melrose Abbey

RCAHMS

1 **Melrose Abbey**, from 12th century Founded by Cistercian (white) monks having originated from Rievaulx in Yorkshire, then moved from their initial location at Old Melrose (eastwards towards the Tweed) to that at Melrose (Little Fordell) more suited to their agricultural habits. Subject to much sacking, looting and rebuilding, most surviving work is 15th century, the high point of Scottish Decorated with the Parish Church, 1618, built over the nave until its removal, 1810, to Weirhill. Restoration of the Abbey remains took place, 1822, by John Smith under the supervision of Sir Walter Scott (Melrose figured as *Kennaquhair* in the *Waverley Novels*, *The Abbot* and *The Monastery*) and at the expense of the Duke of Buccleuch, the then owner.

Despite the efforts of despoilers from both sides of the Border, a wealth of decoration on the building has still survived, much of it at high level on the abbey kirk where the stone carvers, using stone from Dryburgh, *devised and carried out designs of leaf, bud, and flower. They produced the gargoyles shaped like strange uncouth animals or flying dragons that belched out the roofwater, and set up the array of demons, devils and hobgoblins on the buttress intakes and gables. Sculptors or imagers gave the master touch to representations of the Christ, the Virgin, the saints and martyrs that filled the many elaborate niches; and to the angel musicians on the supporting corbels. Heads of kings, queens,*

In 1747 **Dr John Rutherford** experimented in growing turnips on a 2-acre field, fattening two bullocks with the crop so successfully that local butchers would not purchase them, thinking them monsters.

Two Gothic inscriptions refer to a French master mason with responsibilities for the Abbey, and in particular probably for the design of its south gables. Transcribed by an 18th-century minister of Melrose, Adam Gray, one reads
John : Morow : sum : tym : callit was : I : and : born : in : parysse : certanly : and : had : in : kepying : al : masoun : werk : of : Santan droys : ye : hye : kyrk : of : glas gw : melros : and : paslay : of : nyddysdayll : and : of : galway : I : pray : to God : and : mari : bathe: & : swete : sanct : Johne : to : kepe : this : holy : kyrk : fra : skathe.

Dorothy Wordsworth was not taken by Melrose Kirk in the Abbey: *Within these beautiful walls is the ugliest church that was every beheld – if it had been hewn out of the side of a hill it could not have been more dismal ... what a contrast to the beautiful and graceful order apparent in every part of the ancient design and workmanship!*

The Scotts' involvement might have been in some way expiation, for in 1569 Sir Walter Scott of Branxholm had dismantled *the inner queir, uter kirk, the stepile and croce kirk of the same* (the quire, nave, tower and transepts) and carried off the stone, timber, lead, iron and glass. Accused of this in 1573 he ingenuously responded that he had removed the materials to save them from the English. To be fair, the English in 1544 and 1545 had fired the town, destroyed the monastery, and desecrated the Abbey Kirk and its tombs, and little or no rebuilding had taken place.

Commendator's House

The great abbeys of Melrose, Jedburgh, Kelso and Dryburgh built up flocks and established an export trade with Flanders, France and Italy. There was great demand for wool and skins from Scotland, and the agricultural pattern of the Borders was thus set: sheep in the hills, arable in the valleys. Hope, *A Caledonian Feast*

An 18th-century stone has the legend
> The earth goeth on the earth glistring like gold
> The earth goes to the earth sooner than it wold
> The earth builds on the earth castles and towers
> The earth says to the earth all shall be ours.

lords, ladies, monks, craftsmen, saracens and scolds looked down from their places at each side of the windows, from which their faces have smirked, smiled, scowled, and grimaced throughout the centuries. A pair of binoculars will help to pick up the relevant detail of the piping pig and his party (see colour p.161).

2 **Commendator's House**, 15th century
The abbot's palatium, which in 1590 became the house for the then Commendator James Douglas. The dated lintel is reset in the (modern) south end. Reconstructed, 1590 and thereafter, restored 1936, J Wilson Paterson His Majesty's Office of Works. Museum since 1941. The lean-to **Abbey Doocot** is early 18th century, part of the Priory Farm complex.

The Abbey grounds contain several interesting gravestones. That of the Smith dynasty of Darnick, architect-masons, marked by a great red sandstone column, has clear relevance to the period of 19th-century restoration. But perhaps the most fascinating grave is one which is not marked at all. Bruce's heart is reputed to have been buried at Melrose, and indeed below the chapter-house floor lies *a mummified human heart enclosed in a cone-shaped container of lead. Decomposed iron box straps were found beside the casket, but nothing to indicate its history. Historic Scotland. Open to the public; guidebook available*

Right *The Cloisters.*
Below *Priorwood Garden*

3 **The Cloisters**, 1815, John Smith
Built as manse, two-storey three-bay in coursed squared rubble with droved and polished dressings, piended slated roof. Later 19th century additions.

4 **Priorwood Garden**
Originally part of the policies of Priorwood House (now youth hostel) now National Trust

for Scotland has the (originally gardener's) cottage (and shop!), 1875, Peddie & Kinnear, at its north-west corner, the garden a sanctuary providing one visits it out of season. The wall to Abbey Street is 18th-century, great wallhead scallops filled with 1904 (Lutyens? Lorimer?) wrought-iron adverts for its contents.

5 **The Wall**, East Port, 1988
Clothes the naïvely massive retaining structure of the Melrose bypass with standard concrete masonry blocks. Civic Trust Commendation, 1989. Initial concept built in decorative references (not executed) to the *Waverley Novels*. The simplistic neoclassicism nods to Peter Womersley's University of Hull Sports Centre.

King Robert Bruce (1274-1329) died of leprosy at Cardross Castle, his wish being that his heart be taken to Jerusalem, his body meanwhile buried in Dunfermline Abbey. Sadly the crusading heart reached only Spain, where its steward, Sir James (the Black) Douglas, died fighting the Moors in Andalusia. The heart returned to be interred at Melrose.

Left *East Port*. Below *Bank of Scotland*. Bottom *Corn Exchange*

6 **East Port**, *c*.1830, restored Aitken & Turnbull, 1980
Welcoming piended-roofed two-storey building, a guardhouse which constricts (watch for both traffic and Denys Mitchell's galleon sign for the late 18th-century Ship Inn) to emphasise the spacious **Market Place**, now sadly little more than a traffic island around the **Market Cross**. New (1991) finial replacing that of 1645, an unrecognisably eroded Unicorn with mallet (Mel(l)) and rose, above modern shaft and 19th-century octagonal stepped base. The cross, 1645, replaced an earlier one – a natural focal point in this area which had developed just south of the Abbey's main entrance, where Abbey Street begins.

7 **Bank of Scotland**, 1897,
George Washington Browne
Originally British Linen Bank, strong *free Renaissance* red sandstone stop to the view from Dingleton Road.

8 **Corn Exchange**, 1862-3, David Cousin
Scottish Jacobean three-storey with crowsteps

and strapwork. More mells and roses. To the right on the Ormiston Rooms a large cast-iron **Memorial Clock**, 1892, on ornamental bracket.

9 **Melrose Station**, 1847-9, John Miller
One of the few remaining railway buildings albeit with little railway setting, the restored octagonal high chimneys of the Jacobean block cut a lively skyline. The demolition of south platform and goods building, and the salvaging of the cast-iron urinal (from George Smith & Co's Sun Foundry, Glasgow) to Bewdley, Hereford & Worcestershire, has lost the station much of its context, and even the magnificent lotus-capitalled columns (Blaikie & Sons) and brackets of the canopy struggle to maintain cheerfulness in the face of adversity and the new roadway supplanting the Waverley Line. Conversion, 1986, Dennis Rodwell, restaurant and offices.

11 **Rosebank**, 1814, John Smith
Built for James Curle WS: two-storey three-bay with advanced, pedimented centre bay, coursed squared rubble with ashlar dressings, slated roof. In 1845 Curle was faced with the railway being constructed at the foot of his garden and moved to Harmony Hall.

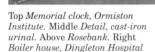

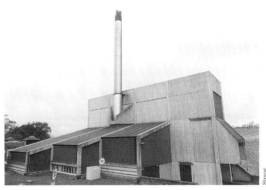

Top *Memorial clock, Ormiston Institute.* Middle *Detail, cast-iron urinal.* Above *Rosebank.* Right *Boiler house, Dingleton Hospital*

12 **Dingleton Hospital**, 1870-2, Brown & Wardrop
Little beyond the utilitarian to recommend its original conception. Peter Womersley's **Boiler House**, 1977, commands respect, a positive landmark, commended for its concrete work, FT Industrial Architecture Award 1978; the same architect being responsible for the flowing timberwork of the entrance hall ceiling.

High Street disappoints: the majority of the buildings scraped or overlain, few original features remain. The discovery of original horranising (fine patterned river-stone [13] cobbling) at **The Pendstead** (1823, two-storey five-bay former United Secession Church behind Messrs Ormiston & Renwick) is surprisingly the work of Anne Carrick and R McDonald Scott in the middle of the 20th century, their family wheel-barrowing raw material from the Tweed.

[14] **George & Abbotsford Hotel**,
early 19th century
Overblown presence with added second floor, mansard, and painted finish in contrast to the simpler four-bay three-storey **King's Arms** faced in squared rubble with ashlar dressings and Tuscan doorpiece.

Top *King's Arms Hotel.*
Above *Buccleuch House*

[15] **Buccleuch House** (St Mary's School), c.1830
Two-storey five-bay symmetrical front with central doorpiece, fanlight and hood on consoles, tripartite window over, piended slated roof and tall stacks.

[16] **Abbey Park** (St Mary's Preparatory School), c.1820
Two-storey three-bay classical villa with Tuscan-pilastered doorpiece and armorial panel over. Coursed squared rubble with polished ashlar dressings, piended slated roof and substantial late-19th- and 20th-century additions, its classical stable block (also c.1820) converted, 1975, to school use.

[17] **The Greenyards**
Originally common land which town proprietors used for clay, turf, and *the pasturage of their bestial*; now witness to the clash of titans on the rugby field. No doubt one side or the other will raise their eyes during the game to **St Cuthbert's**

St Cuthbert's Parish Church, c.1908

Top *Harmony Hall Stables.*
Right *Harmony Hall*

Parish Church, 1808-10, John Smith, of which only the tower remained after a fire to be incorporated into the reconstruction, 1911, J M Dick Peddie (won in competition with notables including MacGibbon & Ross and J P Alison of Hawick), Georgian Revival not ill-suited to the tower, and which makes the most of the church's position (attractively floodlit *c.*1988) on the Weirhill.

18 **Harmony Hall Stables**, St Mary's Road, *c.*1807 Single-storey classical range with pediment housing blind oculus and fire insurance mark.

Harmony Hall was named after Waugh's Jamaican plantation. He supplied Jamaican cedar for the library and drawing room at Abbotsford. Waugh was known by Sir Walter as *Melancholy Jacques,* apparently a gloomy if wealthy chap.

19 **Harmony Hall**, 1807
Reclusive behind high rubble walls, built in uncertain times, as befits the house of a local joiner, Robert Waugh, who had made his fortune in Jamaica: two-and-a-half-storey-and-basement built of coursed whinstone with freestone dressings, a pedimented centre bay and Ionic porch.

Prior to the construction of bridges, the fords were sometimes crossed by hired stilts, and these were used just downstream of the Chain Bridge site.

Chain Bridge

20 **Chain Bridge**, 1826, Redpath Brown & Co John Stevenson Brown was originally a smith from Lyne in Peeblesshire. Gothick pylons with corbelled and crenellated heads over pointed arched openings. Blacksmith-forged iron chains, suspenders, stress and tension were artfully combined in this footbridge *it is also calculated to admit horses.* Construction work by the Smiths of Darnick who may have designed the accompanying charmingly scaled **Toll-house**, 1826. Bridge completely reconstructed, 1991, with most unsympathetic new deck: this wouldn't have happened to a Chippendale chair of the same date!

21 St Cuthbert's Manse, Tweedmouth Road,
1901, Andrew G Heiton
Scots Baronial with Arts & Crafts detailing,
harled (extraordinarily, painted) with ashlar
dressings, expansively two-and-a-half-storey,
attractively-detailed.

22 Holy Trinity Episcopal Church, 1846-50,
Benjamin Ferrey
Early English, Decorated chancel and
transepts, 1899, Hay & Henderson. Stained
glass transept window, 1900, Kempe; other
commemorative glass by Meyer & Co and
W Wilson, 1963. Adjacent is the **Rectory**,
1847-8, also by Ferrey, now subdivided, and his
contemporary stables, converted to the Old
Abbey School and later to domestic use.

Holy Trinity Episcopal Church

Benjamin Ferrey, 1810-80, was
born in Christchurch and died in
London.

23 RC Church, High Cross Avenue, 1866,
Peddie & Kinnear
Built as UP Church (later Church of Scotland),
1872, three-stage tower with octagonal spire
added. Romanesque four-bay hall church in
snecked bull-faced rubble with stugged and
polished dressings, its principal feature being
the rose window in the road elevation.

St Helen's, Waverley Road, 1806
One of the best of Melrose's many mansionettes,
three-bay one-and-a-half-storey-and-basement,
centre bow, Tuscan pilastraded entrance with
fanlight, cast iron balcony at attic bow, coursed
squared rubble with polished dressings,
piended slated roof with two spectacular rows
of six octagonal chimneys.

25 Waverley Castle Hotel, 1869-71,
James Campbell Walker
Extended 1876, pioneering construction, probably
the earliest mass concrete building in Scotland,
whose pruned and consquently lumpish architecture does nothing for its prominent position.

Left and below *Waverley Castle Hotel*

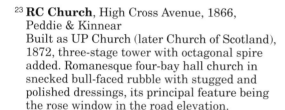

Darnick Tower

RCAHMS

Andrew G Heiton was born Andrew Heiton Grainger, but he transposed his middle name and surname on inheriting and continuing his uncle's practice (in Perth) and Darnick Tower.

Nothing could subdue the warlike aspect of the massive tower, battlements and steeply peaked roof. The castle stands amid its flowerbeds and tree-shaded gardens as grandly and incongruously as a Spanish galleon stranded in a tiny harbour. Lang

DARNICK

26 **Darnick Tower**, 1595

Three-storey T-plan house in warm red sandstone, carrying the bull's head motif of the Heiton family. Hankered after by Sir Walter Scott (no doubt it would be less recognisable today had the *Duke of Darnick* got his hands on it). Restored, 1865, by Andrew G Heiton, the tower has a corbelled and crenellated parapet walk around the attic storey. Shortly after the restoration works, the two-storey east addition was constructed in 1869 (eight years earlier John & Thomas Smith had prepared plans for an extension, but it is not clear if these were they). Given the wall-thicknesses the accommodation contained is not large, but whether by dint of careful Victorian repair or an absence of later *improvement* an ambience of antiquity still persists. With the help of such features as an iron yett from Doune Castle this is also in considerable part due to the enclosing wall which curtails the views of certain insensitive alterations to Darnick village. Fortunately the tower has just enough height to maintain its presence above the wallhead.

27 **Fisher's Tower**

The second tower of Darnick (the site of the third is lost): a roofless shell of 16th-century origin, altered in the 18th century to form a two-storey house. Now even the wallheads crumble, and its architectural interest, almost entirely restricted to the interior of the east gable, seems to survive by its fingernails.

28 **Darnlee**, 1816, John Smith
A mini-mansion for Smith himself, altered 1872, Brown & Wardrop. Original simplicity of form and idyllic setting can be appreciated from points where the rear extensions are invisible.

29 **Chiefswood**, 1820-1, John & Thomas Smith
Built following the acquisition of the then-named Burnfoot property by Sir Walter Scott. Transformed in name and accommodation, Chiefswood became the home of Scott's daughter and son-in-law/biographer Lockhart, who no doubt also enjoyed the fruits of the Monk's Well, formed by Scott with the aid of *salvaged* 15th-century abbey tracery just south of the Huntly Burn, and used by him as a wine-cooler. Briefly (1885-91) the base of the great art collector and apiarist Thomas Gibson-Carmichael before his inheritance of Castlecraig and subsequent removal to Skirling House, where a Chiefswood sundial can still be seen (see p.253).

Top *Darnlee, 1969.* Above *Chiefswood*

30 **Harleyburn**, 1872, Brown & Wardrop
Italianate two-and-a-half-storey symmetry in coursed red sandstone with contrasting dressings, a piended roof, and balustraded balcony over Ionic porch.

Borders General Hospital: Below *Chaplaincy Centre.* Bottom *Main entrance*

31 **Huntlyburn**
A simple two-storey house acquired and *improved*, 1817, by Sir Walter Scott.

32 **Borders General Hospital**, 1988, Reiach & Hall
Pared-down people-factory lacking a pitched roof to hold it down visually in the open vista terminating upon the Eildon Hills. The jury is still out on both the ameliorating effect of David Skinner's landscape works and the long-term merits of protecting the Borders' biggest (and probably most highly serviced) building with a flat roof. A two-tone concrete block

backcloth makes the entrance canopies seem positively frivolous. **Nurses' Residences**, by the same architects, contrast, suggesting that the Great Architect in the Sky dropped a piece of Tweedbank during its creation.

Abbotsford engraved by James Johnston, 1833

The story of the growth of the house, as narrated in the Life of the proprietor, shows it owes all its characteristic and prominent features to Sir Walter himself, working in conjunction with his master mason from Darnick. MacGibbon & Ross

To quote Scott: *The farm-house itself was small and poor with a common kail-yard on one flank and a staring barn ... on the other, while in front appeared a filthy pond covered with ducks and duckweed from which the whole tenement had derived the unharmonious designation of Clarty Hole.* But he recognised the potential of the site at least ... *a small property delightfully situated on the side of the Tweed, my native river ... I intend to build a beautiful little cottage upon the spot.* On the topmost of a series of gravel river-terraces sprouted not an ornamental cottage but an *old English hall such as a squire of yore dwelt in,* and Scott extended its grounds to 450ha by the eventual acquisition and improvement (including much landscaped woodland planting) of three farms. Today's policies are about one-seventh of that area.

Abbotsford, 1817-24

Verily a house designed by a committee, although with Sir Walter Scott as chairman the result was never likely to be camel-like. Scott acquired the farm and farmhouse in 1811.

Abbotsford was built in two principal phases, after some preliminary skirmishings involving William Stark of Glasgow (d.1813), James Skene of Rubislaw, and Edward Blore (antiquarian draughtsman turned-architect in the 1820s to such good effect that he was later known as the *cheap architect* as a tribute to his sound contract management; he completed Buckingham Palace in 1832).

Phase 1, from 1817 to 1819, William Atkinson (formerly a pupil of James Wyatt) was principally responsible for the addition of the breakfast parlour, armoury and dining-room to the original farmhouse, his design talents as a Gothic Revivalist being applied to interior as well as out, with those of George Bullock,

Abbotsford from the air by Air Marshal G McGregor, 1930s

cabinet-maker and sculptor, and Daniel Terry, architectural draughtsman turned actor-manager who acted as Scott's London eyes and ears. Terry's father-in-law was Alexander Nasmyth, landscape painter and designer, whose daughter Elizabeth designed a number of the Abbotsford stained-glass windows. Phase 2 (1821-3, Scots-Jacobean this time rather than Tudor-influenced) involved the same team (with the exception of Bullock who had died in 1818) in the construction of the drawing-room, library, study and great hall, and the clearance of the old farmhouse.

Even without the literary associations of the place, Abbotsford is of primary architectural significance, the *unsung prototype of Scots Baronial architecture which was to sweep across the country after the middle of the century*, surely due in part to Abbotsford's opening to the public from 1833. With the exception of the dining room the interiors are much as Scott left them, an extraordinary mixture of old and new, incorporating *ancient objects and modern pieces of Bullock's furniture*. Today's visitor is able to relate to the comfortable scale of the spaces, and for all its apparent historicism the house was designed from the first to be lit by gas and occupied by a family – albeit one with rather more family heirlooms than most.

Certain features salvage ideas or actual parts from Scottish historic buildings, the interiors too many to mention: the courtyard walls, built 1817-24, by the Smiths (builders of Phase 2), incorporated five medallions from Edinburgh's Old Mercat Cross, and the fountain bowl came from the same source. John Smith sculpted the mounting block in the form of Scott's dog Maida, and there are other features including six Roman stones, the statue, by John Greenshields, of Morris (an exciseman from *Rob Roy*, surely not for venting financial frustrations upon), Gothick conservatory (designed by Scott, *c*.1820), and castellated tower/game larder. The west wing, including the **chapel**, was built *c*.1852.

Tweedbank

Urban expansion having been identified for the Tweed valley, downstream of its junction with the Gala Water, by the 1968 Johnson-Marshall Plan for the Central Borders, a supposed new community was planned for Tweedbank. In reality a dormitory village with little services of

Abbotsford: Top *North Terrace*. Above *South Armoury*

Scott to Lady Abercorn, 1811
I have bought a small farm ... so now I am a Laird and in 1812 we are all screwed into the former farmhouse – our single sittingroom is twelve feet square and the room above subdivided for cribs to the children – an old coal hole makes our cellar, a garret above the little kitchen with a sort of light closet makes bedroom and dressing room decorated – lumbered – my wife says with all my guns, pistols, targes, broadswords, bugle horns and old armour.

Despite his historical and romantic bent, Scott was progressive in other directions, installing his gas lighting and hot air heating systems in 1823, when he wrote to his son that gas *was very clean yet this cheapness is an encouragement for greater liberality not to say extravagance in the use of it. But then your house is twenty times lighter for the same expense so that one gains a great deal in comfort and brilliancy ...*

Tweedbank

Since most of the Border textile towns are located in steepish valleys they tend to spread out rather than up the sides. Unfortunately, the valleys into which their expansion presses are often the most visually attractive and fertile: internal regeneration and rehabilitation (in areas such as Selkirk's riverside, for example) might seem appropriate stewardship.

its own, Tweedbank has never reached the population predictions, departing in some cases desperately from its original proposals in order to obtain development (see colour p.164). The initial phases carried out to the designs of the Scottish Special Housing Association have considerable merit – built around a major water feature created for the purpose, and rising responsively towards the Tweedbank Farm buildings, converted to **community centre**, 1986, Ray Licence. Little of note stands in the industrial estate, but the landscape structure by David Skinner conceals this fact.

Lowood (Bridgend)
Rambling riverside house of at least Georgian and Victorian periods, one-time retirement home, 1839-56, of Robert Reid, Master of Works and Architect to the King.

Above *Old Bridge of Tweed.*
Right *Pavilion*

Crossing to the north bank of the Tweed (not alas now by the perhaps mythical Old Bridge of Tweed illustrated by Scott (and Skene) in *The Monastery* – the bridge-keeper living in the central tower with a drawbridge to front and rear), **Pavilion** is a secluded, somewhat low and lengthily languorous mansion built for Lord Somerville as a sporting lodge, with east-facing pedimented elevation and supporting wings (one of which, unusually cavity-walled, was added before 1837, John & Thomas Smith).

Gattonside is a sunny little village with a plethora of (monkish?) orchards and a medieval

plan which has so far resisted the *improvements* of the roads engineer.

Gattonside House (St Aidans), 1826, John & Thomas Smith
Late-Georgian mansion of middle size which deserves better than to be surrounded by the sea of 20th-century architectural flotsam and jetsam which now occupies its policies.

The Rig, 1956, Peter Womersley
His own house and office, framing one of the orchards which characterise the history of the village. The house is south-facing, open plan, of modest proportions. Any guests were accommodated in the southern section of the office, which stepped up the slope, the entrance and reception so glazed as to show to best advantage an intricate modern sculpture.

RIAS Collection

EARLSTON
The **Old Earlston Bridge**, the **Rhymer's Mill**, an early **lintel** behind the Main Street frontage (garden shop), and a **thatched** (*Floother's*) **cottage** are all interesting features to be discovered within the town. Of the more obvious structures of note, one at least must be looked out for, the **Rhymer's Tower**, a small whinstone keep, in ruins, whose internal red sandstone corbels and vestigial vault are still recognisable features, just visible behind the late 20th-century commercial detritus associated with the A68. Now held by the Edinburgh Borderers Association.

Earlston Parish Church, 1892
A stone which marks that *Auld Rhymer's race lies in this place* was transferred to the *new Kirk* in 1736, and then to this most recent Victorian version in red sandstone where it is

Much abused urban form, with unsympathetic expansion and infill effectively disguising its historic origins, Ercildoune or Earlston's most famous resident was **Thomas Learmont – True Tammas** or **Thomas the Rhymer** – a poet and seer whose youth was punctuated by a seven-year spell in Fairyland after falling asleep under the Eildon Tree where he met and kissed the Queen of the Fairies. Returning older and far wiser, he was famed for his predictions over the remaining seven years before he vanished for good. Or so the story goes. The Rhymer's prophecies were collected and published in 1603. One of these was the accurate prediction, in 1286, of the accidental death of Alexander III.

Thomas Rymour of Ercildoune witnessed a charter of Petrus de Haga, c.1260-70, and in 1294 Thomas of Ercildoune *son and heir of Thomas Rymour of Ercildoune* conveyed lands to the hospice at Soutra.

Left *The Rig*. Below *Rhymer's Tower*

RCAHMS

Above *Earlston Parish Church*.
Right *Carolside*

somewhat dominated by carved memorials to the owners of (the local) Park Farm. Some good early gravestones elsewhere in the kirkyard, and an attractive set of gatepiers, 1819, with iron overhanging lamp bracket between, to the street frontage.

Leadervale

Slightly two-faced Regency house, the principal front to the south with Ionic columned porch, the garden front to the east double-bowed. The balustraded **Park Bridge** ornamentally links Leadervale's policies with those of **Carolside**, *c*.1800, a gem-like three-storey-and-basement Georgian mini-mansion with single-storey bow-ended wings, twinkling on the valley floor in its former deer park setting.

The Norman features of Legerwood Church survived *the fury of despoilers and the bite of neglect* (Lang) because the chancel arch was blocked up by the Kers of Morriston as part of their burial ground. The 1898 restoration which revealed the Norman work was financed by W van Vleck Lidgerwood, British Chargé d'Affaires at the Brazilian court as well as *head of an Airdrie Iron Works*.

Legerwood Church

Birkhill, 18th century

Extended simply eastwards, *c*.1850, the house stands above the A68, its harled and painted finish, two-storey five-bay front and steeply pitched roof stubbornly responsive to its somewhat exposed, though south-facing position. A stone wall and arched gateway face the old roadway to the east.

Legerwood Church, rebuilt 1717 and 1804

Nave 17x6m *having been frequently repaired and altered, it now presents no features of interest*, but has a Norman chancel 6x6.5m, with 4m ornamented chancel arch (complete with 12th-century grinning demon) and slim round-headed windows. Restored, 1898.

Corsbie Tower, 16th century

Substantial small tower 12x8m of which two sides only remain, 2m-thick walls with curved corners, not dissimilar to Cranshaws in scale. **Corsbie Farmhouse**, late 18th century, two-storey five-bay harled and slated with some additions to side and rear. **Corsbie Doocot**, square type, demolished, *c*.1970.

LAUDER

A burgh to an ancient plan, with the central space subdivided by line of building known as **Mid Row**. From the **East** and **West High Street** run rigs to the lanes which encircle the burgh and define it with the help of a considerable amount of stone walling. A genteel place in recent years (with the advent of more regular communications to Edinburgh) the lanes have been renamed **Castle Wynd** and **Manse Road** from their original titles of **Upper** and **Lower Backside**.

The west end of Mid Row is stopped by the dominant **Town Hall**, 18th century (the Mercat Cross was originally at its foot), first floor is the town hall, forestair first walled then railed, ground floor part-vaulted burgh prison until 1843.

Corsbie Tower

In 1669 the benefits of the roads being recognised, all males between 15 and 60 were required to work on them for six days a year for three years, and then four days a year. This (inadequate) system lasted until 1763 when cash levies, rather than labour, became the norm.

Black Bull, 18th century

Former coaching inn, enlarged 19th century, long frontage with main feature a Palladian window with Gothick astragals. Scotch-slated roof, conceivably once thatched.

Black Bull

13, 31-33 West High Street, worthy, if ordinary, 19th-century burgh houses empty and heading for dereliction for over 20 years (owners could not be traced) before Borders Regional Council grasped the nettle and compulsorily purchased them *c*.1986 for repair and improvement through the joint National Trust for Scotland/BRC Little Houses Improvement Scheme.

18-24 West High Street, 1989, Benjamin Tindall Architects

Nineteenth-century frontages (one with oriel window feature) sensitively repaired and

In 1649 *the witch of Lauder* was one of a number arrested for witchcraft, which she at first denied, then on sentencing *confessed*. Just prior to her burning at the stake she witnessed ... *I declare that I am as free of witchcraft as any child: but being delated by a malicious woman, and put in prison under that name of a witch, disowned by my husband and friends, and seeing no ground of hope of my coming out of prison nor ever coming in credit again, through the temptation of the Devil I made up that confession on purpose to destroy my own life, being weary of it, and choosing rather to die than to live ...* and so died.
Prof. George Sinclair, *Satan's Invisible World Discovered*, 1685

22-24 West High Street

James III *had a refined and cultivated mind, but was unfitted to rule a country like Scotland and to keep in order its turbulent nobles. He spent his time in the society of architects, painters and musicians ...* Chambers Biographical Dictionary

Earl of Lauderdale to Sir William Bruce 1673: *I would have it decent and large enough, with a handsome little steeple; if any of the timber of the old church will serve, it will be so much the cheaper, but I can say now no more till I see the draught which you promise me, and I would have both plan and perspective.*

Below and right *Thirlestane Castle.* Bottom *Proposals for Thirlestane Castle by Robert Adam*

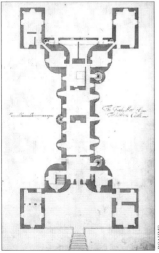

revived for the Scottish Historic Buildings Trust.

Lauder Church, 1673, Sir William Bruce Built for the Duke of Lauderdale by this gentleman architect, *the Kit Wren of Scotland.* Greek cross plan, central crossing tower over four pointed arches, becoming octagonal above roof level. Walled graveyard enclosure (watchhouse built after bodysnatching raid, 1830) entered past rusticated gatepiers which stand over-proud following the stupid slighting of the walls, c.1979. The duke was an ambitious builder who wished to remove the former church from its site close to the castle as part of his grand scheme of improvements. It was from the earlier church, in 1482, that James III's commoner favourites, including the architect Cochrane, were dragged by envious nobles led by Archibald *Bell-the-Cat* Douglas and hanged from the (earlier) Lauder Bridge.

Thirlestane Castle, c.1590, the east-west, turreted block, most unusual in linear form, at centre of large 16th-century English artillery fortification. In 1670-7, Sir William Bruce, supervised its transformation to *palace* through remodelling by Robert Mylne for the Duke of Lauderdale, using foreign craftsmen who had worked at his English mansion, Ham House, and plasterers fresh from contracts at Holyroodhouse in Edinburgh. Exquisite heavy plasterwork (some early 17th century on the top floor, and

some of 1674 by English plasterers John Houlbert and George Dunsterfield, and Thomas Alborn of Glasgow), but above all, marvellous long processional axis through (public) Great Apartments, dining room, drawing room, to bedchamber, dressing room, and private closet. Ante-chamber with its doors the finest small 17th-century space in Scotland. Alterations, 1840-1, William Burn and later David Bryce, give it its particularly lively skyline. Elaborate wrought-iron **Eagle Gates**. Freestanding crowstepped-gabled stable courtyard, 1841, William Burn (colour p.164). *Thirlestane Trust; open to the public. Includes Border Country Life Museum / Toy Museum; guidebook available*

Harryburn, 1834

Two-and-a-half-storey three-bay house with billiard room and stabling to rear, all in the local dark whinstone, with sandstone dressings, slated roof. Cast-iron first-floor balcony, built off slim columns. *Chuckie* **lodge** remarkable for its coursed pebbles finish set within thin sandstone margins: cast-iron gatepiers, iron gates with anthemion pattern.

Norton, 17th century

Old stone barn, probably built as a house, surely its only future if this building's survival is to be encouraged.

Norton, 1975

Justicehall, Oxton, 18th century

Long slim rectangular house one room deep in coursed rubble, rendered, centre gabled pediment and chimney, skewputts on end gables.

Airhouse, 18th century; demolished, 1990

Two-storey five-bay house, central pilastered doorpiece and slated roof, with single-storey Palladian-windowed flanking pavilions.

Plan view of end panel, low dining room, Thirlestane Castle

In 1671 Lauderdale wrote to his brother: *As to the marble chimneys, I am far advanced, for I have bargained for six already for Thirlstane Castle, and three of them are fairer than any I see in England, and I have got pennyworth – two I have paid for this day, much finer than my Lord Chancellor's, larger and cheaper above a fourth than his. I lighted on them by chance in an Italian merchant's hand, who let me have them as he paid for them in Italy, with the customs and charges ... I shall fit marble chimneys for the whole two lower stories in Thirlstane Castle ...*

Before the [Lauder] Common was *wholly enclosed, and when the marches were marked by cairns, there was a periodical riding of the marches, and the pockets of the recently admitted burgesses were loaded with stones in order that they might, as each cairn was reached, add their stone to the cairn; and the practice was only stopped when it was found that the pockets were pre-occupied by bottles containing* **refreshers** *for use at the cairns. Lauder: a series of papers by Robert Romanes of Harryburn, privately printed 1903.*

Channelkirk Parish Church of St Cuthbert, 1817, James Gillespie Graham
Mortsafe, Gothick pointed windows and battlemented gables, with a fine view commanded down the valley, but by an unfortunate juxtaposition the kirk appears to have its own tennis court. The Saint was a shepherd-boy here, saw a vision one night and presented himself the next day at Old Melrose Priory to join up.

Heriot Kirk, rebuilt 1875,
James Maitland Wardrop
Gothic Revival, random rubble harled, Pointed tracery and lancet windows, slated roof with belfry.

Borthwick Hall, 1853, John Henderson
Scots Baronial three-storey harled block with string-courses, angle-turrets, crowstepped gables and slated roofs.

Above *Memorial, Channelkirk Parish Church.* Right *Borthwick Hall.* Below *Memorial, Heriot Kirk*

After I heard the melancholy news of the loss of the battle [of Prestonpans] I with my wife and two daughters went into England, and lay by accident at Cannall [ie Channelkirk] when one of the defeated regiments of [Hanoverian] Dragoons came there. As many of their officers came to lodge under us in the same house, we thought Hell had broken loose, for I never heard such oaths and imprecations, branding one another with cowardice and neglect of duty.
Sir John Clerk of Penicuik, 1745

Raeshaw Lodge, 19th century
Long one-and-a-half-storey harled block with eight pedimented dormers, slated roof, and two-and-a-half-storey block added at the south end.

Carcant House, mid 19th century
Scots Baronial two-and-a-half-storey and three-storey caphoused tower and one-and-a-half-storey wing.

Old Crookston House, from *c.*1450
Eastern portion initially, the western more modern (17th century). Two-and-a-half-storey, harled, with crowstepped gables and slated roofs with piended dormers. **Borthwick Memorial**,

Crookston, *c*.1810, dressed stone pyramid on an inscribed pedestal. **New Crookston House**, 1816-19, enlarged 1860-3, Brown & Wardrop, Jacobean, two-and-a-half-storey, triple-ridged slated roof and flowing gables.

Above *Old Crookston House.*
Left *Burnhouse*

Burnhouse, *c*.1810
Two-and-a-half-storey-and-basement five-bay Georgian mini-mansion, centre three bays projecting and pedimented, central classical doorpiece reached by balustraded stair, piended slated roof. **Burnhouse Doocot**, early 19th century, roofless, circular plan in coursed rubble, 463 nestholes partitioned in brick. **Torquhan House**, 1823, is two-storey but otherwise the mixture as for Burnhouse. Flanking Palladian-windowed offices.

Above *Burnhouse Doocot, 1975.*
Left *Mitchelston Farmhouse and windmill, 1924*

Mitchelston Farmhouse, 18th century
Traditional two-storey-and-basement harled dwelling with gabled skews. An 18th-century circular **windmill** in random rubble was demolished here to make way for a new mid 20th-century shed.

STOW
Stow Kirk, St Mary of Wedale, 1873-6, Wardrop & Reid
Gothic Revival, situated commandingly above

The old Kirk had a relic of St Mary, and was the centre of one of Scotland's two ancient territorial sanctuaries for criminals. Derivations of the place-names *Stow* (place of religious assembly) and *Wedale* (valley of the shrine) may suggest its religious importance as far back as the Northumbrian Kingdom.

the A7 as it snakes along the haugh-edge. Octagonal spire set on three-stage west tower with pinnacled angle turrets. Cruciform plan with polygonal apse. Rock-faced masonry, pointed windows, and slated roof.

Old Kirk, late 15th-century
Ashlar oblong kirk, repaired 17th century in when rubble and south aisle added, belfry 1794. Round-arched doorway, pointed traceried window in west gable. In use until the new kirk was completed, now an ivy-clad ruin.

Top *Stow Kirk and Pack-Horse Bridge*. Middle *Pack-Horse Bridge*. Above *Bowland*

The pack-horse bridge allows only one beast to cross at a time, and has low, almost non-existent parapets which the panniers can clear without difficulty.

Pack-Horse Bridge, 1654-5
Three segmental rubble arches constructed by the Kirk Session to carry those of a religious persuasion (and no doubt the rest) across the Gala Water.

Bowland, 1811, James Gillespie Graham
Castellated, corbelled and crenellated two-and-a-half-storey mansion with piended slated roofs and porte-cochère. Rear addition, 1890, George Henderson, demolishing the old ?17th-century house to which Gillespie Graham's building had been added. Small oblong 18th-century **doocot** in random rubble with lean-to roof and timber dormer. Entrance lodge and gates, 19th century, castellated and crenellated, with lattice windows, hood-moulded, linked by large and small pointed arches to a fake tower. Sundial, 1708, cuphollows, tabulated for every day of the year.

Torwoodlee Broch
Dating from about the time of Christ, only vestigial remains are left, set within a ramparted oval fort around 100m diameter, the broch walls 5.5m thick with a 12m internal diameter, excavated, 1891, by J S Curle of Trimontium fame, and again in 1950 under the auspices of the Society of Antiquaries of Scotland.

Torwoodlee Tower

RCAHMS

Archaeology, which in the past was rather more concerned about the discovery of objects, has progressively expanded the significance of the object's context as the archaeologist's technical and scientific skills have increased. Today, through such methods as pollen, carbon dating and chemical analyses, it is possible to be far more informed than previously, when only relative position and the object itself could be obtained and compared. With this progress comes the recognition that further enhancement of archaeological study techniques is likely to be made and that once the archaeology is disturbed or destroyed, a non-renewable resource has been lost. Consequently, these days it is only when archaeology is threatened that excavation is likely.

Torwoodlee Tower, 1601

Replacing an older Pringle keep sacked in 1568, whin and ashlar, constructed on a south-facing, terraced site. Main building, 8x20m, with vaulted ground floor, now a ruin, courtyard to the east, from where a falling axis leads to **Torwoodlee House**, 1784, three-storey-and-basement Georgian rectangular well-proportioned block with flanking two-storey pavilions linked by curved screen walls, the whole in whin with red sandstone ashlar dressings. Robust alterations, 1864, Peddie & Kinnear, central two-storey porch extension and the incorporation of the original (south-facing) vestibule into the drawing-room, thus effectively re-orienting the house. Within the entrance hall are stone panels, one from Buckholm Tower, 1582, the other from Torwoodlee Tower, 1601.

Buckholm Tower, 1582

Three-and-a-half-storey, vaulted ground floor, 11 x 7m rectangular tower, whin rubble with ashlar dressings, with projecting stairtower, courtyard and gateway. Overlooking the Gala Water, in 1956 the Tower had *only recently become ruinous* (RCAHMS Inventory).

GALASHIELS

A burgh of barony in 1599, the early settlement was south of the Gala Water, adjacent to Old Gala House, home of first Pringles then Scotts. The principal occupation was weaving, and the town developed rapidly from the end of the 18th century filling the

In *The Heart of Midlothian* Scott noted that *the hilly pastures of Buckholm ... which the author now surveys ... are famed for producing the best ewe-milk cheese in the south of Scotland.*

Buckholm Tower

Douglas of Galashiels

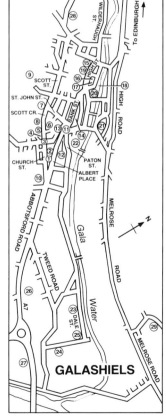

Top *Burial-aisle.* Above *Galashiels Parish Church.* Right *Church Square and Mercat Cross*

GALASHIELS

valley with slate-roofed stone-built structures more remarkable in the main for their utility than their elegance.

1 Churchless churchyard with solitary **burial-aisle**, 1636, to house the Scotts of Gala, extraordinarily, its curtilage now with a serrated edge due to the partial slighting of the graveyard wall, almost as inconsiderately as that of Lauder. Reroofed with stone flags in 1992. The church that this aisle related to was built in 1617, marking the change in parish centre from Lindean to Galashiels. The kirk was demolished in 1813, being *dangerous and unhealthy and totally unfit for divine service* according to John Smith in 1811. Smith built its replacement, the **Galashiels Parish Church**, 1812-14, in semi-Gothick, using the OP Church's pulpit and fittings. Demolished 1960 after being closed since 1931.

2 **Church Square**, 1960, Peter Womersley Comprehensive rectilinear redevelopment, on the site of the church and environs, still keeps a fair sense of scale although signs of individual *improvements* are nibbling away at this. Spawned a series of less convincing clones across the town which luckily managed to contain them. Saltire Award 1963.

3 **Mercat Cross**, dated 1695, but restored 1887 and 1987, until, like George Washington's axe, it has become more of a historical concept than a reality.

4 **The Hall**, Scott Crescent, 17th-century core The Hall was a place where merchants

purchased the woollen goods made in cottages in and around Galashiels. Its historical significance belies its undistinguished appearance of 19th-century overcoat.

5 **Old Parish and St Paul's Church**, Scott Crescent, 1878-81, George Henderson Gothic Revival, its main feature is a dizzily articulated steeple, 57m (190ft) high, finished in 1885, at the south end, which sadly has lost some of its rich detail in the interests of public safety and economy. Open interior with pointed arches on red granite columns separating nave and aisles. Good glass, including some by Douglas Strachan, and a notable memorial tribute to Queen Victoria, 1902, George Henderson. **Halls**, 1927, Jeffrey Waddell.

Old Parish and St Paul's Church

Other memorials of note in Old Parish and St Paul's Church include those to James Pike, 1899, Ballantine & Gardiner; James Gloag, after 1899, Douglas Strachan; Alexander Rutherford, 1901; James & Christina Smith Wood, 1906; Walter Lamb, after 1906, Douglas Strachan; Revd David Hunter, after 1911, Douglas Strachan; Walter Cochrane, Willowbush, 1911, A Ballantine & Son.

Old Gala House

6 **Old Gala House**
Topsy building which conceals its charms from the road. A tower house was built here in 1457, but there are no visible remains of this. Organic development, from north to south, as a sequence of building from 1583, c.1611, mid-18th century, and 19th century, with, for good measure, a transformation of the interior to museum, 1988, Page & Park. Painted ceiling, dated 1635, discovered 1952. Decorative plaster ceilings, possibly by the plasterer of Ednam House, Kelso, with Persephone and the four ages of woman in the dining room, and in the hall the Galashiels symbols of plum-tree and fox. Unconvincing mural, 1988, by Rob Hain. Excellent Clapperton exhibition depicting the career and talents of this notable sculptor.

7 **Scott Park Lodge and Gates**, 1881
Richly decorated composition as befitted the main entrance to Scott of Gala's 1872 **New Gala House** by David Bryce, utilising carved stone armorial panels, dated 1583, from Old Gala House, as his client no doubt wished to

To Sir James Pringle *his house did we go, and there were we wondrous courteously entertained .... there are of the Pringles for some eight miles up Gallowater, gentlemen all of pretty seats and buildings .... He hath a very pretty park, with natural walks in it, artificial ponds and arbours now a-making. He hath neat gardens and orchards, and (so have) all his tenants through his care.* Christopher Lowther, 1629

Dorothy Wordsworth remarked in 1803: *The village of Galashiels pleasantly situated on the banks of the stream, a pretty place it has once been but a manufactory is established there, and a townish bustle and ugly stone houses are fast taking the place of the brown roofed thatched cottages of which a great many yet remain, partly overshadowed by trees.*

New Gala House

The Hon Colin C P Tennant/RCAHMS

New Gala House was adopted during Second World War as home of St Trinnean's School from Edinburgh, to be translated to St Trinian's after Sapper Ronald Searle met two schoolgirls in Kirkcudbright in 1941.

house himself in something more fitting and less overlooked. The Bryce house was a fine building if lacking the dynamic presence of, say, Hartrigge. Demolished 1985, the armorial stonework having preceded the rest of the building, this time following the laird to Hollybush.

8 **Old Folks Home**, Scott Park, 1983, Borders Regional Council
Brick and tile building of pleasant *domestic institutional* scale and appropriate redness, particularly when seen with its neighbour the Old Parish Church. Nevertheless, this is still *helicopter architecture* in a park setting.

9 **Swimming Pool**, Scott Crescent, 1983, Duncan Cameron & Associates
Concealed in the woods the laminated structure and twin shallow ends are the most remarkable features of this specimen of municipal pride. BRC Architectural Award 1984.

10 **St Peter's Episcopal Church**, Abbotsford Road, 1853, John Henderson
Early English chancel and aisle, hall and school added 1881, George Henderson. Church Hall, 1889, Hay & Henderson. Stained glass by Heaton, Butler and Bayne.

11 **Cornmill Square**
The corn mill was demolished and cleared away but the lades were creatively transformed, 1912-13, Sir Robert Lorimer, into a horranised and balustraded water feature, well worth peering into, with stone boys astride dolphins around an elaborately carved column.

12 **Burgh Chambers**, 1867
Clock-tower and **War Memorial**, added 1924-7, Sir Robert Lorimer, strengthens this

Cornmill Fountain

Strang

two-storey gushet block, incorporating a fine equestrian **statue** of a dour mosstrooper, a Border reiver, by Thomas J Clapperton. Cool, sophisticated, brick office extension, 1975-6, Aitken & Turnbull, to the north-west on Paton Street. Across from the reiver are **busts** of Burns and Scott by, respectively, F W Doyle-Jones of Chelsea, 1912, and T J Clapperton, 1932.

13 **Library**, 1873, George Henderson
Three-storey ashlar, extended 1890, its gabled central projection giving it a civic presence to which the adjacent **sheltered housing**, replacing a redundant church, fails to respond.

Bank Street and **Bridge Street** were laid out by George Craig, baron bailie from 1813, as one-sided streets with gardens similar in concept to the Edinburgh New Town. Sadly Bridge Street's gardens were built over, but the Town Council preserved those at Bank Street.

Above *Burgh Chambers and mosstrooper, 1940s*. Left *Royal Bank of Scotland*

14 **Royal Bank of Scotland**, Bank Street, 1946, J R McKay
Built as National Bank of Scotland to 1940 design of Dick Peddie Todd & Jamieson, consistent two-storey breakfronted elevation.

15 **119 High Street**, 1888, J & J Hall
Built for the Galashiels Co-operative Store Company, red sandstone on a prominent corner site. Literal high point of commercial development in Galashiels. Good corner building rather let down by its neighbours. A less charitable view would be that it is a touch overblown, but no matter. Fine roofline to which corner turret and anthemion-topped cast-iron dormers are major contributors. Less impressive at ground level requiring some sensitive shop-front treatments.

16 **St Ninian's Church of Scotland**, High Street, 1844
Built as the East UP Church, enlarged 1868, Corson & Atkin. Romanesque in rock-faced

In 1813 a wire bridge was built in Galashiels by Mr Richard Lees, one of the best-known pioneers of the woollen trade in Gala, assisted by a blacksmith (perhaps J S Brown) and a description of such a project from an American journal. (The first US suspension bridges of the Industrial Revolution were developed 1801-10 by a lawyer, Judge James Finley, clearly a *hanging judge*.) Their bridge was destroyed by flood in 1838.

Above *St Andrew's Arts Centre.*
Right *Kail Kirk*

John Glas (1695-1773) was born at Auchtermuchty, and from 1719 was minister of Tealing, by Dundee. He founded the (minor) religious sect of Glasites or Sandemanians.

Galashiels Post Office

snecked rubble, gable front to the street with a handy set-back providing a fund-raising piazza.

17 **The Industrial Bank**, 46-48 High Street, 1880, Wardrop & Reid
Built as British Linen Bank, solidly reliable Renaissance corner building, two-storey, five-bay in ashlar, moulded architraves and a piended slated roof.

18 **St Andrew's Arts Centre**, Bridge Street, 1885, McKissack & Rowan
Built as St Andrew's Church (Ladhope Free) in stone of many colours on important site at elbow of street, though later spire reduced to impotent stump – a major loss to the roofscape of this valley town. Good (now concealed) stained glass, 1909, Douglas Strachan.

19 **Kail Kirk**, mid-19th century
Secluded but charming religious structure now used as store in industrial/commercial backwater, originally constructed for followers of Pastor John Glas whose day-long sabbath services included the provision of sustaining kail soup.

20 **Galashiels Post Office**, Channel Street, 1894, HM Office of Works
Primly assertive two-storey, five-bay frontage with octagonal towers and projecting porch, extended 1915.

Market Place survives as a largely useless space (formerly the bus stance) with rosebeds and presence-lacking totem, *Man with a Sheep*, 1971, whose sculptor is identified only by a monogram.

21 **RC Church of Our Lady and St Andrew**, Market Street, 1856-8, William W Wardell
Second Pointed Gothic Revival, random rubble

with sandstone dressings, slated roof over buttressed nave, copper roofs over side-chapels. Extended 1870, Goldie & Childe. Stained glass by Barnet & Son, Leith, with a striking Polish window in memory of expatriates stationed in the area during Second World War.

[22] **Valley Mill**, Paton Street, mid-19th century
Sixteen-bay, four-storey range in whin with sandstone dressings: pediment, bellcote and weathervane removed (along with a fine cast-iron water tank dated 1866) in its conversion to Co-operative supermarket, 1984, Duncan Cameron & Associates.

[23] **Netherdale Mill**, 1857
Remaining part of one of a pair of imposing four-storey mills, whinstone with rough hewn quoins, owned by the Cochrane family after 1866. This dynasty also commissioned houses, Abbotshill (up *Archie's Walk*) for Archibald Cochrane, and Kingsknowes for Adam Lees Cochrane (see p.202).

[24] **Gala Fairydean Football Club Grandstand**, Netherdale, 1967, Peter Womersley
Board-marked concrete of exciting geometrical form produced at a time when it was hoped that the Gala Fairydean FC would attain major league status. They didn't. The drama of the novel structure (Ove Arup & Partners, Engineers) has not been matched by the quality of maintenance, care and respect this building should engender. Apart from anything else, a sparkling stand might be worth a goal of a start in home games.

Valley Mill, 1980

The textile industry's cyclical nature is not new. In *c.*1829 Galashiels *greys* and *blues* went out of fashion, and instead the manufacturers tried out *Shepherd's Tartan*, the black and white check still worn by Border shepherds. Sir Walter Scott and other leaders adopted the material and it caught on.

Arup's office in Scotland was established in 1960 with work on Ninewells Hospital (see *Dundee* in this series). They brought with them (and developed) considerable experience and expertise in concrete design which, in the hands of Peter Womersley, resulted in architectural sculpture.

Gala Fairydean Football Club Grandstand

[25] **Scottish College of Textiles**, Netherdale, R Forbes Hutchison & George R M Kennedy
A contrast with Womersley's work across the car park but far more representative of the institution of the time: the auditorium is a fine period piece though perhaps more 1950s than 1960s.

Lucy Sanderson Cottage Homes

Strang

The Cottage Homes were named after the wife of a mill owner. Just how the earliest occupants (remember they were likely to be folk who had spent the best years of their lives in the bedlam of textiles manufactuary) reacted when confronted with the major mural panorama of just such a place can only be imagined: at least, though, they could raise their eyes to the hills at the gable ends.

Phyllis Bone (1896-1972) was the first woman to be elected to the Royal Scottish Academy. She carved the animals on the Scottish National War Memorial in Edinburgh, the most popular and accessible, to the younger visitor at least, of that monument's attributes. *The favourite is probably her panel of the Tunnellers' Friends depicting canaries and mice, but her recumbent lion and unicorn at the entrance are ridden with enormous pleasure by children of the 1990s.* Ian Gow

26 **Lucy Sanderson Cottage Homes**, 1930-3, Mears and Carus Wilson
Early sheltered housing around an imaginary Border village green, planting by Meriel Hansen, complete with clock-tower and hall. Originally to be harled, the whinstone finish was apparently adopted to provide work for local masons. Sandstone dressings and Westmorland slates complete the romantic composition with the aid of carved stone features – including a fox and a lamb – by Phyllis Bone and Pilkington Jackson. As if this ensemble was not artistic enough the hall's barrel-vaulted interior was given murals of Border life and myth by W R Lawson and Miss M Caird (see colour p.216).

27 **Kingsknowes**, 1868-9, William Hay
Mill-owner's expansive sandstone Scots Baronial house, now hotel, with fine chimneypieces and interiors reputedly by Italian craftsmen. Exquisite domed cast-iron and glass conservatory, MacKenzie and Moncur, manufacturers, perched above the Tweed (see colour p.213).

28 **Woodlands**, Windyknowe Road, *c*.1855
Principally as recast, 1885, George Henderson, externally, if anything, Elizabethan, fine plasterwork and some stained glass internally. Contemporary Mackenzie and Moncur

Woodlands

Mrs E S Phillips/RCAHMS

conservatory. First house with electric lighting in Galashiels (colour p.216); 1896 (dated finial) **lodge** and **offices** complete the ensemble.

Below *St John's Church, Langlee.*
Bottom *Hillslap*

Langlee follows the logic of the valley situation where expansion tends to ooze along rather than up. Unfortunately, the visual impact of this large-scale and somewhat monolithic expansion is considerable, and it can even be seen from Scott's View. Much is Scandinavian-influenced, social housing of the late 1960s and '70s, by Wheeler & Sproson (see
²⁹ also **St John's Church** here, 1972, Anthony Wheeler), and the SSHA's own architects.

Strang

East of Langlee, up the valley of the Allan or Elwyn Water, stand a trio of tower houses in close proximity, Hillslap, Colmslie and Langshaw, whose broadly contemporary construction may reflect a perceived need to plug a possible invasion route in unsettled times, or just a punctuation on the direct route to Soutra.

RCAHMS

Hillslap (formerly **Calfhill**), 1585
Model for Sir Walter Scott's *Glendearg* in *The Monastery*, five-storey 9x9m L-plan tower house with corbelled stair turret built off a diagonally planned arch which shelters the entrance below. Vaulted ground floor with shot-holes, and Tudor hood-moulded lintels over many of the openings showing an English design influence at the least. Carefully repaired and rebuilt as a labour of love by Philip Mercer, architect, for his family use. BRC Architectural Award 1990.

Glendearg
A lonely tower … of small dimensions, yet larger than those which occurred in the village (of Kennaquhair *or* Melrose), *as intimating that, in case of assault, the proprietor would have to rely upon his own unassisted strength. Two or three miserable huts, at the foot of the fortalice, held the bondsmen and tenants of the feuar.*
Walter Scott, *The Monastery*

Colmslie, later 16th century
Rectangular Borthwick tower house of which really only the ruinous basic 12x8m shape remains, and that only at squatly proportioned ground (to aid defence there was no ground-floor access) and first-floor levels.

A Scots Act of Parliament, 1535, proposed that the proprietor *sall big ane sufficient barmkyn upon his heritage and landis, of stane and lyme, contenand three score futis on the square, ane eln thick and six elnes heicht for the resett and defens of him, his tennents, and his gudis in troublous tyme, with ane toure in the samen for himself gif he thinks it expedient. And all other landit men of smaller rent and revenue big pelis and greit strenthis as they plese for saifing of themselfs tenentis, and gudis; and that all the saidis strenthis, barmkynis, and pelis be biggit and completit within twa years under pane.* (But it is doubtful if this Act was ever passed – MacGibbon & Ross)

In the Borders the peel tower was a miniature of the Norman keep: its entrance at first floor, or by a narrow winding spiral stair, its ground floor below vaulted to act as a fireproof byre or store. The first floor the public; the second floor the private rooms. As a type these buildings were absorbed or abandoned in the middle 17th century, for they were defenceless, sitting targets against artillery.

Langshaw 16th century
Larger but equally dilapidated L-plan house, 21x13m, extended 17th century to the east, and with semicircular stair tower attached to its north elevation. Extensive derelict walled garden enclosure.

Glenmayne, Selkirk Road, 1866, Charles Kinnear
Asymmetrical Baronial house about a five-storey tower, built for John Murray, a Galashiels pelt-monger, and followed within three years by garden walls, a reservoir and ice-house, and a conservatory and vineries. **Library**, 1913, Robert Lorimer, accompanied by staircase decoration and a set of entrance gates.

Probable site of abbey founded by David I at Lindean, 1110, which later moved to Kelso to leave a more substantial mark, **Lindean church**, removed to Galashiels from here in 1622 when the *old vicar's church of Lindean* had been abandoned for some 36 years. Ruins and old graveyard remain.

Lindean Mill, *c.*1841
Cornmill and sawmill converted to fine glass works and offices, 1983 and earlier, Ray Licence, losing the machinery but retaining the character and shape of the buildings.

Right *Glenmayne*. Below *Lindean Mill*

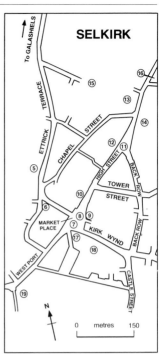

SELKIRK

Location of a royal castle from 12th century, and the focal point of the royal hunting forest, Selkirk's eventful medieval existence slumbered latterly until at the beginning of the 18th century it was *ill-built, irregular and decaying*. But the population of Selkirk more than quadrupled 1791-1891, and large increases in the manufacture of woollens came after 1836. It would seem almost that Galashiels overspilled. Railway (branch line from Galashiels), 1854. Certainly from 1855 there was no holding the Selkirk mills. Thus the town is a medieval plan (irregular, focused on Market Place, narrow streets) largely fleshed out by Victorian buildings. The top half of the medieval town was cleared and redeveloped, 1960s, Sir Frank Mears & Partners, gaining a Civic Trust Award in 1971.

In 1540 James V granting a burgh charter described Selkirk as *often burned, harried and destroyed*, accessible as it was *to England, Liddesdale, and other broken parts*.

Hume/RCAHMS

Ettrick Mills

The Riverside industrial area was where the overspill was deposited, most prominently at **Ettrick Mills**, 1836, 1850 and later, John & Thomas Smith. Huge symmetrical range about gabled pediment, attic Palladian window and clock, range-ends terminated by projecting gables. **Linglie Mills**, mid 19th century, four-storey range with central projecting gabled feature and oculus. **Yarrow Mills**, 1867-92, tall range and central gabled projection. **Forrest Mills**, 1838 and 1868, bellcote on four-storey block. Recent decay and indifference makes this a major planning challenge, as are much of its surroundings. New buildings in the vicinity are

In 1714 there were 187 houses in Selkirk, a population of about 700 folk. Glasgow had a population of about 14,000 at the same time.

A day oot o' Selkirk's a day waistit.
Wattie Dobson, Deacon of Incorporation of Tailors

Selkirk was not always well served by roads: *the town of Selkirk did not possess a single cart till after 1725*. Handley

Pant Well
In 1706, after a drought, Campbell the plumber was paid £95 Scots for *casting the ditch for the pypes, building a little lodge round the font and a big trough at the Cross for gathering water.*

Right *County Buildings and Court House.* Below *Market Cross.* Bottom *Court House before 1957*

not encouraging, so refurbishment, repair and conversion must be promoted.

5 **County Buildings and Court House**, Ettrick Terrace, 1868-70, David Rhind
Precipitously sited, solidly imposing, linked by underground passage to the **Old Jail**, 1803, now converted to public library.

6 **War Memorial**, 1922, Sir Robert Lorimer
Recessive cross, steps and balustrade composition which should have had a better site, bronze plaque of *Victory and Peace* by Thomas J Clapperton.

Market Place
Here once stood an ancient market cross (demolished 1765) and tolbooth, as well as the
7 stalls of the old flesh market. Today the **Pant Well**, 1898, Peddie & Washington Browne (the Pant was an overflow trough to catch the water from the well), may incorporate part of the original cross shaft.

9 **Court House**, 1803
Imposing even without the knowledge that Sir Walter dispensed justice here 1803-32. The spire is 33m (110ft) high to its weathervane.

8 **Statue of Sir Walter Scott**, 1839, Handyside Ritchie
Erected by the *Gentlemen of the County*, the

statue shows Scott in the dress of Sheriff, and the pedestal carries the arms of Scott, the arms of Selkirk, a winged harp and a Scots thistle. A new base (Dick Peddie & Walker Todd) was added to the front, 1932, perhaps to keep vehicles at bay.

10 **County Hotel** (formerly the Grapes), 13 High Street, early 19th century Coaching inn whose Victorian front used to bely the interest in its Georgian stable courtyard. Alas now following stable demolitions and alterations the most remarkable thing is the statue of **Red Dog Souter**, the greyhound, built into the wall.

At the junction of High Street/Back Row is the
11 splendid **Mungo Park Monument**, designed and carved by Andrew Currie, 1859. Thomas Clapperton sculpted the bronze panels, 1905, of Park's travels in the Niger regions, and at each corner added at popular request, in 1913, to the original design, voluptuous life-size figures of *Peace*, *War*, *Slavery*, and *Home Life in the Niger*.

Much of the **High Street** has its interest in details, particularly the tiled shopfronts of the Buttercup Dairy Company and J A Waters (Butchers), and above the Southern Reporter office the memorial to Tom Scott (1854-1927, mentor of William Johnstone, 1897-1981, both artists of distinction). Opposite Back Row is the
12 **Roman Catholic Church**, 1866, George Goldie.

St Mary's West Church, Chapel Street, 1889, John B Wilson
Early Decorated Scottish Gothic. Red sandstone, notable tower was a major element in the prospect of Selkirk from the south-west, Early Decorated Scots Gothic style. Demolished, 1982.

14 **Lawson Memorial Church**, R Baldie, 1880
Early Gothic style with spire 130ft high.

13 **Victoria Halls**, Scotts Place, 1895,
Hippolyte J Blanc
A blousy Renaissance style in red Hailes (Edinburgh) sandstone, giving pride of place to the **(Fletcher) Memorial** *to the Selkirk men killed at Flodden*, 1913, Thomas J Clapperton. **J B Selkirk Memorial Plaque**, 1931, Thomas J Clapperton. Blanc also designed the Masonic Halls, Back Row, in 1897.

RCAHMS

Mungo Park Monument

Mungo Park was born at Foulshiels in 1721, four miles upstream from Selkirk. After a medical education in Edinburgh, and apprenticeship to a surgeon in Selkirk who was to be his father-in-law, he travelled to West Africa in 1795. Returning, he married and practised medicine in Peebles until 1805 when wanderlust struck and he journeyed once more to the dark continent, drowning at Boussa on the Niger.

James Duncan Ltd, tile & marble contractors, were the chief firm in Glasgow supplying and fitting encaustic tiles between 1865-1965: their client, the Buttercup Dairy Company, ceased trading in 1949 (see Innerleithen).

Back Row was the principal street of sutors (burgesses). Since the main trade of the town for many years was the manufacture of thin- or single-soled shoes, the term *Souter* is now synonymous with shoemaker, and indeed a native of Selkirk. In 1694, Selkirk's total population was 715, of whom 47 were cordiners (not all necessarily making shoes). In 1745 the Selkirk Souters provided 2000 pairs of shoes to the Jacobite army, but this investment did not pay off.

Strang

Right *Victoria Halls*.
Above *Halliwell's Close*

In 1629 **Christopher Lowther**
described the OP Church's
predecessor as a *very pretty church,
the form of it a cross house, the
steeple having at each corner four
pyramidical turrets. The
Hammersmen and other Tradesmen
have several seats, mounted above
the rest, the gentlemen below, the
Tradesmen in the ground seats. The
women sit in the high end of the
church, with us the choir. There is
one neat vaulted porch in it. My
Lord Buccleuch's seat is the highest
in the church and he hath a proper
[ie private] passage into it at the
outside of the vaulted porch.*

Willie Creech (1745-1815) was an
Edinburgh bookseller who first
published an Edinburgh edition of
Burns, who had great problems
receiving his royalties, hence Burns'
*Lament for the Absence of William
Creech, Publisher.* Creech was Lord
Provost from 1811 to 1813.

15 Viewfield, early 19th-century
Classical, one-and-a-half-storey-and-basement
eight-bay, pedimented doorpiece and low
pitched slated roof. The birthplace of Andrew
Lang, 1844-1912, poet, essayist and collector of
folk tales, now old folk's home.

16 St John's Scottish Episcopal Church,
1867-9, J M Wardrop
Good interior with later carving designed by
Sir Robert Lorimer, and stained glass by
Herbert Hendrie.

RCAHMS

**17 Halliwell's House Museum & Tourist
Information Centre**, Halliwell's Close
Eighteenth-century (at least) range of
vernacular buildings with cobbled close,
incorporating a local museum and a notable
collection of ironmongery amassed by the last
of this trade (which had been practised on the
site since 1828) in the frontage property.
Converted 1982, Borders Regional Council
Architects.

18 Old Parish Church, 1748
Repaired several times, especially 1829. Only a
shell set in the graveyard, having been
abandoned after a fire and on construction of a
new version in Ettrick Terrace, 1860-3, Brown
& Wardrop. Note too the inscribed marble slab
erected in the West Port, 1884, to mark the site
of the Forest Inn where, in 1787, Burns wrote
the *Epistle to Willie Creech*.

19 The Haining, 1794
Plain classical house built on to a simpler 18th-

Antonio Canova (1757-1822) was
the finest sculptor of his generation,
counting among his patrons popes,
kings, and the Emperor Napoleon.
He was a friend of Gavin Hamilton,
the Scots archaeologist and
antiquarian painter, and carved the
Stewart Pretenders' cenotaph in St
Peter's, Rome, 1817-19.

Left *The Haining, 1972.* Below
Stable block, The Haining

century one. The former remodelled and
enriched, 1819-20, Archibald Elliot, the latter
burned down, 1944. The arcaded portico and
persiennes are Elliot's, the garden statuary by
Canova, the lakeside landscape setting
magnificent. Second World War service took its
toll of the Haining's interiors. The **stable block**,
with Doric columned entrance and horse's skull
over, is also by Elliot *c.*1819, residential
conversion Fergus Lenaghan, 1983. Adjacent lie
the **bear and wolf enclosures** (one owner had
served in Russia). Within the grounds lies the
long-demolished medieval **Selkirk Castle** on
Peel Hill, currently unrecognisable under its
cloak of trees. Arched gateway from the West
Port contemporary with the house and as
carefully detailed and proportioned.

Fletcher is said to have been the sole
survivor, from 80 Selkirk men, of
those who fought at the Battle of
Flodden, 1513, returning with a
captured English flag which he first
raised defiantly and then cast down
thinking, no doubt, of the price of war.

The poet **J B Selkirk** was **James
Brown** (1832-1904), whose best
known work is *Selkirk After
Flodden.* The J B Selkirk memorial
plaque quotes from the poem:
*Then I turn to sister Jean,
And my airms about her twine,
And I kiss her sleepless een,
For her heart's as sair as mine.*

Heatherlie Church, 1874, Wardrop & Reid
Built as Chapel of Ease. Early Decorated in
Prudham freestone, with green Westmorland
slates. Stained glass memorial windows, 1916
and 1919, Douglas Strachan.

Bannerfield, 1945-64, Basil Spence
Extra-mural suburb with all the virtues and,
sadly, the vices accompanying such
monocultural development.

Aikwood (Oakwood) Tower, 1602
Possibly later than 1602 given its lack of
serious defences. Three-and-a-half-storey
11x7m rubble-walled oblong house with close-
fitting roof punctuated by two corbelled square
turrets at the east and west corners.
Marvellous joggled lintel chimneypiece, with
masons' marks, in the first-floor apartment.
Repaired and converted after years of decay,
1991-2, William Cadell and Partners, for Sir
David and Lady Steel. Adjacent site of first-
century Roman fort.

Heatherlie Church

Ettrick Bridge Chapel, 1836-9, William Burn
Plain church building but with excellent war
memorial lychgate to the road frontage.

Kirkhope Tower, probably 17th century
Square 8x7m five-storey tower built virtually
from available field stones. Vaulted ground
floor, first-floor entrance, barmkin to the front.
An earlier version was burnt by Armstrongs in
1543. Restoration about to be put in hand, 1994.

Kirkhope Tower

Adjacent to Ettrick Kirk stood a
village of over 50 houses around a
stronghold known as **Ettrick
House**. In *c.*1700 the *improving*
laird cleared the lot and built
himself a fine mansion-house:
Ettrick-Ha' stands on yon plain,
Richt sore exposed to wind and rain;
And on it the sun shines never at morn,
Because it was built in the widow's
corn;
And its foundations can never be sure,
Because it was built on the ruin of the
puir;
But or an age is come and gane,
Or the trees owre the chimley-taps grow
green,
We winna ken where the house has
been.

Whether due to wind or rain or
inadequate foundation the Hall did
not survive into the 19th century.

Tushielaw Tower, *c.*1600
Tower ruins in courtyard form. In 1530, the
Laird of *Truschelaw* was Adam Scott, (having
feued the forest stead and lands from the king
in 1507) but this *King of Theivis* was convicted
of taking blackmail and executed in Edinburgh
*to terrifie others – and they were heidit, and
their heidis fixed upon the Tolbuith of
Edinburgh.* (New Statistical Account)

Thirlestane Tower, late 16th century
Tower fragments (originally vaulted ground
floor and at least three storeys high) behind
the later house, 1820, demolished 1965, an
unresolved neoclassical and Gothick ensemble.

Thirlestane House, 1965

Gamescleuch, c.1570

Tower ruins, vaulted ground floor, hall on first floor, only vestiges of second floor. Traditionally built for Simon Scott but never occupied as his stepmother poisoned him on the eve of his marriage.

One mighty sheep-walk, wave upon wave of long, green, rounded hills, whose rich grass feeds enormous flocks of Cheviots, and now cropping trees too, Ettrick Forest was the Crown's – deforested from the time of James IV, but its sheep stells not constructed until c.1830.

In the pastoral counties of Peebles and Selkirk the shepherds' wages (c.1800) were commonly forty to forty-five sheep, a cow kept throughout the whole year, a house and garden, and a stone of oatmeal every week.
Handley

James Hogg was no simple shepherd: he was known to enjoy an oyster supper. *A month without an R has nae richt being in the year. Noo gentlemen, let naebody speak to me for the neist half-hour ... Hae the kettle on the boil, and put back the lang haun' o' the clock, for I fear this is Saturday nicht, and nane o' us are folk to break in on the Sabbath.*

Ettrick Kirk

Deep in rural isolation, square tower, 1824, memorial stone of 1619 built into its main elevation. Unspoilt interior with laird's loft, pulpit and fittings, and memorial bust (Lord Napier & Ettrick), 1900, Pittendreigh Macgillivray. In the graveyard lie the Ettrick Shepherd James Hogg (1770-1835), Tibbie Shiel (1783-1878) and Thomas Boston (1676-1732).

Left *Ettrick Kirk.* Below and bottom *Monument to the Ettrick Shepherd*

Monument to the Ettrick Shepherd,

Ettrick Hall, 1898, Andrew G Heiton Neoclassical obelisk, with rams' heads at the corners, bronze medallion, 1898, Hubert Paton, and the earlier, humbler, red sandstone block discreetly stuck to the base at the back, marking the site of James Hogg's cottage birthplace.

Monument to the Ettrick Shepherd, 1860,

Andrew Currie
A seated James Hogg, in shepherd's garb on a grassy knowe, in his right hand a shepherd's staff, in his left a scroll inscribed *He taught the wandering winds to sing*, at his feet sheepdog Hector. Inscribed pedestal.

Tibbie Shiel's Inn, 19th century; alterations,

1945, Dick Peddie McKay & Jamieson
Associated with various literati including David Brewster, De Quincey, Lockhart, Christopher North, and of course James Hogg.

The Highland & Agricultural Society, founded in 1784, *inter alia* sought to encourage agricultural improvement. It awarded James Hogg, the Ettrick Shepherd, three guineas for an essay on the diseases of sheep.
Handley

Sir Walter Scott's great-grandfather was the grandson of Wat of Harden.

Below *Dryhope Tower.*
Bottom *Yarrow Parish Church*

Megget Reservoir, 1983,

W J Cairns & Partners (see colour p.216) Engineering work by Robert H Cuthbertson & Partners. BBC Design Award, 1984, an astonishing public tribute to a piece of thoroughly well-integrated design which proves, as if proof were needed, that change can occasionally be inspirational. In this case it had to be, of course, since the valley bottom was flooded, losing the area's stock wintering capacity (replaced by a large over-wintering shed) and the ruined, late 16th-century, Cramalt Tower.

In Yarrow Church until after the Second World War ministers pronounced the Benediction to a seated congregation, a practice called *cheatin' the dugs*, designed to accommodate the shepherds' dogs which sat with the congregation reverently through the rest of the service. Such ingrained habits had their drawbacks though. At the Disruption of 1843 one farmer's dog apparently refused to follow his master to the Free Kirk a mile up the valley, but continued to worship with the Established Church.

Dryhope Tower, 1613

Possibly a rebuild since an order was made by James VI against Wat of Harden for its demolition in 1592. Dour four-storey four-square tower house, 1788, now roofless and crumbling within its vestigial barmkin. The home of Mary Scott, the *Flower of Yarrow*.

Yarrow Parish Church, 1923,

A N Paterson & Stoddart
Crowstepped gabled, apse-fronted T-plan, memorial windows, 1927, Douglas Strachan. The kirk moved to a more central location here, 1640, from a site (St Mary's of the Lowes, 1292 and earlier) overlooking St Mary's Loch. Rebuilt, 1771, destroyed by fire, 1922. In graveyard two 17th-century table-stones, good later monuments and ironwork. Cheerful sundial, 1640, instructing *watch & pray / Tyme is short.* Manse, 1811.

Top *Window head, Drochil Castle.*
Above *Kingsknowes Hotel.* Left *The
Yair*

Top *Peebles Hydro*. Middle *Bellcote, Stobo Church*. Above *Carolside*. Above right *Broughton Place*. Right *Bernat Klein Studio*

214

Top *Traquair House.* Above *Peebles Kirk and Swimming Pool*

Top *Lucy Sanderson Cottage Homes*. Above *Interior, Megget Dam*. Top left *Stained glass, Hawick Library*. Middle left *Detail, Woodlands*. Left *Neidpath Castle floodlit*

Hangingshaw, 1846

Two-storey Jacobethan house of rambling character on wooded south-facing site of 15th-century tower house (a stronghold of the *outlaw Murray*) and 18th-century and earlier mansion, destroyed by fire, *c.*1765. Terraced gardens, *c.*16th-century, with their ancient yews and hollies, and neoclassical pavilion, *c.*1930s, are still splendid features.

The *outlaw Murray* according to balladry came before James IV on charges of treasonably occupying the Ettrick Forest. *Thir lands are MINE!* the outlaw said; *I ken nae king in Christentie; Frae Soudron (English) I this Foreste wan, when the king nor his knightis were not to see.* A sensible compromise left Murray making feudal obeisance to King James, and the monarch appointing the reiver *Sheriffe of Ettricke Foreste, surely while upward grows the tree.*

The *Flower of Yarrow* was the daughter of Philip and Mary Scott of Dryhope, and married to Sir Walter (Wat) Scott of Harden.

The **Revd Robert Russell** (1766-1847) described Yarrow kirk thus: *The windows were small, and the light insufficient: there was no ceiling; and, on great days, the exposed rafters afforded seats for the adventurous youth, who perched on them like on hens on their baulks.*

Newark Castle, from 15th century

Massive (3m-thick walls) rectangular tower house (first mentioned in 1423), standing on a natural stronghold, reinforced by a 16th-century barmkin. An older castle (the *Oldworck*) was in the vicinity of this *Castel of Neworck*, but no trace remains. From first floor to wallhead Newark is the builder-work of Sir Thomas Joffray, 1467, having passed back to the Crown (it was the royal hunting-seat in the Ettrick Forest) from the Earls of Douglas in 1455. The royal coat of arms on the west gable may mark the grant to his Queen Margaret of Denmark the Lordship of the Ettrick Forest by James III in 1473. In 1547-8, the English took the barmkin, burnt the stables, but could not capture the house: they came back the next year and did so. In 1645 100 prisoners from the battle of Philiphaugh were slaughtered in the courtyard, and Cromwell's troops occupied it in 1650. Anne, Duchess of Buccleuch (1651-1732) and wife of Monmouth, lived here after his death. The apocryphal site of *The Lay of the Last Minstrel*, by Sir Walter Scott, the Castle was deroofed in the 18th century and accessible stone facings

Left and below *Newark Castle*

James III was not always so generous. He imprisoned his brothers, the Duke of Albany and Earl of Mar, the latter dying in captivity.

As if the slaughter of captured Royalist combatants after Philiphaugh was not bad enough, a few of their followers (mostly women) and their children were incarcerated in the Selkirk Tolbooth, three months later only to be brought out into the Market Place and shot.

At the **Battle of Philiphaugh** in 1645, the Marquis of Montrose, commanding the forces of the king, was surprised by Covenanters' forces under General David Leslie, and defeated. Within the grounds of the present house stands a rustic stone pyramid, the Covenanters' Monument, built by Sir John Murray (1817-82).

were robbed. This damage was substantially if crudely repaired in the 19th century.

Mungo Park's Cottage, a stabilised, roofless shell, was where the explorer (1771-1806) was brought up as the seventh child of a tenant farmer. In the late 18th century the road ran above Foulshiels, not as now.

Bowhill

Walter Francis, 5th Duke of Buccleuch, 1806-84, owned some 1750 km² (676 square miles) of Scotland.

Duchess Charlotte-Anne was not taken with Burn's visual skills, believing, for example, the clock-tower so bad that he *should pay us to take it down.*

Philiphaugh

Bowhill, from *c.*1708

Acquired by the 2nd Duke of Buccleuch in 1747 (so that his son Lord Charles Scott could stand for Parliament in Roxburghshire or Selkirk) from the Jacobite James Veitch. Landscape improvements followed in the later 18th century, but the house was not occupied by the 3rd Duke. When the 4th Duke succeeded in 1812, though, his commitment to the estate was considerable. William Atkinson virtually built a completely new house, 1812-13, on the south elevation in a manner not likely to endear itself to a Civic Society or Planning Authority today, an east wing following immediately, that to the west by 1819.

William Burn, principally in 1831-2, replanned and reordered Bowhill into a classic Victorian country house plan, with its family wing, darkly brooding in its whinstone with sandstone dressings. Landscape layout, Thomas Gilpin, 1832, creating lochs and using Newark Castle as a feature ruin in the picturesque landscape. Drive-carrying bridge at Faulshope, 1834, John & Thomas Smith. Monument to Sir Walter Scott, 1835, Rickman & Hussey.

J MacVicar Anderson, nephew and successor in Burn's practice, carried out the last major works, 1874-6, adding chapel, billiard-room, and smoking-room. Eclectic interiors which reflect the sources and resources of the Dukes of Buccleuch & Queensberry. Small Theatre, 1989, Law & Dunbar-Nasmith Partnership. *Adventure playground; open to the public*

Philiphaugh

Present house, 1964, Sir William Kininmonth after the demolition of the old, a large and picturesque white-harled Jacobean pile remodelled, 1874, by James Maitland Wardrop, who also designed the 1877 lodge.

Bernat Klein Design Studio, 1970, Peter Womersley

An uncompromisingly modern exercise in brick, glass and concrete, this building is as exceptional to look from as to look at, with more than a touch of the architect's Far East work and travel on display, and well suited to Bernat Klein's nature-inspired textile creativity: simplicity, neutral colours for the design and display of textiles, and *architectural integrity*. In the client's view the approach from the north is the most successful, a private wooded pathway from his house over a bridge to the studio's first floor. This bridge was an ingenious late addition to the building since a separate fire escape from the first floor was insisted upon by statutory authorities. RIBA Award, 1972 (see colour p.214).

Detail, Philiphaugh

Philiphaugh was the seat of Lord Murray. As early as the 1830s it was open to the public. William Morris remarked, *The beauty and elegance of the hall and public rooms make it one of the most interesting and attractive residences in the Scottish borders.*

Peter Womersley (1923-93) was a Yorkshire-born architect. Not the world's greatest draughtsman, he had a special understanding of the 3-D qualities of buildings, informed by sketch sections and models. A sun worshipper, he well understood the principles of building orientation, modelling and texture. Arguably the most creative architect/designer in Scotland in the 1960s and early '70s.

Bernat Klein was born in Senta, Yugoslavia, in 1922, to parents who ran a textile business. In Jerusalem he converted from a religious education to an art school one; in his first exams at Leeds University he failed in all twelve subjects. But inspired by the Festival of Britain he set up in business in Galashiels in 1951. In a long career as Scotland's foremost textile designer, his designs *inter alia* used by the greatest fashion houses, his business typified the cyclical nature of the textile industry. And his interest in creativity and design across all fields is exemplified by his patronage of Peter Womersley.

The same architect/client relationship had earlier produced **High Sunderland**, 1957, a rigidly geometric pattern of white-painted wood and glass which frames and acts as a foil to its landscape setting. The apparent restrictions of the basic *cage* are not noticeable within the house, where the extended plan with its part-sunken living room takes maximum advantage of the aspect.

Left Bernat Klein Design Studio.
Below High Sunderland

Top *Sunderland Hall*. Above *Yair Bridge*

In 1722 John Hodge described Fairnilee as *a very fine house with fine orchards, avenues, parks and planting very pleasant.*

Alison Rutherford (1713-94) of Fairnilee was, despite being widowed and poor, a kind of midwife to the Enlightenment, friend of Burns, Hume, and Scott's mother, amongst many others. She bore her troubles with élan: *Sudden death has been very fashionable of late* (i.e. in 1792). *I go piecemeal. I am deaf, blind, and lame, but content, because I know God made me, and knows best how to take down His own works.*

Right *Fairnilee, c.1910.* Below *Old Fairnilee*

Sunderland Hall, 1850, David Bryce; additions, 1885, Peddie & Kinnear
Possibly tower core, Georgian house, transformation (with use of Denholm Quarry red sandstone). **Stables, coachhouse & lodge,** *c.*1872. Largely Georgian terraced garden layout.

Yair House, 1788 (see colour p.213)
Built to accommodate Pringles vacating Whytbank. Alexander Pringle, *pressed by the expenses of a numerous family* had to part with Yair Estate in 1759. His son, with East India Company profits, bought back the Estate and built the square mansion, centre-bayed front and balustraded parapet, in one of the best locations, fronting the River Tweed, in the Borders.

Yair Bridge, 1760, possibly William Mylne
Three-arched bridge over the Tweed with refuges above cutwaters.

Fairnilee, 1904-6, John James Burnet
For A F Roberts, Selkirk cloth manufacturer. Burnet's best house, topped with Westmorland slates, walled terraced gardens with pergolas.

Old Fairnilee, late 16th century
Long rectangular three-storey-and-garret house with corbelled turrets to the south-west. A picturesque addition of *graceful degradation* to the grounds of Fairnilee, where Alison Rutherford (later Mrs Cochrane) wrote her version of the *Flowers of the Forest*.

Caddonfoot Church, 1863, David Rhind
Plain but finely detailed low rectangular kirk, extended, 1875, by the same architect. Stained glass by Herbert Hendrie. The adjacent **War Memorial**, Sir Robert Lorimer.

Somewhat implausible site of famous vineries, established 1869, (8km of hot water pipes and

6600kg of grapes/year) which succumbed in 1959 to the loss of the railways, an adverse microclimate from tree-felling during World Wars I & II, and rising energy prices, **Clovenfords** has little today to commend it beyond the **statue of Sir Walter Scott** set in the forecourt of the not unattractive **Clovenfords Hotel**.

Clovenfords Hotel with statue of Sir Walter Scott

Whytbank, 16th century
Pringle keep with terraced gardens below the courtyard. Inhabited until 1790, roofless by 1823, consolidation and considerable rebuilding, from 1990, John Reid.

Ashiestiel (Low Peel) Bridge, 1848, John & Thomas Smith
Built of whinstone, on construction this was the longest (40m) single-span rubble arch bridge in the world.

In a (futile) attempt to create order out of apparent chaos, in 1587 the Scots Parliament legislated that *landlords and bailies of the lands on the Borders ... where broken men have dwelt or presently dwell* had to attach themselves to lowland landowners who would act as surety for good behaviour on the relevant Border land, the idea being that a victim of such *broken men* could sue the surety (who himself would then seek redress from the Border landlord, the latter also subject to further legal financial penalty).

Peel House, 1920s

Peel House, 1909, Kinross & Tarbolton
Scottish Baronial mansion of exceptional design and constructional quality (interior plasterwork by Grandison of Peebles), which survives its spell as hospital only to be threatened with an outbreak of residential zits in its policies. Built for W R Ovens, seed merchant in Leith.

Ashiestiel House, from 1660
Oblong core recast and enlarged on at least four occasions, most notably in Victorian times when it took on its 19th-century appearance of crowstepped gables and dormers. Home of Sir Walter Scott, 1804-12, where he wrote *The Lay of the Last Minstrel*, *The Lady of the Lake*, *Marmion*, and part of *Waverley*.

Elibank Castle (formerly Eliburn), 16th century
Whin rubble ruin originally 20x7m rectangular plan, with basement and second floor vaulted,

According to the *Transactions of the Highland & Agricultural Society* (1872), it was a proverb in Peeblesshire that no month in the year save July was safe from frost.

Sir Gideon Murray owned Elibank from 1594. Wealthy and well-connected, Border balladry would have his ill-favoured daughter *Muckle-mou'd Meg* married off to an unsuccessful reiver, William Scott of Harden (son of Auld Wat) who took three days to decide in favour of the large-lipped lass (surely a 17th-century supermodel) as the alternative to Murray's gallows. But in fact contracts of matrimony do exist, the first dated 18 February 1611 (Auld Wat could not sign *becaus I can not wryt*) and the marriage itself was celebrated on 1 May.

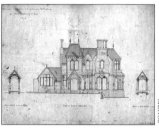

Top *War Memorial*. Above *West (entrance) elevation, Stoneyhill, drawn by F T Pilkington, 1867*

The village of Walkerburn *does not have a pleasing aspect to the passer-by, but viewed from the station it has great beauty, and the setting is rugged and imposing.* Third Statistical Account

In the Seventh Annual Report of the County Sanitary Inspector for Peeblesshire (1897), he trumpeted that *a great improvement has been effected in Walkerburn Village by the erection of a public urinal.*

The Kirna

of at least four storeys, set above *hanging garden* terraces and overlooking the Tweed. Very dilapidated, Elibank was a ruin in 1722.

Holylee, 1825-7, John & Thomas Smith
Built for James Ballantyne of Old Holylee following his marriage in 1821. Austere late Georgian three-storey five-bay mansion, dated 1827, with a serene Ionic portico. 300m-away stands **Old Holylee**, the residence of Ballantynes from 1734 to 1827, an oblong 13x7m two-storey exercise in harled rubble. The adjacent Holylee Quarry was a source of large thick slate principally quarried for pavements.

WALKERBURN

War Memorial, 1923, James B Dunn
Roadside enclosure of concrete and white granite, with bronze inscriptions and statue of a greatcoated *Tommy* by Alexander Carrick.

Stoneyhill, 1868, F T Pilkington & Bell
For John Ballantyne, mill owner and plainly progressive patron of Pilkington in this area. Music Room, 1890, James B Dunn. Free composition of Early French Gothic with a wealth of detail, most bordering (just) on the decorative side of grotesque, and with a pair of symmetrical lodges and stables. Ceiling paintings by Spanish artist Cuadras were obliterated during its spell as convent.

Museum of Woollen Textiles/Ballantyne's (Tweedvale) Mill
Complex dates from formation in 1855, with the Museum's main theme the Victorian tweed industry. **Tweedvale**, 1855, has a later lodge, 1860s, by F T Pilkington.

Ballantyne Memorial Institute, 1904, James B Dunn
Stylish red sandstone gabled hall at the foot of the village.

Urinal, *c.*1897
Cast iron from the Saracen Foundry (Macfarlane's) of Glasgow. A unique survivor in the Borders. Ladies should approach this rare object with care.

The Kirna, 1867, F T Pilkington & Bell
A *unique and handsome* house with rich stone patterning and several built-in maintenance burdens at roof level in the form of unusual

drainage arrangements. Two-storeys-and-attic, asymmetry a feature, with ornate mouldings, whin rubble with ashlar dressings and detail.

INNERLEITHEN
Just a kirk hamlet until around 1790, comprising thatched cottages, irregularly spaced. Brodie's mill at Caerlee was set up in 1788, and with the medicinal spring receiving publicity on the publication (1824) of Walter Scott's *St Ronan's Well* the town developed apace. The north/south straggle down the Leithen Water was subordinated to a new east/west main street of *rather new good-looking houses*, and the beautiful village green was appropriated, feued, and built upon.

There is some good local authority housing on the plain, part of the burgh housing scheme, from 1920, Dick Peddie & Walker Todd, including an elongated and extended 20th-century version of Traquair House.

15-19 Pirn Road
No 15 bears the date of 1774 on the door lintel, and may have been an inn, with the remainder of this little group originally stable buildings.

Top *Local authority housing.*
Above *15-19 Pirn Road*

Caerlee Mill (Ballantyne's Cashmere), 1788 Alexander Brodie was a native of Traquair, who made his fortune as an ironmaster in Shropshire, an intimate of Thomas Telford. His five-floor mill did not meet with great success in his lifetime but sparked off the growth of the Innerleithen woollen industry.

Robert Smail's Printing Works, High Street Shopfront extolling the more commercial aspects of the heritage, but passing through this one finds a major lade system which at one time powered at least eight separate industrial enterprises. That preserved since 1986 by the National Trust for Scotland was not latterly

While on the face of it there seems little connection between iron production and the woollen industry, the technology of using water power to drive machines was very similar, in the case of the metal to operate bellows for smelting and hammers for working. Multistorey textile mills had vertical drive shafts so that power could be taken off at any floor.

Top *St James's RC Church*. Above
Parish Church. Right *St Ronan's Well*

water-powered, of course, but the mechanical
presses and typesets are fascinating, and the
social history contained within the printing
firm's sample books must be someone's thesis
material. *Open to the public, guidebook available*

Further down, the lade served an interesting
group of adjacent enterprises: **Meikle's Saw
Mill**, a converted 18th-century farmsteading
(saw mill and water wheel); a turbine
generator house and **Hogg & Robertson's
Engineering Works** (demolished 1990, but
water wheel and oil engine house remain).

St James's RC Church, High Street, 1881,
Mr Biggar
Fourteenth-century English Decorated Gothic,
snecked rubble with sandstone dressings, 30m
broach spire on tower, stained glass James
Ballantine & Son. Presbytery and School, 1876.

Parish Church, 1865-7, F T Pilkington
Won in competition with David MacGibbon and
David Bryce. Proposed tall spire never built.
Chancel added, 1888-9, J McIntyre Henry (who
also designed the church hall). Cupola *c*.1920.
Fine stained glass. The fragment of a 9th-
century decorated cross set at the front
elevation was found in the foundations of the
earlier parish church in the course of its
demolition in 1871.

St Ronan's Well, 1826, W H Playfair
On the slope of Lee Penn, at the mineral
spring, the pump room building was originally
erected by Lord Traquair, housing subscription
reading rooms with newspapers and select
library (perhaps to take one's mind off the taste

St Ronan's Border Games were
established by the Edinburgh Six-
feet-high Club, 40 gentlemen of
suitable size.

The chemical composition of the
water here is put down to
St Ronan's actions:
> *Battlin' gamely, wi' his back*
> *Yerkit to the wa',*
> *Bauld St Ronan cleek't the Deil*
> *And gi'ed his leg a thra.*
>
> *He gi'ed his leg a thra',*
> *The crafty Cleikum thra',*
> *The spot he fell's a sulpher well,*
> *Ye'll taste it in the spa.*

and effect of the medicines) ... *a salubrious mineral spring, ... eminently beneficial in cases of scrofulous disorders, inflammations of the eyes, and various diseases originating in impurities of the blood ... The gay loungers at the watering-place came habitually to take an interest in the Games and in 1827 42 noblemen, knights and gentlemen joined in instituting an annual competition for prizes in all gymnastic exercises* (New Statistical Account). Reconstructed 1896, refurbished 1991.

Leithen Bridge (Cuddy Brig), 1701
Single span of rubble masonry, built across the Leithen Water with funds from the vacant stipend.

St Ronan's Mill, 1846, Robert Hall & Co; demolished, 1981
Early *modern* factory designed for wool spinning of George Roberts & Son of Selkirk. Eleven-bay four-storey main block, whinstone rubble harled back and sides, droved ashlar dressings to openings and quoins. Water-powered via a 550m lade from the Leithen Water.

Dr Fyfe describes the waters (of St Ronan's Well) *as particularly beneficial in cases of Bile, Stomach Complaints, Scurvy, Cutaneous Disorders and General Debility of the System*. He adds, *PS – In cases of sterility the Innerleithen Spa has been found of the greatest service; and Married Ladies, who had long given up thoughts of having a family, by taking a regular course of the waters have found themselves in a state which* 'Ladies wish to be who love their Lords'.

In 1685 **the Vacant Stipend Act** ensured that any available stipend must be used by the patron *for pious urges and in building and repairing bridges, repairing churches and maintaining the poor* on pain of removing his right of selecting the parish minister.

RCAHMS

Pirn House, 1700
Pavilion wings added 1746. It was demolished in 1950, following wartime acquisition by Innerleithen Town Council, and the site is now occupied by a school.

Pirn House

Leithen Lodge, *c*.1876
Built for John Miller, civil engineer, who bought the estate in 1852, the 16th-century Lee fortalice being quite uninhabitable. Reconstruction, 1889, Sydney Mitchell & Wilson, and in progress, 1992. **Kennels**, **stables** and graceful **footbridge**. Good **sundial** in garden.

James Smith, who *ruined himself (financially) by a Drowned Colliery near Musselburgh* had 18 children by his first wife, who died aged 37 of twins, and 14 by his second, whom he also survived. One of his sons was christened Climacterick Smith, being born in his father's seventieth year.

Montrose, defeated after Philiphaugh (1645), knocked in vain for shelter – the 1st Earl pretended he was not at home: though accused by Montrose of treachery, he at least saved self and house from General Leslie's Covenanting Army.

William the Lion, 1143-1214, in an effort to press the Scots' title to Northumberland, invaded but was captured in 1174 near Alnwick. He agreed to be a vassal of England, through the Treaty of Falaise, revoked in 1189 at a payment of 10,000 merks to Richard I.

Below *North elevation, Traquair House, drawn by R A C Simpson.* Bottom *Traquair House, 1963*

Williamslee Farm, probably early 18th-century house, with steep slated roof, thackstanes, and good byres. **Woolandslee Tower** remains of small tower group, the tower *c.*16th century, vaulted ground floor only remaining, now altered and extended into a sheep stell.

Traquair House

In part of the royal Ettrick Forest, originally a tower-house strategically located on a bend in the river (realigned *c.*1640 by the 1st Earl of Traquair to prevent undermining of the house). Core probably 15th century, main block extended to its present form through 16th and 17th centuries. Alterations, 1695, James Smith, who prepared plans for remodelling (not proceeded with), new courtyard, and gardens with pavilions (see colour p.215).

Jacobite sympathies ensured a period of relative poverty in the 18th century when other lairds were building classical mansions. Accordingly Traquair now contains a wealth of early architectural features, and its asymmetrical front elevation makes it as fine an example of complexity and contradiction as Castle Howard ever was – and at a more human scale. The Palace of Traquair was by repute the favourite residence of Scottish Kings (in 1176 William the Lion granted Glasgow's Burgh Charter here) and the oldest continuously inhabited house in Scotland. The products of the **brewhouse** are to be recommended. The **Bear Gates**, 1737-8, bears added 1745 (closed in 1796 after death of 7th Earl's wife), were the original

gateway of Tully Veolan, in Scott's *Waverley*.
Walled garden, 1749. A number of interesting
garden buildings here, particularly the **lodges**
and the **rustic summerhouse** (thatched), 1834.
Open to the public

Traquair Parish Church, rebuilt 1778
Interior recast, 1821 (W H Playfair plans of
1840 exist for work on church). **Memorial**,
1877, by John Steel. An odd combination of
faiths, with the Roman Catholic Stuart of
Traquair **burial aisle** forming a T with the
Kirk. See the tailor's tombstone in the
churchyard. **Manse** rebuilt *c*.1793, two-storey
house, **courtyard range**, with large addition
and extensive repairs, 1814.

Traquair Parish Church, 1964

The Glen, 1854, David Bryce
Sumptuous Scottish Baronial for Charles
Tennant of the St Rollox Chemical Works,
Glasgow. Named after the Tennants' farm in
Ayrshire. The Bryce house replaced the old
plain farmhouse (demolished *c*.1853) which
W H Playfair had sensitively extended in 1821.
Additions 1874, internal reconstruction after
fire, 1905, Robert Lorimer, and further work by
Syrie Maugham later. **Lodge**, 1854. Good Arts
& Crafts (Lorimer?) garden gates, 1914. Many
fine estate buildings, including summerhouse,
coachhouse, dairy, pighouse, and kennels.

The St Rollox chemical works was
founded to make bleaching powder
and became *the biggest chemical
works in the world.*

Robert Burns knew Charles
Tennant's grandfather as *Auld Glen,
the ace and wale of men* after the
Ayrshire farm he worked. The
Tennants' fortune was latterly built
on their alkali chemical works,
which boasted *Tennant's stalk*, a
130m-high chimney, built in 1842.
Charles Tennant was aged 29 when
he acquired the Glen, and 31 when
it was built.

Cardrona Tower, *c*.16th century
Roofless L-plan ruined peel tower for the
Govan family, probably three storeys and attic,
of whin. Ground floor vaulted, turnpike stair
on the west corner forming the foot of the L.
Still almost entire in 1794, despite the Tower's
being vacated after 1685 when the Williamsons
(see p.235) acquired the property.

Cardrona, 1840, William Burn
Attractive Victorian mansion built to replace
an earlier version of 1715, which was relegated
to use as offices. To the north a **doocot**, *c*.1700,
with penthouse roof and crowstepping.

Kirkburn Church, 1921
Memorial Chapel to Cree of Kailzie. Contains
stone lintel inscribed *Hous for Prayer, 1614*
(salvaged from the earlier kirk), formerly used
as a mantelpiece in the nearby old toll-house,
and stained-glass window, 1919, by Douglas
Strachan. Adjacent, stabilised **remains of
earlier church** and graveyard: the church was
new built in 1614, but parish suppressed 1674.

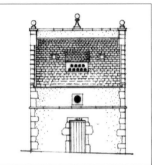

Top *Kailzie, 1958.* Above *Kailzie doocot*

Edinburgh-born **David Roberts**, 1796-1864, was a scenery painter at Drury Lane before making his mark with pictures shown at the Royal Academy. Biblical and classical subjects were enhanced by his visits to Mediterranean countries: he became a Royal Academician in 1841.

The Horsburghs of Horsburgh were the oldest family of landowners in Innerleithen parish: after more than 700 years of *traceable history* (Burnett), the direct male line died out in 1911 on the expiry of Lt-Col Horsburgh.

Kailzie, 1803; demolished 1962
Built for John Nutter Campbell, a Glasgow merchant. *A plain two-storey mansion*, additions and alterations, 1914, Peddie & Forbes Smith. **Home Farm** & **steading** presumably *c*.1800, the latter containing a water-powered saw-mill, wheel and machinery largely intact. Entrance lodges, 1802, additions (principally dormers), 1920, J M Dick Peddie. **Stables** comprise delightful range with some Gothick details *c*.1800. **Doocot**, 1628, is a lean-to type with crowstepping and ball finials. Gardens (*open to the public*) with **sundial**, 1811, and Regency glasshouse.

Scotsmill, 1802
Large pyramidal grain-drying kiln. Adjacent **miller's house**, 1812, Gothick details surviving conservative restoration, 1985, by Kanak Bose. **Whitehaugh**, late 18th-century farmhouse, painted stonework.

Haystoun, 1660
L-plan house built on foundation of old tower, enlarged in 18th-century, and became factor's house and farmhouse in 1795 when Hay family built Kingsmeadows. Conversion back to country house, 1925, Orphoot, Whiting & Bryce.

Glenormiston House, 1805
Replaced the then cleared Ormiston Tower of *c*.1600. Extended 1824, remodelled 1846 for William Chambers, eventually demolished in 1956. In the course of the demolition, wall-paintings by David Roberts (presumably commissioned by Chambers) were discovered. The still-surviving Victorian entrance lodge combines grandly with the iron screen railings.

Nether Horsburgh Farmhouse, 17th- and 18th-century core
Two-storey three-bay, harled with quoins, pitched slated roof, with later additions which include the almost obligatory coursed whinstone outbuilding range to the back. **Nether Horsburgh Castle**, 16th century, a secluded, ruined, three-storey, oblong tower house of which only three sides remain.

Horsburgh Castle Farmhouse, probably 18th-century core
Two-storey, harled, slated roof, irregularly extended, with a large farm steading to the back. **Horsburgh Castle** is a shell of a small L-plan,

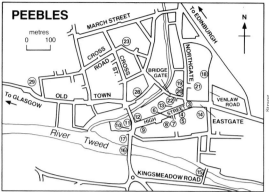

Kerfield

16th-century, tower-house, main block 9x10m, wing containing turnpike stair, its remains *injudiciously* patched in the 19th century.

PEEBLES
County town, a douce place as befits its rural setting on both banks of the Tweed, the valley being open here and running primarily west/ east with the Edinburgh road off to the north. South-east of its junction, a long garden wall and a brace of picturesque lodges, are the evidence of the existence of **Kerfield**. A brewery was first on the site in the latter half of the 18th century: its success was followed by the erection of the pilastered **Kerfield House**, *c.*1800, and the removal of the brewing concern to Edinburgh left the House and policies in a more conventional relationship, now compromised by 20th-century housing of little architectural merit.

Peebles Hotel Hydro, 1878-81,
John Starforth
Impressively French Renaissance in red Dumfriesshire sandstone. Burnt, 1905, while a

As quiet *as the grave – or Peebles*
Lord Cockburn

The town is small, *and but indifferently built or inhabited, yet the High Street has some good houses on it. There is a handsome stone bridge over the Tweed, which is not a great river here, though the current is sometimes indeed very violent. The country is hilly, as in the rest of Tweeddale, and those hills cover'd with sheep, which is, indeed, a principal part of the estates of the gentlemen; and the overplus quantity of the sheep, as also their wool, is mostly sent to England, to the irreparable damage of the poor; who, were they employ'd to manufacture their own wool, would live much better than they do, and find the benefit of the Union in a different manner, from what they have yet done.*
Daniel Defoe, 1723

A positive attitude by Hydro patients was recommended: *Hopefulness on behalf of the patient is most desirable, and a cheerful outlook should always be encouraged. Patients who are continually worrying about their business or household matters are not likely to get well quickly. Mental excitement must be avoided ... Discussing one's own or other people's particular ailments is a baneful habit, and must be on no account indulged in.*

Peebles Hotel Hydro, 1890s

Top *Mercat Cross*. Above *Chambers'
Institution*. Right *War Memorial,
Chambers' Institution*

In c.1800 the coach *Willie Wilson's
Caravan* took 10 hours to crawl from
Peebles to Edinburgh, a distance of
20 miles.
Handley

The opening ceremonies of the
Institution extended over an entire
week. On the Wednesday, the 59-
year-old William Chambers
attended the celebration ball and
*tripped upon the light fantastic with
steps evidently remembered since his
dancing school days.* But the
Thursday concert, also much
enjoyed, took place without him, *the
labours and anxieties of the
preceding days having quite knocked
him up.*

northern extension was being built.
Replacement building, 1905-7, James Miller
(architect of the Turnberry Hotel) as a neo-
Georgian, American railway hotel, dormered,
red tiled roof over an expansive three-storey
composition (see colour p.214).

3 **Mercat Cross** was originally an octagonal shaft
carrying a sundial, 1699, with copper weathervane, 1662, taken down and sold, 1807, shaft
erected in court of Chambers Institution, 1857,
re-erected on new pedestal at junction 1895,
relocated eastwards Schomberg Scott 1964-5.

High Street was laid out in the 16th century
on the peninsula formed by the Tweed and
Eddleston Water. Prior to this the **Old Town**,
thatched houses, burning peat, lay chiefly on
the north bank of the Eddleston. In 1846 the
High Street was lowered 2-3ft over its length,
drains built, *unsightly* projecting buildings and
stairs removed.

4 **Chambers' Institution**, principally 1859
Traditionally known as the Dean's House in

reference to an earlier religious ownership, later passing to the Hays of Yester and the Dukes of Queensberry. William Chambers (Lord Provost of Edinburgh in 1865) acquired it in 1857 for *purposes of social, moral and intellectual improvement* and presented it to his native town as a free gift in 1859, after its substantial alteration to form public lending library, reading room, rooms for private study, art gallery, county museum and hall. The art gallery has reproductions of the Parthenaic Frieze, and the Alexandrian equivalent by Danish sculptor Bertel Thorvaldsen, 1770-1844. Enlargement, 1912, George Washington Browne.

5 Within the courtyard framed by the Institution stands the **War Memorial**, 1922, Orphoot & Whiting; sculptor Thomas Beattie. Great bronze panels by the Bromsgrove Guild Mosaic-work based on 12th-century mosaics of Monreale (cross and mosaic by Prof G Matranga of Palermo).

Local government reform is sadly unlikely to be as immediately beneficial as a former Peebles Burgh Council standing order that *if any member of the Council be not present at the meeting after the prayer be said and calling of the roll, without a lawful excuse or licence had of before from one of the magistrates,* (he) *shall pay for the public use* (the Common Good fund) *two shillings Scots*: members in 1664 also had to *buy and wear hats at all occasions when they are called to wait upon the magistrates, and when they come to the Council.*

Thorvaldsen was born at sea, the son of an Icelandic carver of ships' figureheads.

High Street
In 1671 residents were instructed not to *keep any midden or muck upon the King's causeway, at any time hereafter, under this certification ... it shall be lawful for any neighbour within the same to intromet* [ie tamper with] *and lead away such muck* (to spread on his own ground!) *found upon the said street, lying above eight days time, for his own use.*

Left and below *Town House*

6 **Town House**, 1753
Real architecture, with burgh arms pediment, and generally substantial civic proportions.

7 **Corn Exchange**, 1860, to the rear. The Corn Exchange's function was superseded with the coming of the railway to Peebles in 1868.

8 **Cornice Gallery**, 1987
Just south off the High Street, down a close marked with a hanging sign. Demonstrates the

Above *Marriage lintel, Parliament
Square*. Below *Parish Church*.
Bottom *Sheriff Court*

art and craft of a long-established firm of
architectural master-plasterers, Messrs
Grandison. There is even the opportunity to
try your hand at casting if you dare.

9 **63-67** High Street (Parliament Square), 1759
Leading to a cobbled square (within which is a
marriage lintel dated 1743 bearing mason's
compasses and square) and thence to a close
(the *Stinking Stair*, perhaps due to the impact of
a brewery and tannery at its foot in days gone
by) stepping down to the river. It is perhaps too
fanciful to imagine that there might have been
any connection between John Buchan's book
The 39 Steps and this stair just across the road
from his family's legal and commercial practice
at Bank House. Parliament Square is so-called
because following the Battle of Neville's Cross in
1346 (at Durham) the Scots Parliament met in
the vicinity to determine their response to the
English capture of King David II.

Peebles Castle was regularly used as a royal
residence. It was last mentioned in 1685, and
in the 18th century used as a quarry. In 1783 a
church *elegant and substantial, ornamental to
the town*, was built on part of the old castle
site, which had in the interim been used as a
bowling green. This church was largely (his
plan was not entirely followed) the work of
James Brown, the architect and developer of
George (named after his brother) Square in
Edinburgh. The old kirk was demolished, 1885.

10 **Parish Church**, 1885-7, William Young
A spectacular stop to the High Street, 13th-
century Scots Gothic with dominant crown
tower feature. Stained glass, 1890, by Cottier &
Co of London. William Young was the London-
based Scots architect of Glasgow City
Chambers and the War Office, London.
Guidebook available

11 **Sheriff Court**, 1848, Thomas Brown
Elegantly Tudor, originally prison and
courthouse, alterations, 1892, Peddie & Kinnear.

12 **Bank House**, site of Chapel of the Virgin,
post-Reformation
The Town Chambers until 1753. Present
building (surviving only in part due to crude
road-bridge widening) associated with the
Buchans. In the close beside and behind 82
High Street is a **marriage lintel**, dated 1648.

¹³ **24-28** High Street, 1724
House of the Turnbull family, notable for its
inscribed stone *God provides a rich
inheritance – WT 1724* and details of the baker's
trade – guild symbols (4), the shovels and
swaffles (cloth mops). The steeply pitched roof
betrays an 18th-century thatched origin, but
the present Westmorland slate is 20th century.

¹⁴ **Leckie Memorial Church**, 1875-6,
Peddie & Kinnear
Fourteenth-century Gothic on a fine terraced
situation. The massive broach spire is 42m
(146ft) high. Less dramatic but beautifully
formed, the adjacent **St Peter's Episcopal
Church**, 1830-3, William Burn. Chancel &
organ chamber, 1882, Hay & Henderson.
Memorial window, 1936, Joyce Meredith.
Across the road **former Free Church**, 1871-2,
John Starforth.

Top *Carved trade stone, 24 High
Street.* Above *Leckie Memorial
Church.* Left *Priorsford Bridge*

The Burgh Council provided
consumer protection by establishing
trading standards: in 1667 five
Peebles bakers were fined 10 merks
apiece *for baking and selling of
wheat bread lighter than the table.*

¹⁵ **Priorsford Bridge,** 1905
Attractive iron suspended structure, erected by
public subscription. In 1817 John Stevenson
Brown, originally from Lyne, of Redpath &
Brown, ironmongers of Edinburgh, built a 33m
span here for Sir John Hay.

¹⁶ **Tweed Bridge**, *c*.15th century
Strangely, dated IV II 26 (1426?). Until the

David II was the only son of King
Robert Bruce, whom he succeeded
aged five. He spent seven years in
France, 1334-41, while the English
were in the ascendancy. Thereafter
in English hands for 11 years, he
was only released subject to a
promised (king's) ransom of 100,000
merks over 10 years: despite a raft
of taxation only half had been paid
after 14 years (when David died). In
1363 he had tried to buy off secretly
the outstanding sums in return for
the recognition of Edward III as
successor if David had no male heir:
the Scots Parliament, hearing of
this in 1364, rejected it out of hand.

18th century the only bridge over the River Tweed above Kelso. In 1663 stones were taken from the ruined St Andrew's Church for its (re)building. Three additional arches, 1799, John Hislop. Increased in width from 8ft to 21ft, 1834, John & Thomas Smith, and to 40ft, 1900, McTaggart, Cowan & Barker. Look underneath to see evidence of the widenings, and note the dolphin lamp standards, survivors of the 1900 works.

17 Swimming Pool, 1983, Morris & Steedman Low-lying form held down by its hipped roof which visitors from Peebles' hinterland may feel has an agricultural feel (and why not?) and an ascetic self-effacing nature (correct for the site overlooked by the Parish Church) relieved by the yellow steelwork (see colour p.215).

18 Old Burgh Wall, 1571, Thomas Lauder, Mason Interesting remnant complete with tower and cannon-ports, but surely not of any real defensive significance. Across the car park (formerly the railway yard) is **Venlaw** built in commanding position (site of Smithfield Castle) c.1782, with baronial additions c.1900, now **Venlaw Castle Hotel**.

19 Masonic Hall, Northgate, 1716 Two-storey, rendered, with a fine Gibbsian doorway – rustication and a broken pediment.

20 5-7 Northgate, mid-18th century One-time residence of (Dr) Mungo Park (1771-1806), explorer and missionary. Two-storey, harled, centre-columned doorway. Surgeon Park arrived here in 1801, after his expedition to the Niger, but could thole only two years – *He confessed to Scott that he would rather brave*

Africa and its horrors than wear his life out in toilsome rides amongst the hills for the scanty remuneration of a country surgeon (Lang).

21 Cross Keys Inn, 1693
Three-storey L-plan main block, note the cinquefoil-carved triangular dormer pediment built into the west wall of the outshot. Originally townhouse of Williamson of Cardrona (initials WW in roof slates) then inn named the Yett i.e. the Gate due to arched approach from Northgate. Scott is supposed to have based Meg Dods in *St Ronan's Well* upon the innkeeper Miss Marion Ritchie.

22 Burgh Killing-house, Dean's Wynd
Probably 18th century or earlier, in use until 1908 (now an open store), a high rubble wall with lean-to killing-booths within, and the burgh crest carved in the lintel above the gateway to the wynd which links High Street and Bridgegate.

23 Cross Kirk, from *c.*1260
Remains of nave and west tower of Trinitarian (Red) Friary founded in response to discovery of ancient cross and burial urn. Post-Reformation, used as Parish Church from 1569 to 1784, then as quarry(!). *Historic Scotland Guardianship Monument*

In Rosetta Road a fine trio of 20th-century buildings with adherence to traditional values. **RC Church**, Rosetta Road, 1913 and 1951, Reginald Fairlie. **District Council Offices**, Rosetta Road, 1935, Dick Peddie & Walker Todd, interior work by Scott Morton & Co, on the site of W L Moffat's Combination Poorhouse of 1857. **Kingsland School**, 1901, Robert Wilson.

Top *Cross Keys Inn*. Middle *Cross Kirk*. Above *Kingsland School*. Left *District Council Offices*

Opposite: Main *Swimming Pool*. Small from top *Dolphin lamp standard, Tweed Bridge; Old Burgh Wall; Detail, Masonic Hall; Detail, 5-7 Northgate*

On 7 May 1261 *in the presence of honest men, kirkmen, ministers and burgesses, a certain magnificent and venerable cross, enclosed in a box inscribed 'The Place of Nicolaus, Bishop' was exhumed.*
John of Fordun

Sir Ralph Abercromby (1734-1801) was born in Menstrie, and served in the 3rd Dragoons, 1756-63, in the Seven Years' War. MP for Clackmannanshire, 1774-80, he rejoined the Army in 1793, became a major-general, and died victorious over the French at Aboukir Bay.

St Andrew's Church: Right *in 1790.*
Below *Tower.* Bottom *Gravestone*

Rosetta, 1807
Regency mini-mansion in whinstone rubble with ashlar dressings for a surgeon who had earlier served in Egypt in the Abercromby expedition which *salvaged* the Rosetta Stone. A replica is built into the porch. Contemporary **stable courtyard** castellated range similar to that of Kailzie.

Biggiesknowe (originally Brighouse knowe) was a place of handloom weaving, which cottage industry was superseded by factory production. These humble cottages didn't just 28 produce woollen goods though. **No 14** was the birthplace of John Veitch (1829-94), Professor of Philosophy, poet and historian of the Borders. **No 18**, 1796, was the birthplace of William (1800-83) and Robert (1802-71) Chambers.

Much of the Old Town narrowly avoided terminal blight caused by an insensitive proposal to widen the road to Glasgow. Although there is still scope for further infill, much of the success of its appearance today can be put down to the initiative of the Eildon Housing Association whose selection of architects Aitken & Turnbull, with their urban renewal experience from Hawick's Howegate, has paid dividends in a handsome revival, 1989, of the north side of the street.

29 **St Andrew's Church**, founded 1195
Originally a plain western tower of rubble freestone, attached to a rather small and somewhat undistinguished church. Despite its limited accommodation, it contained 11 altars in 1543 when it became collegiate. In 1548 it was burned by the English, and probably never was properly restored.

In 1650 enough of the church remained to house horses of Cromwell's forces besieging Neidpath. Presently a fine example of the difference between repair and restoration. *It has been so completely restored or transformed by the late Dr Chambers, that it is now of no interest whatsoever as a specimen of the ancient architecture of Scotland* (MacGibbon & Ross). William Chambers (who had masterminded the restoration of St Giles' Cathedral, Edinburgh, in 1879) provided the funds, and the *restoration* plans, 1883, were by George Henderson (of Hay & Henderson), scraping away the vaulted interior floors, and adding about 3m of *appropriate* Norman pitched stone roof with crowstepped gables and corbelled cornice. Good gravestones, some from the 17th century.

Chapelhill, from 16th century
Small 9x6m tower was starting point for this harled and painted two-storey house, which in its single-storey courtyard range has an imported datestone of 1696 over the kitchen door.

Winkston, from 1545
Rectangular 10x7m tower house dated 1545 and 1734, converted 18th century to laird's house, more recently as dairy and storehouse concealed behind present two-storey three-bay 19th-century farmhouse.

Top *Hope stone, 1704, St Andrew's Church.* Above *Lintel, 1545, Winkston.* Left *Winkston, 1964*

Dickson of Winkston is the only recorded Provost of Peebles (thus far) to have been assassinated, in 1572.

In 1665, **Peebles Burgh Council** ordained that, *Hew Black, for his miscarriage, brawling last Tuesday, breaking several doors, offering injury to several of the inhabitants, and his cursing, swearing and imprecating, to be put in the stocks at the cross next Wednesday, and to lie there the space of one hour, with a paper upon his face written in great letters, and there after to be banished this town, and if he be seen or found in the burgh at any time hereafter, without a call or public authority, then to suffer death as an adulterer.*

The winning design for the monument came from south of the border, from Rickman & Hutchinson, but was set aside in favour of the *native* proposals of Meikle Kemp, who submitted his entry under the pseudonym *John Morvo*. Meikle Kemp (1795-1844), a shepherd's son, helped his father until he was 14, when he trained as a millwright and carpenter. He worked in England and France, studying Gothic architecture, joining an Edinburgh office in 1826. Sadly, before the Scott Monument was completed, Kemp drowned in the Union Canal.

Below *Scott Monument, drawn by George Meikle Kemp.* Right *Cringletie House.* Bottom *Mural panel, south-east front, Cringletie House*

At Redscarhead stands the **memorial to George Meikle Kemp**, designer of the Scott Monument in Edinburgh. The memorial (1932) was erected here where Kemp was apprenticed to a millwright.

Cringletie House, 1861-3, David Bryce
Delightful baronial mansionhouse, now hotel, in red Dumfriesshire sandstone, replacing the old mansion by something *on a better scale*. The interiors are not too Bryce-like, having been designed around very fine salvaged mid-18th-century chimneypieces. Adjacent is an 18th-century **Doocot**, of square plan, rubble with sandstone quoins, and slated conical roof.

Harehope, 1723
Small (laird's) house, two-storey, harled with slated roof, next to the later farmhouse of the same name.

Milkieston Toll was part of the turnpike road which opened in 1770, as indeed was Eddleston. **The Tollhouse** is single-storey, with a stone-gabled centre porch. Tolls in Peeblesshire were abolished in 1866.

EDDLESTON
Village founded about 1785 as a single street of whinstone cottages, now terminated by (on the west) the former **railway station** (1855) and **station house**. To the east lies the **Parish Church**, with its Flemish bell dated 1507. The present kirk dates from 1829 rebuilding, and was restored in 1897 and vestry added after a fire. Note the 18th-century sundial on south-west corner. The **Horseshoe** (dated 1862) was, unsurprisingly, originally a smithy.

Black Barony, Darnhall
Sixteenth-century tower-house core, recast possibly by Robert Mylne or Sir William Bruce by the end of the 17th century. The peculiarly

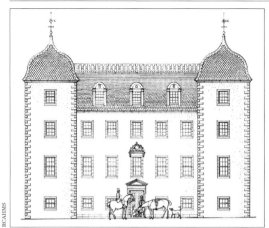

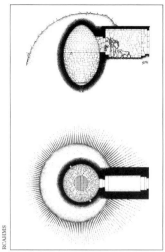

Scots character provided by this period's front elevation with twin bell-cast roofed corner towers has proved strong enough to cope with Victorian enlargement, family wing 1855, bachelors' wing 1877, conversion to a hotel in the 1930s (billiard room, 1930s, Sir Basil Spence), and an uncompromising upgrading, 1987, Dick Peddie McKay, but little historic detail remains. Icehouse.

Portmore House, originally 1850, David Bryce
Preliminary designs produced by William Burn in 1833, this red sandstone baronial mansion in Elizabethan style was destroyed by fire April 1883, rebuilt, 1884 David & John Bryce, and substantially restored latterly (1982, Cameron & Gibb and (more fire) 1986). Crowstepped lodge which lingers at the roadside beside striking (if isolated) ornamental gatepiers with ball finials.

Neidpath Castle, 14th century
Dominating the narrow gorge, massive L-plan, 18x12m, 18m to the parapet, with walls over 3m thick, and vaulted to the third floor (of five), enlarged 1654 (with addition of stables and terraced gardens), while retaining its ancient character – the epitome of Borderland. The gateway keystone carries the goat's head on coronet crest of the Hays, Earls of Tweeddale. In 1795 *Old Q* (the dissolute 4th Duke of Queensberry) cut down the timber around the castle to impoverish the estate before it descended to the heir of entail, the 8th Earl of Wemyss. Fortunately *Q's* gardener, Mr Spalding, managed to salvage the lectern-type

Left *East façade, Black Barony.*
Above *Icehouse*

Sir John Murray of Darnhall, knighted 1592 by James VI, was known as *The Dyker* for his enclosure of the previously open lands of the estate by stone walls, the first in Peeblesshire.

Portmore House, Eddleston, 1 May, 1884
I write this so that if ever it is found in after years it may let the finder know how long it is since the corridor ceiling and frizie was put up and by whom it was done and how long it took for to do it. The master's name was James Annan, plasterer, who has a shop in Edinburgh, Perth and London. Men's names that done the ceiling and frizie, Leonard Grandison, native of Prestonpans, William Hunter, native of Hawick, James McKillop, apprentice, native of Edinburgh. Time taken each was 297 hours and the money was at the rate of six and a half d an hour in Edinburgh and here the same. Hoping that it will be picked up some day from yours truly.
Leonard Grandison
Foreman Plasterer
(found 2 October 1980 in a tin above the ornamental corridor ceiling at Portmore by Leonard Grandison's grandson's workers from the family firm now based in Peebles)

Astonishingly, *Old Q*, **William Douglas**, 1724-1810, 4th Duke of Queensberry, Earl of March and Earl of Ruglen, despite being *famous as a patron of the turf, and infamous for his shameless debaucheries ... died unmarried, worth over a million sterling.* Chambers Biographical Dictionary

sundial, which eventually found its way to the Chambers Institution and from there back to the castle (see colour p.216). *Open to the public*

Neidpath Viaduct, 1864

Marvellous seven-arched curved skew viaduct which adds to the grandeur of its setting, unlike many bridges of today. Redundant now, but originally carrying the Symington, Biggar & Broughton Railway.

Neidpath Viaduct

Gear room, Kirkton Manor Mill

Manor Bridge, 1883, Blyth & Cunningham Graceful five-arch structure, which replaced the ford across the Tweed. **Old Manor Bridge**, *William Duke of Queensberry designed this work and William Earle of March his second sone built the same Anno 1702.* Since the Manor church was in ruins and the charge vacant the minister's stipend was used to pay for this bridge over the Manor Water.

Kirkton Manor Church, 1874,

Brown & Wardrop
Bull-nosed red sandstone oblong building with apse and gable bellcote. Bell dated 1483. Stained-glass windows, 1893, Ballantine & Gardiner and, 1931, Margaret Chilton. Headstone of David (Black Dwarf) Ritchie, erected 1845. **Manse** 1804, T-plan two-storey three-bay harled, with quoins, possibly incorporating earlier building.

Kirkton Manor Mill and smithy,

respectively late 18th and mid-19th century Retaining water-driven milling machinery and forge.

Hallyards, principally 1897, Robert Lorimer
The oldest portion of the house was
demolished, leaving the early Victorian
addition at the south-east end. Original plan
was to build anew but costs restricted scheme
to Lorimer's extension. Pedimented **stables**,
1791. High-walled **garden**, *c.*1800; **statue of
the Black Dwarf**, 1836, Forrest.

Black Dwarf's Cottage, 1802, David Ritchie
Known as the Black Dwarf, Ritchie built
himself a cottage here of alternate layers of
rock and turf, with a thatched roof. Around
1802 this fell into disrepair, and a new one was
built on the landowner, Sir James Naesmyth's
orders, for Ritchie and his sister, with a
division wall to separate the dwellings. While
Bow'd Davie lived the house was thatched.
Later it was slated.

Castlehill Tower, 16th century
Ruined oblong tower, 11x9m, of boulder rubble
with walls 2m thick, built off a rock outcrop.
Only ground and first floors survive at all, both
vaulted, the former two cellars, the latter as a
remnant.

Top *Stables, Hallyards.*
Above *Castlehill Tower*

David Ritchie (1740-1811) was
about 1m tall, the son of a Stobo
slate-quarrier, and had sold brushes
in Edinburgh. Retiring to the
country, he received Sir Walter Scott
in 1797 (while Scott was visiting
Adam Fergusson at Hallyards): *The
Black Dwarf* was published in 1816
after Ritchie's death.

Barns House, 1773-80, Michael Nasmyth
A Georgian mansion with Ionic porch, altered
fenestration and a fine contemporary suite of
stables/offices. Nasmyth was a successful
Edinburgh builder, and father of Alexander
Nasmyth, the painter, whose talents were
recognised by Allan Ramsay. An architect as
well as an artist, success in this latter field was
limited to landscape topics, for Nasmyth Jnr
had liberal political views which were not
shared by the aristocracy.

Alexander Nasmyth (1758-1840)
might be best known for his portrait
of Robert Burns: but his landscape
paintings, for example, of Culzean,
are particularly evocative of the
romantic and picturesque.

Barns House

Right *Stables, Barns House.*
Above *Barns Tower*

Each tower in the Tweed valley was within sight of the next: the beacons would blaze if southern marauders were detected, and the Borderers then rallied in defence of their neighbours.

Barns Tower, later 16th century
Oblong 8.5x6m, whinstone rubble with sandstone margins, dated 1488/9 on (recent) door lintels; converted for use in 18th century by retainers (presumably on completion of Barns House in 1780). Ironically less strongly constructed than the now ruined Castlehill, three floors and attic, the ground floor vaulted, the gabled roof a modern substitute for the original parapet. Possibly the oldest grated iron yett in Scotland – or a late 18th-century replica. Dated 1498, which is unlikely to be accurate, and the working of the date almost certainly is not. A wrought-iron tripod beacon stand from here, with a cast-iron conical container, is in the Chambers' Institution, Peebles.

Haswellsykes, mid-18th-century farm group – courtyard range behind two-storey three-bay slated roof farmhouse with single-storey flanking piended-roof wings. The New Statistical Account declared that *this farm exhibits the finest model of agricultural management which is to be seen in the county.* Unfortunately to an extent these buildings have been been obscured by more modern farm structures.

Lyne Church

Lyne Church, 1644
Rectangular plan with gable bellcote, 1644, dated oak pews and pulpit have survived. Stone font found in wall of church. Windows glazed, 1830. Harling removed. Porch and belfry date from 1889, as does most of interior.

Hallyne House, *c.*1830, Mr Turnbull
Two-storey three-bay, coursed whinstone with raised sandstone quoins. Former Lyne Manse, with irregularly aligned ground-floor windows. Stable range to rear.

Drochil Castle, *c.*1581
For the Regent Morton who was unable to enjoy it, being executed in that year in connection with the murder of Lord Henry Darnley, husband of Mary Queen of Scots in 1567. Subsequently, though, the 5th and 6th Earls considered it occupiable, so the tale that it was never completed seems mythical. A marvellous, massive ruin, at the junction of Tarth and Lyne Waters, 25x21m in whinstone rubble (which may have been harled) with red sandstone dressings, it has an exceptional plan with a central spine corridor (possibly derived from those of Chenonceaux and Chambord, *toute une masse*, or alternatively a double pile version of Huntly, *c.*1560), with an economical pair of 8m diameter towers, the north-east one corbelling from round to square, producing a Z-plan, enfilading all four elevations. Close inspection of the gunloops shows some redenting, to stop the embrasures from funnelling shot into the towers. Note also the fetterlock (a leg-iron) in the centre of the tympanum, the Earl's emblem as Warden of the Borders. Simpson attributes this sophisticated palace design to William Schaw, who became

A **royal palace**, *or seat of a nobleman, once the first man in Scotland, next the king: It is a prodigious building, too great for a subject, begun by the Earl of Morton, whose head being afterwards lay'd in the dust, his design perish'd ... The great Earl of Morton, Regent of Scotland, ... the same that brought the engine to behead humane bodies from Hallifax in Yorkshire, and set it up in Scotland, and had his own heed cut off with it, the first it was try'd upon.*
Daniel Defoe, 1723

James Douglas, Regent Morton, was a younger son who succeeded through his wife (daughter of 3rd Earl) to the title and estates of the Earl of Morton. A party to the assassinations of David Rizzio and Lord Darnley, at one time he was in the pay of Elizabeth Tudor.

North-east tower, Drochil Castle

Gunloop, Drochil Castle

from 1583 to his death in 1602 James VI's Master of Works (see colour p.213).

Drochil Farm, *c*.1824
Two-storey-and-basement, painted, contrasting quoins and dressings, piended roof, sitting rather uncomfortably under the shadow of its older neighbour, from which materials were taken and carried as short a distance as possible!

Newlands Old Kirk
Ancient roofless shell dating from the 13th century, reconstructed in the 14th century, and further altered (doorway dated 1705) better to fit Presbyterian worship (focused on pulpit rather than altar). Interesting blacksmith's tombstone in kirkyard, which is also last resting place of Dr Pennecuik, author of *A Description of the Shire of Tweeddale.*

Newlands Old Kirk

Newlands Manse
At its core the manse of 1740, but externally it wears the garb of the 1839 repairs, two-storey harled and painted. The manse stable has a 13th-century coffin slab and dated stone of 1600 built into it.

Datestone, Newlands Manse

Newlands Parish Church, 1838, James Currie
T-plan, coursed red sandstone, crowstepped gables, lattice glazing, with original pulpit and fittings. Later alterations P MacGregor Chalmers.

Approaching **Stobo** village from the north should be noted **Easter Dawyck** farmhouse, built using stones from the old peel tower on the site by order of Sir Walter Scott's father, who factored here in the latter stages of the 18th century.

Stobo Church, 1863, John Lessels
Remodelling of a parish church of great antiquity (probably Norman) with openings from *c.*1600. The north transept, restored in 1929, James Grieve, probably dates from the 14th or 15th centuries (see colour p.214). Interesting carved medieval slabs inside church, and good gravestones of 17th and 18th centuries in churchyard. Harled and painted **Manse** (now Glebe House) dates from 1791, with Victorian addition. Manse **stables** in whinstone probably *c.*1800.

Stobo Castle, 1805-11,
Archibald & James Elliot
Similar plan form to Inveraray (a square block, corner towers and a central hall lit by clerestorey openings). Porte-cochère and other alterations, 1849, John Lessels. Garden terraces and more alterations, *c.*1907, Peddie &

Stobo Church

The Aberdeen Ecclesiological Society spoke for many when it reported that *No disapprobation can be too strong for some things done at the 'restoration' of the Church of Stobo, where in 1863 an Edinburgh architect actually removed the ancient Norman chancel arch in order to insert a modern pointed one.*

Stobo Castle

Washington Browne. The landscape setting of the castle (now health farm) may owe much to the improvements of James Montgomery who acquired the estate in 1767. The castle's robustly antique Gothic exterior clothes a refined classical sequence of rooms. Also of interest are the Adamesque **Castle Mill** and the **Home Farm**. **East Lodge Cottages** are a pair of late 18th-century cottages in local whinstone, with good ornamental gates and screen railings. West of the Castle lies Quarry Hill, from whence a dark blue *slate* similar in colour to that of

Stobo slate is actually not slate at all, but dark grey-blue micaceous shale up to 500 million years old. Its heavy, hard, slate-like composition is due to pressure over this long timescale, and indeed some of the shale contains fossils. Stobo slate or *scaillie* was difficult enough to extract and then transport by pack-horse. In the railway era the quarry's product could not compete with the more regular, uniform and lighter Welsh slate.

William Burn, 1789-1870, was born in Edinburgh and trained with Sir Robert Smirke in London. Burn's successful Scottish country-house practice expanded into England, and he worked from London after 1844. *His unhappy restoration of St Giles', Edinburgh (1829-33) has been as far as possible undone. Chambers Biographical Dictionary,* 1935

The Arboretum is over three centuries old, the earliest silver firs (some still standing) planted in 1686. Three of the oldest European larches in Scotland survive from a planting in 1725. Many other rare and old trees can be seen here, including the Weeping Spruce introduced from Oregon by F R S Balfour in 1908. Spring and autumn visits are particularly pleasurable in the Garden and Arboretum.

Ballachulish was worked for many centuries, for Craigmillar Castle in 1661, for instance.

Dawyck House, 1832-37, William Burn
A mixture of Scottish Baronial and Elizabethan after the old house of Dawyck burnt down in 1830, with fine contemporary Italianate terraces. Baronial extensions, 1898, by John A Campbell and, 1909, Robert Lorimer. The glorious formal setting was principally laid out by the Naesmyth family, starting in the first half of the 18th century, and the tree-loving Balfours in the 20th century. The **Arboretum** is now an out-station of the Royal Botanic Garden in Edinburgh. Some fine policy buildings include Burn's **Chapel** (1837, reroofed 1898, with insertion of three-light window by Whall, and replacement of the pre-Reformation font and bell salvaged from the previous kirk on this site, suppressed in 1742). *Arboretum open to the public; guidebook available*

Excellent supporting buildings, all just 20th century. **Stables**, centre-gabled courtyard form, entered through brick-arched pend and marked with its own ornamental gates and piers. **Garden cottage**, picturesque single-storey with pentice dormers and porch, leaded windows. **Bellspool cottages**, 1800, but likely explanation is that this row of buildings include architecturally salvaged material. Centre gables, flanking wings, rustic porches. **Main lodge**, Picturesque, with ornamental porch, entrance gates and piers.

Tinnis Castle

Notable 15th- or 16th-century ruin of around 20m square, with 5m diameter towers at each

Right *Dawyck House.* Below *Stables*

Tinnis Castle

corner, built within an Iron Age fort overlooking Drumelzier Haugh and **Merlin's Grave**, from a secure and precipitous site. Large mortared masonry lumps, well-scattered, confirm its destruction by gunpowder in the 16th century, as part of a family feud between the (Drumelzier) Tweedies and the Flemings. Tradition identifies it as the castle of Dunthalmo, who was attacked and slain by Ossian at its gate. Can reality have been less full of such incidents?

Ossian was the poet son of the third-century Gaelic hero, Fingal.

Drumelzier Village contains a whinstone L-shaped range of cottages, complete with smithy, which may be 18th century.

Below *Bellcote, Drumelzier Kirk.* Bottom *Drumelzier Kirk*

Drumelzier Kirk, principally 1872 It may have medieval origins, but little of these have survived the drastic Victorian alterations, which apparently did not follow the motto of the Tweedies (*Thol and Think*), but rather their family crest, the bull's head. The tablet on which both appear is a replacement of 1911, but the vault of 1617 has survived, along with a small *c.*1700 belfry with pyramidal finialed bellcote. Stained glass, 1926, by Marjorie Kemp, one window showing a portion of Dawyck House. **Tinnis House**, formerly Drumelzier Manse, was built in 1787, but has undergone substantial repairs, latterly in 1911. The timber **Drumelzier Parish Hall**, 1939, is by Sir Frank Mears.

Drumelzier Castle
Mere remnant of the largely 16th-century defensive structure from which Tweedie of Drummelzier (*sic*) led his powerful and turbulent clan. Obtained by marriage in the 14th century, only the angle tower and a portion of the main building now remain.

Drumelzier Castle

Below from top *Cardon; Quarter House; Mossfennan House; East Stanhope old mill.* Right *East Stanhope Farmhouse*

According to Chambers, when Drumelzier Castle fell into ruins, it became a *convenient quarry* for building-stone for the farm-steading called **Drumelzier Place**, amidst which it rears (not so high these days) its spectral form.

Wrae Castle
Another stronghold of the Tweedies. Only a rubble stair-tower remains, like a great standing stone.

Cardon, early 19th-century
Harled and limewashed farmhouse, two-storey three-bay, slated roof, with lower offices wing at side and extensive farmbuildings in the valley bottom which, as Quarter, it overlooks.

Quarter House
Eighteenth-century core picturesquely converted around 1860 into a harled and painted, low-gabled mansion with a turreted porch.

Mossfennan House, later 18th century
Bracketed by Victorian extensions to result in a languid composition, a long low harled building with quoins, piended slated roof and pilastered doorpiece.

East Stanhope Farmhouse
Originally 18th century, with the crowstepped front overblown projection a 19th-century addition, and an interesting mill building (boulder quoins, triangular slate wall ventilators) to its rear.

Polmood, 1638; primarily *c.*1887
Gabled house (crowsteps and sills all dressed in lead reflecting the rainfall here), Westmorland slate roofing, rosemary tile ridging, limewashed harl. Fine **lodge**,

contemporary, whinstone with red sandstone dressings, Westmorland slate roof, rosemary tile ridging, marking the access to the house across a river bridge. **Lectern doocot** to east, perhaps from 17th century but remodelled 19th century.

Crook Inn

Apparently in existence around 1604, *the oldest licensed premises in Scotland* (Gordon), and a posting-house and inn for several centuries, its most striking features are now the 1930s windows on the single-storey flat-roofed infill block, the persiennes on the two-storey Georgian block, and the wrought-iron gate set between crooks in a drystane double-coped dyke across the A701.

Top *Polmood*. Above *Lodge, Polmood*. Left *Crook Inn*

Polmood used to be a royal possession. Its charter reads *I, Malcolm Kenmure King, the first of my Reign, gives to the Normand Hunter of Powmood, the Hope, up and Down, above the Earth to Heaven, and below the earth to Hell, as free to thee and thine as ever God gave it to me and Mine, and that a Bow and a broad Arrow when I come to hunt in Yarrow, and for the mair Suith I byte the white Wax with my tooth ...*

Tweedsmuir Parish Church

Bield, 1726 & 1821

Two-storey, L-plan, harled and painted, piended slated-roofed farmhouse, with lying-pane glazing. For many years a coaching-inn, with an open courtyard.

Tweedsmuir Parish Church, 1875,
John Lessels

On a dry-stane-dyked mound which may be natural or pre-Christian. Norman, T-plan, gabled with tower and broach spire, whinstone with red sandstone dressings and spire, doorway inspired by Dryburgh, and war memorial made from oak tree planted by Scott at Abbotsford. Covenanter's grave in kirkyard. Just as thought-provoking memorial to men (more than 30) who died in progress of Talla Water Works.

Tweedsmuir Manse, 1798

Large, plain, two-storey house, datestone 1662 built in from previous manse.

Above *Control tower, Talla Reservoir*. Right *Keeper's house*

Talla Reservoir, 1895-1905
Reservoir system, linked by an aqueduct 36 miles long to Edinburgh consumers. To aid the 650 men employed in the construction a railway was laid up the valley, and removed on completion. Contemporary **keeper's house** and workers' houses, J & A Leslie & Reid.

Nether Whitslade is a pleasant row of three Victorian cottages converted into one house, the original doorways marked by gables.

Whitslade House
Two-storey, harled, pitched slated roof with modern dormers, an 18th-century house with later alterations and extensions, and the remains of the old 16th-century peel tower, only the vaulted ground floor, 8x6m in plan, nearby. **Whitslade Cottages**, a fine range of 18th-century cottages, are part of the courtyard of offices behind the house.

Kilbucho Place 16th century origins
Largely late 17th century in appearance however, crowstepped gables, traditional dormers, and corner turret, as a typical laird's house. Early inscribed pediments are built in. **Entrance gate** framed by acorn-finialed square rusticated 18th-century piers.

Hidden away in a secluded valley setting reached via ruinous farm steadings, **Kilbucho Church**, now ruined, abandoned c.1810, survives as a post-Reformation (18th-century?) shell standing on the eastern half of an earlier building within its sparsely populated graveyard.

Kilbucho Place

Brigadier-General William Davidson was MP, Lieutenant of Cork, and a noted gambler who carelessly managed to lose all his estates but Kilbucho, which his heirs had to turn into a farm.

Kilbucho Old Manse, 1751
Seventeenth-century lintel inserted over the back door. One of the best examples of a Georgian T-plan manse, harled and slated, with

its twin pavilion outbuildings framing the south front, and spiral stair half-round to the rear.

Hartree, 1775-1790
Discordant composition of Georgian origin (absorbing earlier tower fragments), Victorian incorporation, and modern desecration, requires sympathetic selective demolition.

BROUGHTON
Along with the brewery has some pretty ranges of 18th- and 19th-century cottages reconstructed here (many by James Grieve in the 1930s and 1940s), parts of the old village planned in an English character.

Top *Kilbucho Old Manse.*
Above *Hartree*

Left *St Llolan's cell, Broughton Church.* Below *Broughton Church*

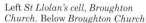

Broughton Church, 1617
Ruin not much more than one whinstone rubble crowstepped bellcoted gable, tin lean-to to inner face. Renovated 1726, abandoned 1803 when new church built at Calzeat. Gable built off *St Llolan's cell* or, more likely, a burial vault possibly 14th century, the cell having been *restored* from virtually a single arch. Kirkyard entered via a pair of immensely heavy cast-iron gates. Gravestone of Revd Hamilton Paul (see p.252, Easter Calzeat), 1854, with a fiddle carved upon it.

Broughton School, from 1876, though principal character is that of 1937 addition (including fine gates and railings) by Reid & Forbes, harled and painted, grey sandstone margins, and Westmorland slate roofs.

Broughton School

John Buchan, 1875-1940, was novelist, historian, biographer, Conservative MP, Governor-General of Canada and Lord Tweedsmuir from 1935.

Hamilton Paul was better known for his interest in literature and music than his eloquence in the pulpit, as a writer himself penning a song *Jeanie of the Crook* about Jeanie Hutchison of the Crook Inn.

Right *Easter Calzeat.*
Below *Broughton Place houses.*
Bottom *Broughton Place with urn*

Calzeat War Memorial, unveiled by John Buchan in 1920, lonely position on the edge of the open view to the west, this obelisk built of grey whin quarried locally at Gameshope.

Calzeat Church, 1803-4, Thomas Brown
After the merger of Broughton, Glenholm and Kilbucho parishes the church, according to Buchan, was *practically rebuilt* in 1886 by Robert Bryden, who came from Broughton, and thereafter *strikingly renovated* in 1937. Now **John Buchan Centre**, set in a sea of red chippings. *Open to the public*

Easter Calzeat, 1815
Former manse: two-storey, harled, three-bay with central projection, quoins and piended slated roof, it owes its setting to the incumbent Revd Hamilton Paul, who reclaimed the glebe from the bog and planted trees.

Broughton Place (Broughton Gallery), 1938, Rowand Anderson Paul & Partners (Basil Spence)
Accessed via a *genuinely* aged range of farm buildings, and past a restrainedly traditional U-plan group of new Spence houses. A great, harled neo-17th-century tower-house, decorative stonework by Hew Lorimer. Now houses the Broughton Gallery. On site of previous house (owned until 1762 by *Apostate* Murray, Secretary to Prince Charlie), burnt down 1773. **Garden house** guarding a concealed tennis court, a surprising feature:

Broughton Place: Above Door knocker. Left Garden house

John (Evidence) Murray, 1715-77, was Prince Charlie's secretary during the 1745 Rising. He returned to Broughton disguised as a drover after the disaster at Culloden, and, too frightened to enter Broughton Place, went to his aunt's at Kilbucho Place. This lady insisted the *drover* dine with the family, which made the servants suspicious, and he was seized at his sister's house at Polmood. He saved his own life by turning King's Evidence, and indeed succeeded to the baronetcy in 1770.

this walled garden has a delicious layout, which also features an enormous urn (see colour p.214). *Open to the public*

SKIRLING

Pretty village with its core around the village green. **War Memorial**, Robert Lorimer, red sandstone, rusticated ashlar plinth with Lorimer monogram, stone flags, square shaft topped with cross. Village Green cottage ranges include the **Piper's House**, so-called because of the Piper statue built-in, perhaps from Skirling Castle which was finally cleared around the Piper's date of 1810.

Skirling House, 1912, Ramsay Traquair Decorative ironwork by Thomas Hadden announces this richly decorated house in the Arts & Crafts tradition (of which Lord Carmichael was a great supporter, even to the extent of sharing the ironwork with Hadden) despite its darkly boarded exterior. Yet a conversion from farmhouse for Carmichael, after financial problems relating to the working out of the family (New Hailes) quarry, forced him to dispose of Castlecraig and his Burrell-like collection. Traquair managed to fit in a 16th-century Italian ceiling Carmichael refused to part with. An earlier plan had been produced in 1906 for a large baronial house by Robert Lorimer (for whom Traquair had worked). Two good **sundials** (one dated 1793

Sir Robert Stodart Lorimer was the son of Prof James Lorimer, professor of international law.

Lord Carmichael was a particular enthusiast for the bee, and founded the Scottish Bee-Keepers' Association in 1891.

Below *Detail, War Memorial.* Bottom *Ironwork, Skirling House*

Carmichael monument, Skirling Parish Church

from Chiefswood, Melrose) set in a sheltered Edwardian garden layout of great charm.

Skirling Parish Church located on its own circular churchyard mound, this rebuilding dates from 1720, renovated 1893 and later for Carmichael, who was also responsible for Hadden's fine wrought-iron gates. **Manse**, from 1803, remodelled in 1837, is harled and painted, with piended slated roof.

Kirkurd Church, 1766
Much recast, harled, T-plan, with gabled bellcote. The square, piended-roof watch- or alms-house is dated 1828, and the graveyard contains good monuments, the most prominent being that of the Gibson-Carmichaels. **Kirkurd House**, 1788, former manse with Victorian twin gables and a large walled garden.

Kirkurd Old Church
Abandoned in 1766 when the new church was built, perhaps related to the acquisition of the estate by Carmichael of Skirling in 1752. Interesting carved gravestones (earliest 1614), and a small pointed barrel-vault, possibly the lairds', perhaps 17th century.

Right *Castlecraig*. Below *Iron beastie, old entrance porch, Castlecraig*

Castlecraig, dated 1798
Three-storey classical mansion, remodelled, 1905, Sir J J Burnet, after the Carmichael fortune declined and the house was sold to James Mann, a Glasgow industrialist. Copper sundial dated 1725 on stone baluster shaft. **Lodges**, also of 1798, although their accompanying screen walls, stylish wrought-iron flower-adorned railings and gatepiers are Edwardian, possibly Burnet's responsibility although the metalwork could also be attributed to Lord Carmichael and Thomas Hadden.

Netherurd House (New Cairnmuir),
1791-4, possibly Robert Burn
Designed in conjunction with the owner.
Palladian mansion, three-storey pedimented
block, random rubble with buff sandstone
dressings. Additions, 1856, include rear wing
terminating in a turret. **Netherurd Home
Farm** with its raised entrance arch feature,
cupola-topped, is contemporary with the
House. **Whalebone arch** entrance was rebuilt
in the 1960s when the road was realigned.

Above *Lodge, Castlecraig.* Left
Principal façade, Netherurd House

Left *Whalebone arch.* Below *Kirkurd
War Memorial*

Kirkurd War Memorial takes the form of an
unusual conical stone monument erected by
Lady Carmichael.

Blyth Bridge Old Mill, 1817
Still carrying on the datestone the information
meal per peck this year – 2/6. The mill wheel,
1.2m x 4.6m diameter, has survived the
conversion to an inn.

Scotstoun

RCAHMS

Scotstoun, *c.*1770
Long slim plan, one room deep, pedimented
and pilastered three-storey three-bay central
portion; marvellous plasterwork in drawing
and dining rooms, two-storey three-bay *wings*,
all piended. **Scotstoun stable square**, 1770.

Romanno Bridge as a hamlet developed
around a grain mill in the early 19th century,
latterly converted to the tweed. Though the
bridge itself was built in 1774, the adjacent
Romanno Toll-house dates from *c.*1830.

On this popular drove route, in
1832, the Romanno Toll-house
derived more than 50% of its income
from cattle passing south.

There were coal mine workings
too at Macbiehill, the mine being
entered by a spiral stair. This
allowed children (from the age of
six) to return to the adjacent
cottages for their *pieces* at
lunchtime.

Halmyre House
Substantially extended and remodelled in
1856, the lower storey contains two vaulted
apartments, suggestive of 16th- or 17th-
century origins as a fortified house. Large
walled garden.

Kaimes House, *c.*1920
Built for Sir Ronald J Thomson. Additions/
alterations, 1931, Dick Peddie & Walker Todd.

Below *Macbiehill*.
Bottom *Macbiehill limekiln*

RCAHMS

RCAHMS

Macbiehill, 1835, William Burn
Incorporated ancient tower-house. Demolished,
1950s. Harled Gothick-windowed piended
slated roofed **lodge**, *c.*1820, with late 18th-
century rusticated gatepiers. **Macbiehill
vault**, square mausoleum of the Beresfords,
ashlar, *c.*1768, repaired 1974. Macbiehill
limekiln, early 19th-century, two-draw kiln,
with extensive workings in the vicinity.

Lamancha House, from 1663
Originally Grange (of Romanno), name
changed due to 18th-century owner who had
resided (presumably happily) in Spain.
Lengthened and improved *c.*1736, the major
transformation occurred after 1831, when coal-
pits were sunk, and limekilns, brick- and tile-
works were built on the estate. Reduction and

Lamancha House

remodelling, 1927, J Drummond Beaton. Note the unique 17th-century **sundial**, *fugit hora*, lectern-shaped dial set on a basket of fruit, all on a later pedestal. Urn-topped rusticated entrance piers. William Boucher, Adam's rival, drew up a scheme (1728-33), incorporating parterre, canal, and avenue, completely impractical on the boggy site. His client scrawled across the (unpaid) design bill *Moss wher the Divel wont grow* and *No part of this plan execut nor would the Brute alter though often desird to do it.*

Below *West elevation, Whim house.*
Bottom *Portico, Whim House stables*

Whim House, 1734

Neoclassical pile with major additions and alterations which included a south (library) wing, 1759-61, John Adam. Hotel since 1956, now old folk's home. On impulse the Earl of Ilay acquired the Estate (then known as Blair-Bog) in 1730 with the experimental intention of turning morass into cultivable land.
Doocot, *c.*1740, stump of circular doocot.
Icehouse, *c.*1745, ovoid, ashlar-faced.
Cowden Lodge, stone lodge, alcove between triple windows and **Whim Square**, range of grand offices, attr David Henderson, both late 18th century. Cistern relocated, Gothick pedimented archway.

Spitalhaugh, 1678

Transformed *c.*1860, it is difficult to see beyond this house's present Victorian picturesque (turreted, battlemented and greatly extended) appearance. Contains well-preserved carved stone panels by James Gifford (see Gifford Panels over).

WEST LINTON
Parish Church, 1784
Neat and compact kirk, renovated and reopened 1871 when spire added to belfry tower, Gothic windows inserted. Internal carving by Jane Fergusson (daughter of Queen Victoria's surgeon) and Mrs Allan Woddrop. Stained glass, *c*.1960, Sadie McLellan (or Pritchard). In the kirkyard excellent carved gravestones; gateposts, 1601. Two bee boles set in ruined gable of earlier manse.

Raemartin Hotel, 1789
Two-storey, four-bay, painted, with rolled skews to the main street. Opposite are the **Gifford**

Parish Church: Top Memorial panel. Middle Bee boles. Above Gifford Panels

At the end of the 17th century, there were silver and lead mines in the West Linton area.

Alexander Pennecuik described the more self-important of local worthies thus *the numerosity, pettiness, pride, contempt of industry and consequent poverty of the Lairds and Portioners about Lintoun, have always been the subject of amusement and ridicule. It is a standing joke in the county that at one time there were no fewer than five and forty of them, and that, of these, no fewer than fifteen got assistance from the poor's fund.*

Panels. These delicately carved stone panels were salvaged, 1864, from James Gifford's house when it was demolished. Gifford, a mid-17th-century stonemason, may also have carved the cubical sundial on the south-west corner of the house. The carving of gravestones, and stonecarving in general, was long-established in the village, due no doubt to the good supply of suitable stone. Gifford erected a statue of his wife and family in 1666. It originally served as a market cross but has now found itself atop the **well** and **clock-tower**, as *A lively specimen of natural genius without the assistance of art* according to Armstrong. Originally there was a child's statue at each corner of the square base. Apparently when a fifth child came along Gifford had no alternative but to position it on the top of his wife's head.

Garvald House (Garvald Foot), *c*.1830-40
Classical fronted, with Ionic portico. Offices range entered through pedimented archway with bellcote, built-in doocot in roadside gable.

Medwynhead House, 1797, rubble one-and-a-half-storey, slated roof with crowstepping.

Deepsykehead was a significant white freestone quarry which supplied all Tweeddale. **Limekiln. House**, c.1760, was built for the quarry-manager. Broomieleas was a similar provider of red sandstone, particularly paving flags.

CARLOPS

Village founded, 1784, by Robert Brown, the Laird of Newhall (just over the boundary in Lothian) for cotton-weaving, which with woollen manufacturing in 1800 then declined when steam power overtook water. Highly picturesque group now straddling a dangerous road. This locality was the setting of many literary works, including *The Gentle Shepherd* by Allan Ramsay.

Allan Ramsay Hotel, 1792 (possibly a store for webs of cloth, but an Inn from at least mid-19th century). **Paties Mill**, foundations dug 1801 for farmhouse, originally designed as a woollen manufactory, then converted to a corn mill. **Carlops Mains**, 1804, originally an inn, two-storey three-bay house.

Left *Garvald House, 1974.* Above *Memorial* Wilson Stout, *West Linton Parish Church*

Allan Ramsay (1686-1758) was born at Leadhills to the manager of Lord Hopetoun's mines and the daughter of a Derbyshire mining engineer. Father of the renowned portrait-painter of the same name, he had a prosperous career as wigmaker, satirist, poet, bookseller, librarian and playwright. Not only did he produce miscellanies of (old) songs and poems, but his play *The Gentle Shepherd* (1725) was found in 1856 still to be performed by Pentland peasants for their entertainment. His earliest surviving poem, *To the Most Happy Members of the Easy Club*, was about a drinking club.

Evaluation drawing, west side of Main Street, Carlops

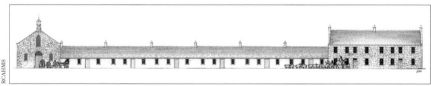

Today we live in difficult times. The steam-roller of progress is flattening out many of our old institutions and there is a great danger of a great decline in idiom and distinctive quality in our Scottish life. The only way to counteract this peril is to preserve jealously all these elder things which are bone of our bone and flesh of our flesh. For, remember, no man can face the future with courage and confidence unless it is solidly founded upon the past. And conversely, no problem will be too hard, no situation too strange if we can link it with what we know and love.
John Buchan (Lord Tweedsmuir) speaking as warden of Neidpath Castle at the Beltane Festival of Peebles in 1935

ACKNOWLEDGEMENTS & REFERENCES

Susie, Sarah and Caroline Strang have put up with various detours and delays in their Borders trips, to satisfy their father's curiosity: I hope they consider the waiting worthwhile. Particular thanks are also due to those responsible for the Buildings of Scotland Archive, a source of much useful data and inspiration; to RIAS staff, particularly Helen Leng, for their harrying and enthusiasm, and to the staff of the NMRS, notably Ian Gow, for hospitality above and beyond the call of duty; and to colleagues, old and new, who have also endured with equanimity my elephantine gestation.

The photographer or photographic source is credited alongside each picture. The RCAHMS has been the principal fount. Others worthy of special mention are Borders Regional Council and Berwick-upon-Tweed Borough Council (from the Berwick Borough Archives in the Berwick-upon-Tweed Record Office).

REFERENCES

Restricted space makes for an unscholarly but I hope adequate bibliography of principal sources. The Buildings of Scotland Archive is a gold-mine, there are numerous individual articles of note, and the Borders is not short of close-focus studies (of varying quality) of localities.

ALISON, James P, **The Parish Churches of Wilton**; BAIRD, **Annals of a Tweeddale Parish**; BERWICKSHIRE NATURALISTS CLUB, **Proceedings**; BILLINGS, Robert, **Baronial & Ecclesiastical Architecture of Scotland**; BROWN, Hume, **History of Scotland**; BROWN, Joe, and LAWSON, Iain, **A History of Peebles 1850-1990**; BUCHAN, J W, **A History of Peeblesshire**; CARMICHAEL, Lord Carmichael of Skirling – **A Memorial Prepared by his Wife**; CHAMBERLIN, Russell, **English Country Town**; CHAMBERS, Robert, **Picture of Scotland, Biographical Dictionary of Eminent Scotsmen** , 1935 (ed); CIVIC SOCIETY, BERWICK-UPON-TWEED, **Various Guides**; CLIFTON-TAYLOR, Alec, **Six More English Towns**; COLVIN, Howard, **Biographical Dictionary of British Architects 1600-1840**; COWE, Francis, **Short Historical Guide to Berwick-upon-Tweed**; DEPARTMENT OF ENVIRONMENT, **Lists of Buildings of Special Architectural or Historic Interest**; DUNBAR, John, **Historic Architecture of Scotland**; GORDON, Anne,**To move with the Times**; GRAHAM, Frank, **Castles of Northumberland**; GROOME, Francis, **Ordnance Gazetteer of Scotland**; HALL, Marshall, **Artists of Northumbria**; HAY, Geoffrey, **Architecture of Scottish Post-Reformation Churches 1560-1843**; HANDLEY, James E, **Scottish Farming in the Eighteenth Century**; HOPE, Annette, **A Caledonian Feast**; HUME, John, **Industrial Archaeology of Scotland**; LAMONT-BROWN, Raymond, **Life and Times of Berwick-upon-Tweed**; LYNCH, Michael, **Scotland, a new history**; MACAULAY, James, **The Gothic Revival 1745-1845**; MACGIBBON & ROSS **Castellated & Domestic Architecture of Scotland**; MYLNE, Robert, **The Master Masons to the Crown of Scotland**; NEWTON, Robert, **Northumberland Landscape**; PEVSNER, Nikolaus and RICHMOND, Ian A, **Buildings of England: Northumberland**; ROYAL COMMISSION ON THE ANCIENT & HISTORICAL MONUMENTS OF SCOTLAND, **Berwickshire Inventory; Peebleshire Inventory; Roxburghshire Inventory; Selkirkshire Inventory**; HISTORIC SCOTLAND, **Descriptive Lists of Buildings of Special Architectural or Historic Interest**; MACKENZIE, Agnes Mure, **Scottish Pageant**; MAIR, Craig, **Mercat Cross and Tolbooth**; McCALLUM, Neil, **A Small Country**; SAVAGE, Peter, **Lorimer and the Edinburgh Craft Designers**; SCOTTISH DEVELOPMENT DEPARTMENT HISTORIC BUILDINGS & MONUMENTS DIRECTORATE, **Descriptive Lists of Buildings of Special Architectural or Historic Interest**; SCOTTISH HISTORY SOCIETY, **Lady Grizell Baillie's Household Book, 1692-1733**; SPENCER, Brian, **New Shell Guides: North-East England**; STATISTICAL ACCOUNTS OF SCOTLAND, **First, Second and Third Statistical Accounts**; TAIT, Alan, **Landscape Garden in Scotland 1735-1835**; TOMLINSON, W W, **Comprehensive Guide to Northumberland**; TRANTER, Nigel, **Fortalices and Early Mansions of Southern Scotland**; WILLSHER, Betty, **Understanding Scottish Graveyards**; WILSON J M, **Imperial Gazetteer of Scotland**.

In addition to the maps, local museums may hold copies of more historic layouts, and these, including the following are recommended: WOOD, J, c.1824 Kelso; 1824 Hawick, Galashiels; 1826 Melrose. AINSLIE, J, 1772 Jedburgh, S.E. Scotland. TENNANT, Walter, 1850 Hawick. SLATER, Commander, 1842 Eyemouth. ROY, General, 1755 Military map of Scotland.

Acanthus In architecture a plant, conventionally treated with symmetrically lobed and scalloped leaves, forming the lower part of the *Corinthian capital* and other types of leaf ornament

Accretions External additions with little or no relationship to the design of the original building

Acroterion Technically, a *plinth* at the apex or end of a *pediment*, for statues or ornaments : more loosely, both the *plinth* and what stands upon it

Aisle Ayle, eyll, an internal subdivision of a church, formed by an *arcade* separating it from the main body of the *nave* or *chancel*, or, enclosed and covered (family) burial-place adjoining church, *mausoleum*

Altars Communion tables

Apse A projection, semicircular or polygonal on plan, from the wall of a church or other building

Apsidal Shaped like an *apse*

Arcaded With a series of arched openings defined by *columns* or piers

Architrave The lowest of the three main divisions of the *classical entablature*, varying to the order employed; *moulded surround* to an opening or recess

Art deco Style of architecture and interior design at its height in the 1930s, characterised by geometrical shapes

Art nouveau Style of architecture and art of *c.*1880 to 1914, characterised by sinuous, sensuous outlines and stylized natural forms

Arts & Crafts Late 19th- and earlier 20th-century movement in architecture and furnishing based on the revival of traditional crafts and the use of natural materials, usually English *vernacular* in character

Ashlar Masonry of large blocks in regular courses worked to even faces and carefully squared edges: the stones themselves are called ashlars and may have a *polished, stugged, droved* or *rock-faced* finish

Ball-finialed Having a *finial* in the shape of a ball or globe

Balustraded With a *parapet* or stair rail composed of uprights supporting a coping or rail

Bargeboards Boards fixed along the edge of a *gable* of a building, to cover the ends of the roof timbers and prevent rain driving in: (surprisingly, therefore) often pierced, *traceried* or carved

Barmkin Outer fortification of castle, also sometimes the area between the outer defensive wall and a central tower

Baronial Style of architecture of the 19th century characterised by neo-medieval features such as towers, *crowstepping, corbels* and *heraldic* panels

Baroque 17th-/18th-century style, developed in Italy, characterised by exuberant decoration, expansive curvaceous forms, sense of mass and delight in both the large scale and the complex in composition

Baroque-nouveau Revival of the *baroque* in a more free and easy, occasionally *mannerist* style

Barrel-vaulted Continuous vault of semicircular cross-section

Bastel-house, bastle Block house, *fortified house,* place of retreat (Old French, bastile = building)

Battered Inclined, as of an external wall surface, usually at its base, the thickness of the wall being progressively diminished

Bay The unit of building between piers or *buttresses*, or defined by windows

Bee bole Small recess in a wall to accommodate a bee skep (a straw hive)

Beehive Doocot Circular *doocot* with a domed roof

Bellcast Slight flattening of roof pitch towards the eaves

Bellcote Open stone (mostly) frame, generally cubical in shape, in which a bell is hung

Belvedere A raised turret from which to view the surrounding scenery: a gazebo

Blazon *Heraldic* coat-of-arms

Block cornice Blocking-course: course of stone laid on top of a *cornice*, crowning the wall

Block and sneck Coursed masonry composed of stones large (blocks) and small (snecks) set in a regular decorative pattern

Blocked Ionic columns *Ionic columns* interrupted vertically by regular projecting blocks, as on the side of a *Gibbs' surround*

Bow-headed Round-headed

Bows Bays

Box pews Church pews completely enclosed with high timber sides, generally panelled, and with a small door for access

Breakfronted With part of the front elevation (usually the central portion) projecting forward of the rest

Broached ashlar Stonework worked to a horizontally or diagonally furrowed surface (a broach is a mason's sharp-pointed chisel)

Broach spire Spire rising direct from tower, not from within a parapet

Bull-faced stonework *Ashlar* with hewn *margins* or edges, but with the centre of the face left rough and proud (projecting beyond the face of the *margins*

Butterfly plan Plan with central stair and axis, and pair of wings

Buttress A projecting support against a wall to stabilise or to counter the thrust of an arch or vault

Byre Farm building where cattle are kept

Cairn Mound of stones erected as a memorial or marker

Cans (lumpig, lumtile) Chimneypots

Cap-house (capehouse, copehouse) Watch turret on top of a *keep* – or small chamber at top of spiral stair, surmounted by a caproof or roof of conical shape

Cartouche A *tablet* with an ornate frame, usually enclosing an inscription or coat of arms

Castellate Construct a fortified building

Cast-iron Iron containing so much

carbon that it cannot be worked or wrought but must be cast into shape

Catslide dormers Ones formed by sweeping a section of roof up from the main plane at a slacker pitch

Catton clay (cat & clay) Walls of wicker or straw finished with clay plaster on both sides: or walls of moulded clay and straw blocks, sometimes built between timber framing

Celtic cross A Latin cross with a broad ring surrounding the point of intersection

Cenotaph Funerary monument (which is **not** a burial place)

Ceramic Fired clay

Chamfered Cut at a 45-degree bevel

Chancel That part of a church, east of the *nave* or *crossing,* in which the *altar* is placed

Channelled Recessed

Chevron-patterned Zig-zag-patterned, from the French word for a pair of rafters in this configuration (in heraldry, a chevron is a charge of pointed *gable* form)

Chimneypiece Also known as a mantelpiece, the frame (wood or stone usually) surrounding a fireplace, frequently including an overmantel or mirror above

Chimneystack Masonry or brickwork containing several flues, projecting above the roof and (usually) terminating in stone *cope* and *cans*

Chippendale-type In the style of Thomas Chippendale, furniture designer and manufacturer: characterised by use of Chinese and Gothic motifs, cabriole legs, and massive carving

Choir (quire) Part of a church, between the *nave* and presbytery, for the choir

Clasping buttresses *Buttresses* notched into the object which they support

Classical A style imitating or inspired by ancient Greece or Rome

Clerestory A lighting storey or range of windows in the highest part of a building, especially the *nave* or *chancel* of a church

Clustered columns A compound shaft, a pier with several column shafts, attached or detached

Cobbled Stone-finished with rounded stones, usually of *whin*

Concrete tile Cast cement-based roofing element fixed to timber battens

Consoles Ornamental *scrolled* brackets, normally in stone or timber

Contextualism A design approach which takes architectural references for a new development sympathetically from its surroundings, in terms of *townscape*, scale, materials or details – occasionally all four

Cooper A maker or mender of barrels

Copes Stone capping to wall or chimney which overhangs allowing dispersal of water

Corbels Projecting stones supporting 'a superincumbent weight'

Corinthian column A *classical* order

featuring an intricately moulded capital with *acanthus* leaves

Cornice Projecting uppermost member of the *classical entablature*; in isolation used as the crowning feature of external walls, or as the demarcation of an attic storey; or at windowheads, over shops, and internally at the junction of wall and ceiling

Corrugated iron A thin sheet of iron given transverse strength by its formation with alternating troughs and ridges

Cotswold Tudor English neo-medieval style loosely based on the domestic details of Cotswold village architecture

Cottages-ornée Artfully rustic buildings, usually of asymmetrical plan, often *thatched*, a product of the *Picturesque* cult of the late 18th/early 19th century, creating arcadian buildings not always in arcadian settings

Crenellated Battlemented, with square indentations at intervals along a *parapet*

Cresting Ornamental finish on a wallhead, beam or roof, usually ceramic or iron

Crossing-tower A church tower above the crossing, that is, that part of a cross-shaped church plan where the *transepts* cross the *nave*

Crosslets Small cruciform openings, possibly *blind*

Crown glass Glass blown in large circular discs and then cut into panes

Crowstepped Of a *gable* having a stepped profile

Cuddy gaol A small cabin (Dutch Kajute) built into the underside of a bridge (perhaps so that the prisoner (a suspected witch) can be positioned securely – above running water)

Cupola Small domically roofed structure crowning a roof or dome

Curtain wall A wall which connects two or more towers or bastions

Cutwaters Projecting elements of bridge piers, usually either v-shaped or semicircular

Decorated 14th-century style of architecture characterised by geometrical *tracery* (*ogee* curves) and floral decoration

Dentilled Carrying dentils, rectangular blocks tightly spaced like teeth, in a dentil course below the main projecting member of the *cornice*

Domestic Institutional A large-scale building disguised as a linked group of houses

Doorcase or doorpiece *Architrave*

Doric A *classical* order with simple fluted columns and plain capitals

Dormers Windows placed vertically in a sloping roof, with roofs of their own

Double-pile plan Plan where an oblong block of double-room width is bisected on its long axis by a central corridor

Double span roof One which is composed of two ridged roofs and a central valley

Dressings Blocks of smooth hewn stone generally as *quoins* or rybats, sometimes also *lintels* and sills

Drip-moulded With horizontal *mouldings* to throw off water

Droved ashlar Smooth stonework finished with a series of parallel lines giving a fine corrugated texture

Dry-dash 20th-century method of *harling* in which the aggregate is thrown on dry and thus sticks on the outside of the mix, rather than being incorporated into it

Dutch-gabled *Gables* of *scrolled* and/or stepped form

Dykes Low walls of stone (or turf, technically) built without mortar

Early English Earliest English Gothic style *c.*1180-1280, characterised by lancet windows and stiff-leaf adornments

Early French Gothic Style of *c.*1140-80, characterised by *pointed* arches and rib vaults

Early Gothic See *Early English*

Eaves course Row or rows of (sometimes contrasting) roof material at the foot of the roof

Edwardian Of the period of King Edward I of England or, more usually, of the period of King Edward VII (1901-10)

Embrasures Small openings in walls or parapets of a fortified building, usually splayed on the inside

Enceinte The main enclosure of a fortress, surrounded by the wall and/or ditch

Encincturing Enclosing or encircling

Enfilading towers Towers from which gunfire can be directed along the length of the main wall(s)

Engaged Tuscan porch A porch with its *Tuscan columns* attached to, or partly sunk into, the main elevation wall

Entablature Collective name for the three horizontal members (*architrave*, *frieze* and *cornice*) above a *column* in *classical* architecture, but frequently found as a wallhead treatment, as a division between storeys or as an impost band at an *arcade*

Eyecatcher A decorative building, such as a mock ruin, usually built on a rise in a designed landscape or parkland to terminate a view or otherwise punctuate it

Façade The face of a building, especially the main front

Faceted Cut like a gemstone

Facings Dressed pieces of timber, sometimes moulded, generally applied to door and other frames to cover joints between timber and the plastered surface of a wall – a type of *architrave*, but simpler and smaller

Fanlight Glazed area above door; if rectangular rather than semicircular, semi-elliptical or segmental, more correctly a transom-light

Fetterlock Kind of padlock, probably originating from fetherlok, a lock which has a feather spring: in heraldry, a handcuff

Finial (Ornamental) top to a *gable*, *pinnacle* or spire

Fire insurance mark Metal plate fixed prominently to building, bearing motif of insurance company so that the appropriate (private) fire brigades could extinguish or ignore the fire with some certainty

First Pointed Gothic 12th-century French Gothic style characterised by pointed arches and geometric *traceried* windows

Fish-scale slates Slates with their lower edges trimmed into a scalloped or fish-scale shape, laid in a decorative pattern

Fleur-de-lis Stylised heraldic lily-flower with three distinct petals

Fluted With rounded shallow concave grooves (on the shaft of a *column* or *pilaster*)

Foil In architecture, a leaf-shaped curve, of three, four, five or more arcs, formed by the cusps of an arch or other opening, or in panelling

Forestair Outside stair usually at street side of house, giving access to the principal apartments on the first floor

Fortified house Defensive dwelling to enable residents to survive guerrilla raids: characterised by secure vaulted ground-floor space for beasts, first-floor entrance and one or more additional floors over, with relatively few (sometimes only one) rooms per floor

14th-century English Decorated Gothic Second of the three periods of *Gothic* architecture, characterised by the use of *ogee* curves

Free Renaissance *Mannerist* or 'proto-baroque', using *classical* elements in vivid, virile, intense, sometimes restless and confused, ways

French Renaissance Style characterised by *classical* elements, freely interpreted, with *mansard* roofs and otherwise lively skylines

Frieze In *classical* architecture, the member in the *entablature* of an order that occurs between the *architrave* and the *cornice*: also applied to a band below a ceiling *cornice*

Gable End wall of building, (usually) at right angles to front wall

Garden front The more private and usually more humanely scaled of the two main elevations of a house

Garden house Summerhouse, plaisance

Gargoyled Carrying grotesque animals or figures acting as water spouts

Gazebo Small *garden house*

Genius loci Particular sense, spirit or qualities of a place

Georgian Literally, belonging to the time of the Georges (I-IV) as kings of the UK

Georgian Revival Neo-*Georgian*

Giant Order Using *columns* or *pilasters* which rise through two or more *storeys*

Gibbsian (of a *surround*) – composed of either alternating larger and smaller blocks of stone set quoinwise, or of intermittent large blocks, often connected by a narrow raised band – named after the architect James Gibbs (1682-1754), an Aberdonian who trained in Italy with Carlo Fontana

Gingerbread gables Showy and relatively insubstantial *gables*

Gothic 'Roll and fillet': style of architecture originally prevalent in Western Europe 12th - 16th century whose chief characteristic is the pointed arch: initially **any** non-*classical* architecture

Gothic Revival Style of late 18th century and 19th century, in a conscious choice of 'medieval' Gothic elements

Gothick window Gothic Revival window, of pointed arch or *lancet* form, sometimes with pointed *tracery* or glazing bars too

Greek Revival Neo-*classical* style, particularly using Greek ornament, pattern, and other architectural features

Gunloops Openings through which to discharge firearms

Gushet Triangular-shaped area of land, or street (Old French, gousset – hollow of armpit)

Ha-ha A sunken ditch to keep livestock out of gardens without the need for a visually obtrusive fence or wall

Half-timbered Exposed timber-framed (structural or otherwise) with the spaces infilled by render, plaster, stone or brickwork

Hammerbeam roof A *gabled* roof supported by timber brackets without tie-beams

Hanging garden terraces Gardens constructed along the contours of a steeply sloping site

Harled Externally finished with *roughcast*, a mixture of lime, sand, small stones and water, cast wet against the wall, to provide a protective covering over rubble or brickwork

Heir of entail One who is to succeed to a property with a fixed line of descent

Helicopter architecture A building or buildings which have been constructed apparently independently of context: usually, but not exclusively, by an architect (or more likely a non-architect) with little or no appreciation or knowledge of the proposed site, as if the building was dropped from the air by helicopter: the opposite of *contextualism*

Heraldic Relating to armorial bearings, symbols and colours of a particular family or place name

Hipped (of a roof) – pitched back at the end rather than being formed with a *gable*

Hog-backed monuments Ridge-backed grave covers, some of the earliest Scottish gravestones

Hood-moulding Projecting *moulding* on face of wall above an arched opening, generally following the arch shape, to shed rainwater from the opening

Hopper *Rain-water head* receiving water from rhones or gutters

Horranising *Cobbling* with small slim stones or pebbles set on edge, often in attractive patterns

Ice house Vaulted or domed chamber,

banked over with earth, which was filled with ice for domestic purposes or commercial fish distribution

In antis In a *portico* when it recedes into a building and the columns range with the side walls

Intersolls Intermediate or mezzanine floors

Ionic A *classical* order characterised by the volutes or scrolls of its capital

Jacobean Generally pertaining to the style of the reign of James VI of Scotland, I of England

Jamb Side part of door, window, or fireplace opening

Joggled lintel A *lintel* constructed of stones indented to prevent them from sliding

Joiner's workshop glazing Timber fixed-light windows with narrow vertical proportions, glazed with overlapping, irregularly rectangular sections of thin horticultural or otherwise cheap, flawed glass

Jougs Iron shackles used for the punishment of minor delinquents

Keep The strongest tower in a medieval castle, sometimes called the donjon

Keystones Central stones of arches or rib vaults

Killing-house Abattoir (usually open, with high walls and killing booths)

Lade Mill-stream, channel for mill stream, a diversion from the main river (Old Scots, mill-race)

Laird's loft Private church gallery reserved for laird (landowner) and family, usually in the *chancel* arch

Lanceted With slender openings with pointed-arch heads (characterising the *Early English* style)

Lattice-windowed Windows with diamond-shaped leaded lights

Lectern doocot Rectangular or square on plan, with lean-to roof sloping downwards, usually towards the (warm) south, sometimes with pigeon port (small *dormer* with *penthouse* roof) in middle of roof

Lenticular truss A bi-convex lens-shaped (in elevation) structural element

Limekiln Large free-standing oven into which layers of limestone and coal or wood were dropped, the fire being lit from below, the lime product being used for agricultural improvement or building mortar, harl, or paint

Lime mortar Mixture of lime, sand and water

Limewashed Whitewashed (generally, although often colour-washed) with lime

Lintels Timber, stone or concrete beams over openings (French linteuil)

Lofts Blocks of seats or pews in gallery of church, originally occupied by important personage, family or guild

Louping-on-stane Stone steps to assist persons to mount horse: mounting block

Lucarne A small opening, usually gabled, in a roof or spire to admit light

Lugged window surrounds Surrounds with 'ears' (Scots lugs), or sideways projecting pieces at their heads

Lying-paned Panes which are horizontally rather than vertically proportioned, fashionable in the period 1815-50

Machicolations Openings in floor of projecting *parapet* through which stones etc can be dropped on assailants

Malt-kiln roof Conical or pyramidal roof like that of an oast-house

Mannerist Style using motifs deliberately counter to their original significance or context: or, sometimes, as a perversely deliberate *classicism*

Mansard Roof in four pitches, with a steep lower pitch and a shallower upper pitch on each side

Manse Dwelling-house of a Scottish minister of religion

Margins The framing of an opening or the angle of a building; most are raised (usually but not exclusively adopted when the building was designed to be *harled*) but some are chamfered and some are backset (i.e. recessed from the plane of the *harl* or *render*)

Marriage lintel *Lintel* stone carrying on the exposed vertical face carved initials (usually of owner and wife) and date of house

Masons' marks Symbols on hewn stones, always on side to be exposed (and generally on specially dressed stones, *lintels*, sills, *quoins*, for example) indicating the mason responsible (so they could be paid pro rata, presumably)

Mausoleum Magnificent and stately tomb (derived from tomb of Mausolus at Halicarnassus)

Moat Wide (water-filled) ditch surrounding a fortified place (Old French **motte** mound)

Modelled Three-dimensional

Modillioned cornice A *cornice* with small brackets, sometimes scrolled, sometimes block-like, set at regular intervals in its *soffit*

Mort bell A bell tolled to alert the community to a death in its midst

Mortsafe Iron frame or grid placed over grave in graveyard as protection against bodysnatchers or 'resurrectionists'

Motte and bailey Mound with defensive enclosure round base

Mullioned windows With upright members dividing their lights

Mural tablet Wall-mounted or built-in inscribed slab

Musicians' gallery Internal balcony, medieval origins, overlooking hall, from which music could be played

Nave The western (main) part of the church, as opposed to the *chancel*

Neoclassical 18th-century style – usually solid, linear, rather severe and precise, in contrast to the late *baroque* and *rococo*

Niches Recesses in walls or *buttresses*, commonly for statues

Norman *Romanesque* architecture, from *c.*1050 to *c.*1200

Obelisk Lofty pillar of square section tapering at the top and ending pyramidally

Oculi Round window (singular = oculus)

Ogee Double curve composed of two curves in opposite directions without a break: used on both arches and roofs

Ogival-roofed Carrying a roof of an *ogee* section

Oriel window A window projected on *corbelling*

Outshots Outbuildings, projections of building or wall

Overshot wheel A mill wheel to which the water from the *lade* is delivered at the top and over, leaving in the opposite direction from which it has come

Palatium A palace; i.e. an oblong building distinct as a structural type from either the hall or the tower

Palladian A *neoclassical* style of architectural design named after Andrea Palladio, its originator

Panelled piers Wall sections finished in a series of flat units

Pantile Clay single-lap hand-made tile in s-shaped section, with a nib to locate it on (timber) tile battens

Parapet A low wall protecting a rooftop walkway

Parterre Formally patterned flower garden

Paterae In *Gothic* architecture, a small ornament usually taking the form of a four-petalled flower, normally set at intervals in a moulding

Pavilions Ornamental buildings, pleasure- or summer-houses, or projecting subdivisions usually terminating the wings of some large building

Pedestals Strictly, the bases supporting *columns*, but usually the bases for a structure or any superstructure

Pedimented Carrying a *classical* form of *corniced gable* or gablet: used at openings as well as a termination to roof structures

Peel tower, Pele tower (Small) houses or towers within enclosures (originally bordered by timber stakes)

Pend Archway, covered way or passage, usually vehicular as opposed to the normally pedestrian close

Penthouse roof Separately roofed structure on the main roof

Pentice dormers Lean-to (monopitch) *dormers*

Pergola Covered walk in a garden, usually formed by double rows of posts or pillars, with connecting joists, covered with climbing plants

Peristyled With a surrounding range of *columns*

Perpendicular Gothic Style of *English Gothic* which followed *Decorated*, from c.1130 to c.1500, characterised by the strongly vertical lines of its *tracery*

Persiennes External slatted window shutters

Piazza basement Colonnaded but integral lower part of building

Picturesque Term defined in the later 18th century as an aesthetic quality in architecture and landscape design: in architecture P- is normally applied to asymmetrically composed buildings of the 18th and early 19th century, particularly in the *castellated*, Italianate and *cottage* styles

Piended *Hipped*

Pilastered Carrying flat versions of *columns*, slim rectangular projections from a wall: without *classical* orders more correctly termed pilaster strips

Piles In *heraldry*, a series of triangular wedge-shaped figures issuing from the top of the shield and pointing downwards: in engineering, long *columns* (timber, concrete or steel) driven into the ground as a foundation for a structure

Pinnacles Vertical structures resembling small turrets

Piscina A basin in which the chalice and priest's hands are washed, usually set in a *niche* or recess to the south of the *altar*, and provided with a drain discharging through the thickness of the wall

Platformed roof Flat roof

Plinth The projecting base of a wall or *column*

Podium A continuous base or *plinth* supporting *columns*

Pointed openings Window or door openings produced by two curves, each with a radius equal to the span

Polished margins Stone *margins* rubbed free from chisel or saw marks

Portico Roofed space, open or mostly so, as an entrance to house or church: usually with *classical columns* and sometimes with a *pediment*

Porte-cochère An entrance provided with a porch under which a carriage (horseless or otherwise) can draw up

Portcullis Defensive castle gate of iron or iron-reinforced wooden bars made to slide up and down in vertical grooves in the entrance-way *jambs*

Principia The headquarters building of a Roman fort

Pylons Rectangular truncated pyramidal towers flanking the gateway to a temple: more usually, any high isolated structure used decoratively or to mark a boundary

Quoins Stones forming corners of stonework, generally larger and/or easier to work and thus better-shaped than those of which the wall is composed

Rain-water head Box-shaped structure of metal, usually *cast-iron* or lead, in which water from a gutter or *parapet* is collected and discharged into a downpipe

Rampart A defensive bank around a fortification

Rat-moulding *Stringcourse* around a doocot which was supposed (incorrectly) to have the function of preventing vermin from gaining access to the pigeons' eggs and squabs

Redenting Stepped cutting (a series

of 'stop-ridges') of a *gunloop*'s outer embrasure to stop it funnelling attacking shot inwards

Refuges (bridge) Recesses for pedestrians projecting from the carriageway or deck, usually placed over the *cutwaters*

Regency The period (1811-20) of the regency of the Prince of Wales (later George IV)

Relief The projection of a proud pattern from a flat ground

Render Smooth coating of cement or *stucco* over masonry

Reredos A screen behind an *altar*

Rhyolite Fine-grained igneous rock

Rigs Strips of land leased for building, usually with a narrow street frontage extended far to the rear 'Lang Rigs': a rig was a measure of land some 6 paces by 240

Rock-faced Masonry worked to a 'natural', rugged appearance

Rococo Elegant, delicate, slightly frivolous 18th-century phase of the *baroque* style, sinuous, asymmetrical and naturalistic, sometimes with Chinese motifs

Roll-moulded With a simple round edging (approximately a circle in section) at the external corner of stones forming door and window openings

Roman Doric More sophisticated, less chunky form of *Doric* order, with *plinth*

Romanesque Style which preceded *Gothic*, characterised by round-headed arches, simple plans, and *barrel vaults*

Rosemary tiles Flat clay tiles, usually red, often laid in patterns and frequently accompanied by decorative clay tile ridging

Rotunda Building or room circular in plan, usually domed, often surrounded by a colonnade

Roughcast External rendering of rough material, usually applied in two coats of cement and sand, on to which gravel, crushed stone or pebbles are thrown while the second coat is wet

Rubble Small shapeless stones usually packed inside walls ('hearting') but sometimes built exposed as rubble walling either uncoursed 'random rubble' or in layers 'coursed rubble'

Runnel Open drain or channel (usually for water), sometimes a narrow pedestrian vennel

Rustic porch Small porch constructed or faced with rough 'natural' materials, such as debranched tree lengths in the place of *columns*

Rusticated In architecture, of masonry in which only the *margins* of the stones are worked, the faces being left rough (e.g. *rock-faced*): of *ashlar*, having the joints emphasised by channelling

Sarcophagus Stone or marble coffin or tomb

Sash Rectangular wooden frame (containing glass) which in the Borders virtually always slides vertically in an outer frame or 'case', the upper sash of a pair sliding outward of the lower

Scissor truss Truss with a pair of braces which cross diagonally between the rafter feet and intermediate points on the opposite rafter

Scotch slates Slates from Scottish quarries, usually blue-black in colour and thicker than the more common (and later into Scotland) *Welsh* or greeny *Westmorland*

Scots Baronial Victorian style of romance and historical invention springing from the writings of Sir Walter Scott, his works at Abbotsford, and the exceptional drawings of Billings, amongst others

Screen walls Walls which simultaneously link architecturally, but more importantly do so while obscuring less attractive or merely piecemeal functions

Scrolled Ornamented with *consoles* or scrolls

Second Pointed Gothic *Perpendicular* style, 15th century

Segmental arch An arch whose arc is less than a semicircle (180°)

Session-house Building or room for meeting of kirk session (minister and elders)

Setted Covered with rectangular-shaped road paving blocks of *whinstone* or granite

Sheep stell Walled shelter for sheep: a fank

Shieling Temporary (summertime use principally) shelter used by folk looking after cattle grazing on high pastures

Shooting-box Small country house or lodge which accommodated a shooting party

Shot-hole *Gunloop* in castle wall (possibly related to boarded or shuttered opening (Old German schot-board) rather than shot

Skewputs Generally, stones shaped to support stones above and at an angle to them, usually the lowest stone of a *gable coping*

Skews Gable coping stones (Latin scutum, a shield)

Snecked stone Rubble stonework constructed with small square stones (snecks) used to break courses

Soffits Under horizontal faces of *lintels* or arches (intrados of an arch is more *classically* correct, rarely used)

Spandrels Areas between an arch and its fellow(s) and the horizontal *cornice* above them

Spiral volute Carved helical ornament, most commonly within the *Ionic* capital

Stepped gable A *gable* with *crowsteps* or 'corbie-steps'

Storey Space between any two floors (in UK, ground-level storey is ground floor, in US the first floor)

Strapped Decorated with *strapwork*

Strapwork Flat interlaced pattern-work originating in Netherlands *c.*1540, popular in Elizabethan and Jacobean England

Stringcourse Horizontal line of projecting *moulding* carried along face of building

Stucco Fine-grained hard plaster used for precise finishes inside or out: for high quality internal decorative work a marble-based stucco was used

Stugged ashlar Stone consistently roughened by use of a pointed hammer or pick: commonly employed from the mid-19th century onwards

Table-stones Flat gravestones (too heavy for one or two 'resurrectionists' to move to get at the corpse?)

Tablet Slab of stone, often inscribed and/or with *heraldic* motifs

Tagged pediments *Pediments* carrying mottos which may group as a well-known phrase or saying

Teind barn *Tithe barn*: large barn where the agricultural tithe (a tenth part of the crop, contributed for the upkeep of the clergy) was stored

Terminal block End building or part of building punctuating a view or providing a full stop on a long block

Terminal piers (on *screen walls*) Piers at the ends of stretches of walls punctuating them or defining the gaps between them

Terracotta Unglazed or glazed fired clay, usually red in colour, used as a substitute for ashlar dressings in late Victorian and Edwardian times, particularly where repetitive moulded decorative detail was required

Tetrastyle Of a *portico*, with four *columns*

Thackstanes Projecting stones at base of chimneyhead which covers the thatch laid on the thackgate or water-table

Thatching A roof covering of straw (usual in the Borders vernacular traditions) or reeds

Three-stage tower A tower stepping as it rises, in three steps, defined by stringcourses, other changes in detail or finish, or an actual reduction in plan

Tithe barn *Teind barn*

Tolbooth Town or market hall, and/or the burgh gaol

Tollhouse Small house at the beginnings of a privately funded road where the collector of tolls for its use would be located

Tooled and margined ashlar Regular stone blocks with broad, regular grooves, their edges smoothly banded

Tower house Compact fortified house, with main hall at first floor or higher, and with further floor(s) above it

Town house Town or burgh council hall

Tracery Pattern of pierced open stonework in a *Gothic* or early *Renaissance* window: in *Georgian* or post-*Georgian* buildings may be of wood and may even be part of a window sash

Transept The 'arms' of a cross-plan church, at right angles to the *nave*

Transitional style Style of ecclesiastical architecture intervening between the *Romanesque (Norman)* and the *Gothic*, current in Scotland between 1170 and 1200

Transomed With a horizontal division (of a window usually)

Tudor-style Architectural style characterised by half-timbered walls and gables with timber *bargeboards*

Turnpike stair Narrow spiral stair

Tuscan Plain and sturdy order of Roman architecture

Two-draw limekiln *Limekiln* with two fires

Tympanum An enclosed space in the head of an arch or doorway, or in the triangle of a *pediment*

Undercroft A vaulted underbuilding, crypt, basement or cellar

Undershot wheel Mill-wheel with *lade* water driving it at its foot

Venetian style Italianate, often *Palladian* style incorporating *Venetian windows*

Venetian window A window having three apertures, of which the central one is much larger than the lateral ones, separated from one another by slender piers

Vernacular buildings Those constructed primarily of local materials, to local details and by local craftsmen, virtually by definition without the involvement of architects

Vestry Room attached to a church where sacred vessels and vestments (clothes) are kept

Vicar's peel *Fortified house* for clergy, in the vicinity of a church

Wallhead Top of the wall, eaves

Watch-house Small stone house constructed within, or with sight over, a graveyard, in order that watch can be maintained over the interred corpses to rebuff the attentions of 'resurrectionists' or bodysnatchers

Waterleaf capitals Conventional leaf-shaped ornament used in the late 12th-century *Transitional* period

Welsh slate Thin blue-black slate of regular size imported from Wales from the 19th century

Westmorland slate Thicker green-grey slate from the Lake District, more common from Edwardian times

Wheel-window Rose window, a circular window with foils or patterned *tracery* arranged like the spokes of a wheel

Whinstone Dark hard fine-grained rock such as basalt

Whitewashed Painted white, originally using a suspension of lime in water

Wrought-iron Pure form of iron, with a low carbon content, able to be worked by hammering and bending into what can be most delicate and artistic non-repetitive shapes

Wynds Narrow streets, lanes, originally perpendicular to gaits (main streets entering a settlement)

Yett Gate, usually heavy iron grille

INDEX

INDEX

ARCHITECTURAL GUIDES TO SCOTLAND

A MAD IDEA: the belief that by the millennium the whole of Scotland can be compressed within 28 vivid, pocket-sized volumes, painting the history and character of each place through the medium of its surviving or demolished architecture.

"Good armchair reading with their exotic mixture of fact, anecdote and personal comment"
– Colin McWilliam, The Scotsman

SERIES EDITOR: Charles McKean

— Currently available —

EDINBURGH by Charles McKean new edition 1992
DUNDEE by Charles McKean and David Walker new edition 1993
STIRLING AND THE TROSSACHS by Charles McKean reprint 1994
ABERDEEN by W A Brogden second edition 1988
THE SOUTH CLYDE ESTUARY by Frank Arneil Walker 1986
CLACKMANNAN AND THE OCHILS by Adam Swan 1987
THE DISTRICT OF MORAY by Charles McKean 1987
CENTRAL GLASGOW by Charles McKean, David Walker and Frank Walker reprint 1993
BANFF & BUCHAN by Charles McKean 1990
SHETLAND by Mike Finnie 1990
THE KINGDOM OF FIFE by Glen Pride 1990
ORKNEY by Leslie Burgher 1991
ROSS & CROMARTY by Elizabeth Beaton 1992
THE MONKLANDS by Allan Peden 1992
THE NORTH CLYDE ESTUARY by Frank Arneil Walker and Fiona Sinclair 1992
AYRSHIRE & ARRAN by Rob Close 1992
WEST LOTHIAN by Richard Jaques and Charles McKean 1994
GORDON by Ian Shepherd 1994

— Forthcoming —

CENTRAL LOWLANDS by Richard Jaques and Allan Peden
SUTHERLAND & CAITHNESS by Elizabeth Beaton
DUMFRIES & GALLOWAY by John Hume and Judith Anderson

ARE YOU BUILDING UP THE SET?

The RIAS/Landmark Trust series is winner of the *Glenfiddich Living Scotland Award 1985*
These and other RIAS books and books on World Architecture are all available from RIAS Bookshops at 15 Rutland Square, Edinburgh EH1 2BE, Tel 0131-229 7545
and 545 Sauchiehall Street, Glasgow G3 7PQ, Tel 0141-221 6496